The
STORY
of
MARY

By
AN AMERICAN
(William L. Spencer)

The Black Heritage Library Collection

BOOKS FOR LIBRARIES PRESS
FREEPORT, NEW YORK
1972

First Published 1885
Reprinted 1972

Reprinted from a copy in the
Fisk University Library Negro Collection

Library of Congress Cataloging in Publication Data

Spencer, William Loring (Nuñez)
    The story of Mary.

    (The Black heritage library collection)
    I. Title. II. Series.
PZ3.S747St 5 [PS2894.S86]   813'.4   72-2124
ISBN 0-8369-9064-1

PRINTED IN THE UNITED STATES OF AMERICA

THE STORY OF MARY.

By AN AMERICAN.

NEW YORK:

COPYRIGHT, 1885, BY

G. W. Carleton & Co., Publishers.

LONDON: S. LOW, SON & CO.

MDCCCLXXXV.

Stereotyped by
SAMUEL STODDER,
42 DEY STREET, N. Y.

TROW'S
PRINTING AND BOOKBINDING COMPANY,
NEW YORK.

CONTENTS.

		Page
I.	Justice !	9
II.	A Gentleman,	18
III.	Free and Equal,	26
IV.	A Happy Family,	34
V.	A Free Ballot,	41
VI.	She whom He Pitied,	43
VII.	Planning for a Future Move,	54
VIII.	A Dream Realized,	58
IX.	"The Yaller Gal,"	66
X.	Three Missing,	73
XI.	Through Your Own Blood,	78
XII.	She Believed in Him,	81
XIII.	A Free Man,	93
XIV.	A Pure Maid,	100
XV.	A World of Delight,	107
XVI.	On to the Rescue,	114
XVII.	Her Snowy Nest,	121
XVIII.	A Terrible Combat,	125
XIX.	Stepping Heavenward,	128
XX.	Mary,	134
XXI.	Two Men,	143
XXII.	"Cause o' Suspicion,"	145

Page

XXIII. On Guard, ... 158

XXIV. Renunciation, ... 167

XXV. A Brave Deed, ... 172

XXVI. Little Jim, ... 184

XXVII. Man's Ingratitude, ... 193

XXVIII. Could there come Requital? . . 201

XXIX. In the Dusky Shadows, . . . 215

XXX. The Will, ... 229

XXXI. He is my Father, ... 242

XXXII. She has Betrayed You, ... 254

XXXIII. "The Sperrits o' Hilton's Sins," . . 259

XXXIV. Two Letters, ... 263

XXXV. The Search, ... 271

XXXVI. Dinah, ... 278

XXXVII. "I Hab Done Wid Life," . . . 284

XXXVIII. Have Mercy Upon Him, . . . 296

XXXIX. The Silver in his Cloud, . . . 301

XL. Two Women, ... 310

XLI. A Carpet-bagger, ... 330

XLII. Among the Moonshiners, . . . 338

XLIII. Ike's Love, ... 349

XLIV. "Guard her Weel," 358

XLV. "Once I Spared You," 365

XLVI. A False Alarm, ... 369

XLVII. Out of the House of Bondage, . . 376

XLVIII. Revolt, ... 380

THE STORY OF MARY.

CHAPTER I.

JUSTICE !

"REMOVE the prisoner."

"Not guilty. O God! He is not guilty!"
This cry, and a woman falling senseless, made the prisoner spring forward striving to reach her.

He had been standing as one stupefied, while some quickly spoken words were consigning him to that hell on earth—a convict's life.

Ten years! and for what?

A few stolen pumpkins that were found, stored away behind his little log cabin.

How they came there he knew not. To this he swore.

His lawyer, hastily summoned to defend him, a poor man, from whom could be expected no fees, a negro, whom as such he despised, felt no interest in the case. And he was, moreover, in haste to return to some friends with whom he had been enjoying a little game when the court's order had summoned him.

"Damn the niggers; now that they are not slaves what were they made for?" he had said, keeping the bailiff in attendance as he played his hand and pocketed his winnings.

1*

While in the crowded court room a man, despite his black skin every inch a man, with a bitter feeling of unmerited wrongs, was waiting his defense.

And a woman, poor, pallid creature, her mulatto face proclaiming in its color the wrong done by a white to an unborn child, was close to the prisoner's dock, holding to its rail for help to stand. Her piteous agony, that spoke in the drawn mouth, the dilated, horror-stricken eyes, appealed to every heart in the room. But there were no hearts. Or else the color line rose too broad and high for them to be touched. Men looked on indifferently as this trial progressed. Each, impatient to begin his own little matter, wished the "damned nigger" was in a hotter place than even that court room ; and that was hot enough, the crowd of human beings taking with their breath the little freshness out of the air.

The judge himself, sitting so gravely on the bench, was anxious for the morning to be over, and was thinking of the pleasant shade and jolly companions with whom he was to spend the afternoon. To him "the nigger" was not an interesting phase of humanity. It had beaten him at the last election, when he ran for continuance in an office he abused, but wherein he would willingly have continued to serve his country. Indignant at being displaced by such a "low element" he had registered a vow that he'd "pay it off on every damned black skin in the country." This negro, tried for larceny, gave him his first chance. And if there could be taken the measure of his vexation and the depth of the agony of that condemned man, well might he have been delighted with his success.

The prosecutor in the case had been a man of wealth and influence, a man standing high in the community. He had been robbed of a great many of these pumpkins. They were a new kind he was introducing. A man had been ordered to watch them. He had not seen the thief in the act, but had tracked footsteps to Tom O'Neal's cabin, where, on searching, the missing pumpkins had been found.

In defense, the evidence offered was that the footprints did not correspond to either Julie's or O'Neal's. The footprints had been seen by several friends of the negroes, who testified that they had been made by boots without nails, boots much larger than Julie's and smaller than O'Neal's, whose only boots were heavily nailed. They also testified that they had never seen any pumpkins on Tom's table, nor any signs of pumpkins around the house.

These witnesses for the defense, frightened-looking negroes, had taken their oaths and given testimony in evident terror, as if in each word they were condemning themselves. However, through their nervousness they did not vary in their statements. Not even the rigid cross-examination of Mr. Eaton's lawyer disturbed their testimony.

His questions were so searching, that, to his annoyance, they drew forth a circumstance which, had there been any one present who was interested in the doing of justice, might have changed the result of the case. It was shown that the footprints which did not correspond to O'Neal's or Julie's were evidently those of a person whose right foot was either lame or injured, as there was a uniformity in the shortness of step and lighter impression of the right foot—and that the body servant of young " Mars Eaton " was lame in that foot. This very important fact was glossed over by Mr. Eaton's attorney, and smilingly passed in silence by O'Neal's defender.

When the prisoner, in a few impassioned words, alluded to this, the crowning point in his case, his throat swelled with an indignant sob, and the dread of what was coming sending its cold sweat to his brow, he was, for his audacity, frowned down by the judge, and silenced by cries of " order."

The bailiff, a man of humble station and without influence, whispered in his ear :

" You'll make it worse for yerself, pore devil."

So, with a bursting heart, and every drop of his honest blood turning to ice, he had listened to his condemnation and sentence.

That agonized cry from his wife, that falling figure —and the ice changed to flame.

He sprang toward her, breaking down the slight rail that divided them, and had his arms about her before the bailiff, who had been too full of sympathy to move quickly, caught his shoulder.

The prisoner evidently was a dangerous criminal, for he did not notice the awful touch of the law, but pressing to his breast the woman he held, kept whispering in her deathlike face, "Julie, Julie, my darlin', don't give up. I'm not goin' ter be killed, you know. I'll come back all right." "Oh, God ! is there a God ?" he half shrieked, as grasped by two or three men he was dragged away from that poor fainting creature and despite his struggles—the struggles of a captured lion—he was handcuffed, forced from the room, and thence sent to his torture. For the contractors of convict labor were short of hands, and had left an order for able-bodied convicts. So O'Neal, with the physique of a hero of mythology, was to be shipped at once to his master. Yes, master !

Bodies of heroes buried, whose lives were laid down to wipe out the black crime of slavery, well may ye rise from your graves !

What has your death accomplished ? Freedom ? No— its pretense.

Maimed soldiers, wrecked lives, all lost, all useless. To free from slavery, and then to leave unprotected the rights of the freed—putting them at the mercy of the conquered ! Is it not a fact in history that defeat brings forth the worst of human passions, as victory the best ?— That the longing for revenge crushes out the nobler elements of a people subjugated by force ? And the hands that dare no longer raise their weapons in open battle keep them, tools for the demon assassination.

Become of interest to the curious crowd that moved from side to side, and stood on tiptoe to see " the nigger show fight," O'Neal, overpowered, but still struggling with the blood trickling down his face and, sounding above other noise, an occasional blow of the wooden club to comfort his despair, was bringing these facts in their full bitterness to a one-armed man at the court room door.

He had been passing by the court house on his way to his home that, shaded by trees, looked inviting this hot day, but seeing a group of negroes at the door, and one pale mulatto woman leaning against the wall, he had turned and hesitated.

The day was so hot, and the room so crowded.

He could be of no help. And he thought of his position, scarcely less favored than theirs. A carpet-bagger ! For so he was called in this sunny land of flowers, Georgia.

Conscious as he was of his own impotence, there was something that touched him in the face of the mulatto. An air of refinement unusual, and misery more common, but so intense that the man could not indifferently pass. He had lately been reading in some Northern journals articles from the pens of Southern men who, lifted above the schemes and wrangles of politics, called public attention to certain abuses in the treatment of the negro— which abuses, if they existed, were flagrant wrongs that called aloud for justice. He had tried to keep himself unmoved by these statements, had ridiculed the idea of his protest against any wrong. His protest ! that would be disregarded by his own party in the North and sneered at in the land of his adoption. He had been battling with himself in solitude, and after using all sorts of common-sense reasoning believed he had silenced the voice of his too obtrusive conscience, when here before him this group of negroes added strength to his enemy, and he stopped irresolute. He said under his breath :

"I'm a fool, but I'll just go in and see if the poor devils do have a fair show. I can't help them, log that I am."

So he had waited outside until the negroes had been summoned, and the pallid woman, starting forward, pushed her way through the crowd, close to the prisoners' dock.

He saw the prisoner, a negro handsome enough to have stood for a statue in ebony, turn as the woman approached, while the anxiety of his face softened to affection as he put out his hand and the pale woman, clasping it, kissed it passionately.

He saw this bit of nature, and tried to swallow a something rising in his throat as the woman leaned her pale face against that black hand, and looked up at him with the same affection a white might have shown for her husband. "Human beings !" he thought, and forgot the tears of sympathy that glistened in his eyes as he gave his attention to law and lawyers.

The trial's progress made him curse his helplessness and the "beastly injustice of the whole thing."

He started forward, impulsively putting out his arm as the woman fell to the ground and clinching his hand, swore, trembled, frowned, and had hard work to crush back the mad desire to "help the poor devil fight against such odds." He ground his teeth and stamped, as bleeding, overpowered, the prisoner was dragged from the room, and sneered half in pity, half contempt, as the

negro witnesses, white almost with terror, hurried from
the court-room ; without a look at their senseless half
sister lying under the feet of the crowd.

And.finally, when the judge with an expression of
disdain pointing to the woman ordered the bailiff to "remove that," unable to stand any more, he shouted :

"Be careful what you do, she's in my charge," Then
with his one arm, and vigorous pushings with the other
shoulder, he made his way through the densely packed
crowd, to the helpless creature that in her misery, had
found one human heart to pity her. "In your charge?"
sneered a voice, "when did you turn nigger trader?
And how can you protect anything?" Not noticing the
words, except by an angry glare that made the blue eyes
black ; Dennis Day put his one arm around the insensible
woman, and with the loud "Clear the way," of the bailiff
whose eyes were still full of pity soon reached the door.

Once in the open air, with the sunlight falling well
upon him, and his excitement somewhat cooled, his
thought "what am I to do with her" brought him to a
sudden stop of perfect bewilderment.

He could not leave her here, in the open streets, and
her condition, rendering her misery more pitiable, while
it touched the man's heart, made his taking her to his
cabin almost an impossibility.

There it was, his little house with its one window and
huge trees, looking at him as if it were saying :

"You're a pretty fool, Dennis Day, carpet-bagger !
Hav'nt you already blighted your life, and ruined your
prospects for the negro ? Is this the result of all your
oath that you'd shut your stupid heart to pity ?"

"Well," he spoke aloud, as if answering the thoughts
his house had called forth. "Well, I'm in for it now ! I
can't put her down on the road ! There's not a negro in
sight !" looking up and down the street in the vain hope
of finding one. "I don't know where her home is !

Great God ! I'd take in a houseless dog, I can't do less for a human being." He strode toward the cabin, still carrying the senseless figure.

When he reached his door he looked around, in the hope of seeing some one who would turn the knob. But there was not a soul near. So, swearing at himself "as a fool for losing his arm in a useless war ;" he gently laid the woman on the grass, and opening the door, took her up as if she had been a sister, and putting her on his own bed, threw himself into a chair, tossed off his hat, and wiped his hot forehead.

"Now, what am I to do ?" he asked himself, as the little room, still full of reproaches, seemed to call him once more "a fool for destroying the quiet of his sanctum," and then went on with more hard words. "Yes, yes, a pretty fool, to rush into battle, get wounded, and then rush back again just in time to lose your valuable arm. And now at thirty-eight a maimed, good-for-nothing hulk of a fellow, called a carpet-bagger by the men you helped whip, and deserted by your 'grateful country,' that only laughs when you're insulted. Yet here you go and burden yourself with a sick woman, when it's as much as you can do to earn your own bread and butter !"

Dennis moved uneasily in his chair in a helpless way, trying, perhaps, to touch the sympathy of the four walls staring him out of countenance.

"Well, I couldn't help it ! I'd have been a brute if I'd have done less, and I hope I'm not that yet," he added, hardly thinking now of what he was saying. For his eyes, falling on the bed, noticed the stillness of that figure.

"I never saw a woman faint ! Isn't it time she came to ?" And then starting to the bed he looked attentively at her.

"Could she be dead ?" He leaned over her. No, she was breathing, and now as he stood beside her, began to move. Her teeth pressed on her lips, and a frown contracted her brow. How young and pretty she was—poor, helpless creature—poor cast-away of life! Dennis was too full of pity for any other feeling. Snatching his hat he started off almost in a run.

"Mammy!" he cried, putting his head in the open door of a small house where lived the old colored woman who kept his cottage neat, "Mammy, come quick, there's a woman sick at my house."

"Lor bress de chile, who am you got dar now?" said fat old Mammy, throwing a shawl about her, though the thermometer stood in the hundreds. Without other protection from the sun than the gay handkerchief around her head, she hurried after "de massa" as fast as she could walk.

On the way Dennis told Mammy what had happened.

"What," almost screamed the old woman, "has dey gone an' made a conwict out o' Tom O'Neal? Lor bress you, massa, heam as hones' as de day. His ole massa could a swore to dat. But his massa's dead. Dead, yes a long time. An' now pore Tom's a conwict!"

She groaned slowly, nodding her head, and with the bandanna knotted around her neck wiped away the tears that ran down her face.

"O Lord, Lord, why was we ever born'd? O, take us to de happy lan'."

With upraised hands and eyes, and solemnly half singing, half saying the last words, Mammy went into the house.

Julie, on the bed, with no consciousness in her open eyes, was moaning and contorted with pain.

Leaving Mammy with the sufferer, Dennis took his pipe for company and went out under the trees, puffing away great clouds of smoke, and striving to banish unpleasant thought. But judging from the occasional

nervous motion of his hand, and the frown that contracted his forehead, he was not very successful. These
unpleasant thoughts received impetus from the moans
that came from the sick room, where amid throes of
agony, with wandering uncertain thought, and wild
shrieks of " Not guilty, O God, not guilty," a child was
born—a poor unfortunate of an unhappy race ! And
despite of her grief, despite of despair, " both chile an'
mudder am doin' well," old Mammy said solemnly to
Dennis, as, still sitting under the tree puffing away at
the empty pipe, he looked up to the twilight sky where
Heaven's lights were being lit, to shine down alike on
the just and unjust.

CHAPTER II.

A GENTLEMAN.

THE child throve and grew strong. Unlike most
new-born infants, it seemed never asleep. It
was a solemn-looking little chap of pure copper
color. Dennis would occasionally glance at the ball of
humanity, who, from a roll of flannel gazed with grave
wondering eyes at this strange world, wherein, uncon-
sulted, he had been thrust. The mother with a breaking
heart lived and grew stronger.

Her first conscious word sent Mammy flying, or as
near such rapid motion as her old legs could attain.
" Tom ?" said the wife, gazing at Mammy with eager
searching eyes.

The old woman had much to do to keep from crying.
Out she ran to Dennis, who having vacated his own
apartment had now for sitting-room only the shadow of
the trees. " Lord, Lord, Mars Dennis, yer'll jes hab ter

tell de pore gal. She axin fer Tom, an' bress yore soul I can't tell a word."

Dennis had been passing some very uncomfortable days. The despair of that black man had haunted every quiet moment since the one when he had walked into the court house to see "what justice was shown the negro."

"Confound it, Mammy," he said, impatiently, but not unkindly, "I don't know what to say to a woman, nor how I can tell such a horrible thing as this truth. I don't like to break the poor girl's heart."

"Ah, please go, Massa Dennis. She'll try harder to hold herself in ef yer tells her. Den you say it more nicer. O massa! I ain't got de heart to, wid dem big eyes o' hern, an' dat thin pore face, jest axin' an' lookin' fer Tom."

Dennis was a soft-hearted fellow ; he could not endure tears, even those of an old black woman. So he put his pipe in his pocket, and with his hand nervously closing and unclosing, walked into the room.

Dennis had intended, quietly and gently as he could, to state the truth. Even in the few moments when walking from the garden to the sick room, he had thought over the words he would use.

But there was something about the thin, girlish face, with the soft dark hair twisted in a knot, and in the large eyes, pitiful as a wounded fawn's, that made him feel a great lump rising in his throat and choking him.

She looked at him piteously, and then without uttering a sound her trembling lips formed :

"Tom. Where?"

In vain Dennis tried to clear his throat and speak, the words would not come. This woman's agonized suspense, which he could only deepen into despair, actually strangled him.

He took the chair near the bed, she watching his every movement. He opened his clinched hand and began to speak, but that face was too much for him. He covered his own with his hand, burying his fingers in his thick, light hair, and something like a gasp broke the stillness.

To those strained, listening ears, that waiting heart, the sound told the story of her woe. Perhaps nothing else could have made the blow less deadly than the pity of this stranger who had opened his door to the homeless.

Her face grew ashen, but when, after a moment, she spoke, her voice was soft and gentle as any lady's.

"Sir, God reward you for goodness to the miserable. I knew there was something wrong with my husband. It comes back to me now. A convict! Ten years, they said. Ten years! Ten years!"

The pallid face was flushed with fever, the slight figure tossing and moaning in the bed, once more drifting out of a conscious world into the uncertain lights of wandering reason, but even in that chaos pursued by relentless fate. Now murmuring of her cabin, now singing with tuneful voice, that suddenly ceased its melody to shriek out "Not guilty," the young wife lay there many a day.

"God help her, if there be a God!" Dennis muttered bitterly, as his human heart was torn by this human suffering, which, for him, destroyed the beauty of the world, even the sunlight, that, shining through leafy boughs, fell on the baby in its roll of blankets lying at his feet.

The grave little copper face stared him out of countenance, and seemed to be mutely questioning the usefulness of life.

He thought of the father of this waif, of his unmerited punishment, and the man's heart within his breast beat fast and furious as indignation grew stronger at this fresh instance of inhumanity.

"Of what use was all the fighting?" he asked, looking at his vacant sleeve, and pressing his hand upon his side, where a throbbing pain reminded him of the bullet he would carry to his grave.

* * * * *

After the birth of Julie's child Dennis had striven to send word to O'Neal. He had sought the bailiff in whose eyes he had seen the glimmer of pitying tears.

He walked down to the court house and found the man directing some negroes who were cleaning the grounds. But in this burly fellow, with shaggy eyebrows, heavy with frowns, and coarse rough voice, he could hardly recognize the bailiff. Walking up to him, Dennis introduced himself : "Dennis Day."

"Well, what's that ter me?" the man answered gruffly.

"Nothing to you, more than you are to me. I did not come here for the pleasure of your acquaintance. I came to make inquiries about a negro convicted yesterday."

"And what's that to me either? Once convicted we ain't got no further use fer 'em."

If Dennis had had two hands, he would have doubled them up and flung them at this coarse-voiced wretch. The one left to him did rise with a threatening gesture, but something in the man's face, not a wink, nor a side glance, but a slight change of expression, made him think he was playing a part. And just then out of a side door came the Judge of the previous day.

"Ah, Brown," he said to the bailiff, "on duty?"

"Yes, yer honor. Can I be of any use ter you?"

Brown's hat was off, and his head bent low in salute, as the great man with a "Not now," passed on. As for Dennis, the Judge had sneered "carpet-bagger," and Dennis glanced back in angry contempt. Brown kept his head down, overpowered by his proximity to greatness. But Dennis, watching him, could hardly control his laughter, for as the Judge receded in the distance, Brown closed his eye with the most comical of winks. Tne face so lately frowns and ill-temper, despite its shaggy brows, weather-beaten skin and grizzly beard, gleamed with good humor, while his very rotund person shook with the enjoyment of his own fun.

When the Judge was well out of sight, Brown rose erect, and snapping his fingers, said :

"Brutes, sir, brutes. Perfect brutes, but my bread and butter depends on 'em. It's not so much my bread an' butter, but the chillens'. Ten on 'em, and hearty as young bears. Bread an' butter ! I guess so ! You jest ought ter see it go down them mouths !"

He held back his head, half closing his eyes, and with admiration on his face, seemed at that very moment gazing at the ten hungry little mouths, for whose sake he hid his truer self, and appeared a thing he hated.

Dennis, looking at him, thought of the miserable shifts poverty forces on a man, and wondered, as many a man has done, that the world is ordered as it is. With a short jolly laugh and a hearty " Bless 'em," Brown came back from the picture of his progeny, eating bread and butter, and looked at Dennis.

" Lor, yes, sir, I knows what yer wants. That pore nigger. God bless me, sir, that man's face, that woman's crying, an' the derned wrong o' the whole thing, made me feel jest like throwing up this place. Though it's a good 'un when a feller's not too soft. As fer me, I've got a shaggy ole face that stands me good sarvice, but my heart, its that soft, mush ain't nothin' ter it. I fights agin it, but 'taint no use. Them young 'uns knows it. Lor, sir, but them is knowin' 'uns !"

Again with half closed eyes, Brown fell to admiring his young, coming back once more with a jerk to meet Dennis's look of kindly sympathy.

" Wal, sir," and Brown, trying to laugh, heaved a

sigh instead. "Wall, sir, I hope you'll excuse me, but ever sence yesterday mornin', when that pore nigger was dragged off, as innocent, sir, as one o' my own babbies, I has had ter keep my eyes jest fixed on my young 'uns. I feels that mean to think I stood by an' seed them a hitten the pore devil, an' then carryin' him off ter worse'n death. I tells yer, sir, law ain't jestice. No, sir, it ain't, when it's given ter the poor an' friendless. I'd ha' throwed up the place yesterday, I'd jest ha' done it, but Lord, Lord, however could I get bread an' butter fer all o' them mouths?"

He tried to bring their little faces once more to his eyes, but he could not.

There were tears in those honest eyes, tears of pity for the condemned negro, and he could not see his children's faces, for that unhappy black one.

"'Taint no use," he said to himself, as he passed his hand across his face to brush aside the tears that obscured his vision, and then turned suddenly to Dennis with a grave:

"What's it, sir?"

"I want to send word, or a letter to O'Neal. His wife had a baby last night."

"A babby! Lord! Lord!" and Brown's face alternated between the broadest of smiles and perfect gravity. "A babby! Wal, wal, it 'ud have been better ef they had both on 'em died! I found it in my heart ter wish it for her, as she lay on the floor so still like! An' now a babby! Is it a cunning little chap, I'd like ter see it! Poor little devil! How they comes, the little innocents, jest a livin' when it arn't nothing but trouble afore them!"

From interest to pity and back again to interest, Brown kept up a stream of comments until Dennis asked:

"How can a letter reach the man?"

"Reach him ! pore nigger, I can't tell, sir, as how a letter 'ud reach him. It's all at the mercy o' his keepers, an' that man ain't livin as has found any mercy in a conwict guard."

He told Dennis the convict had been shipped off to the southern part of the State, where Mr. Eaton's son-in-law was working a large coal mine.

"Why, sir, them pore devils is treated worse nor any dogs. Their workin' hours is so long, their wittals so pore and scarce that they dies off quicker nor folks in cholera time. Three years is counted a life sentence. An' mighty few on 'em don't lasts two o' that style o' life. As fer that camp, it's about the wust in the State. An' the head keeper is a reg'lar brute, strong and fierce as a tiger. They'll only take sech brutes fer guards ter the pore devils. An' when we reads o' them a havin' a risin' an killin' off a keeper or two, I jest wonders how many o' their fellers them has seed killed, afore they strikes up sperrit enough ter hit back. I ain't no friend ter insurrection bein's an officer o' the law," and Brown drew himself up, suddenly recalled to the fact that he had been talking against law and order. "But," and he gave a look around to be sure no one was near, "but, 'deed, sir, an' I pities more'n I blames the wretches, ef I am an officer o' fifty laws."

"There ain't no letters allowed them conwicts ; an' it's a fact, ef it was given ter human ingenuity ter conceive a place more everlastin' horrible than them conwict camps, they'd fail, sir, they'd fail. I doesn't b'lieve," he looked over his shoulder and then whispered, " I wouldn't like my ole woman to hear this, or she'd be gettin' up everlastin' prayer meetin's fer my soul, but I doesn't b'lieve any hell is as bad as one o' these conwict camps down here in Georgia."

Brown gave another timid look around, as if fearful that the uttered heresy would bring his wife bodily before him. But finding there was no living creature nearer than the two negroes raking up the fallen leaves, he straightened himself and gave a fat little laugh, as if to say, " Who's afeard ?''

" Is there no chance of getting a pardon for a man so unjustly condemned ?"

"Chance o' a pardon ! The only pardon he'll get 'll be when death comes a tappin' at the windy, an' says. "Come 'long, now you'se free ! Ef yer was a rich man an' a good Bourbon Democrat, yer' be more likely ter get it. Politics is politics, and money goes a long way in all sech matters. But as fer you, I knows yer, sir, Mister Dennis Day, the carpet-bagger."

Brown said this with a twinkle in his eyes, and a comical upraising of the shaggy eyebrows. " Thar's no chance fer yer to do nothin'. The politicians hates yer, and it's only the politicians serves their country in times o' peace. The other fellers ain't got the time or the money ter secure the posts o' honor. Jest now yer don't represent nuthin', but you'se a stickin' in their crops fer all that. They hates you, more'n they hates the niggers. It was only yesterday arter court hours, an' the Judge says ter me, 'Brown, ef yer'll get that damned carpet-bagger in the prisoner's dock I'll give yer a twenty, an' send him ter keep company with the niggers he likes so well.' But sir," and Brown, took off his hat, slowly, shaking his head, " Im afeard them little mouths ud hev ter go hungry a long time afore I'd do that."

The old fellow looked both kindly and honest, and Dennis's left hand went out, impulsively grasping Brown's big one. Brown cleared his throat, bowed and said : "Much obleeged, sir, much obleeged,'' in a manner half comical, half serious. He was moved, for presently the back of his hand gave a quick wipe to his eyes, which, not relieving him, he drew out a gay handker-

2

chief, and performed some vigorous blasts upon his prominent nose.

"One more question," Dennis said. "What is the name of the convict camp where O'Neal was sent? And the name of the head guard?"

"The camp is Osmerillo, the name of the mine. The captain of the guard is called Hilton, and a reg'lar brute he is."

With thanks and "good morning," Dennis was turning away, when Brown's hand caught his arm.

"Sir, Mr. Day, I has taken that fancy ter your face and ways. I knows a gentleman, sir, when I sees him. I knows trash, too, even ef the trash is a jedge. I'd like yer ter see my young 'uns. Come down some arternoon an' give us a call. My house is jest out o' town on the turnpike, an' my ole woman'll be glad ter see yer. Only sence last revival she says pleasure's a sin, an' larfing's folly."

Here Brown's little fat laugh gave his eyes an extra twinkle, and kept his stout body shaking in such a jolly manner that Dennis laughed in sympathy as he accepted the invitation, and promising to call soon, went back to his home—a home saddened by the piteous moanings of the sick woman tossing on her bed of pain.

CHAPTER III.

FREE AND EQUAL.

While Julie still lay unconscious, Mammy told Dennis her history and Tom's.

"Dey both had massas, an' dey lobed 'em. Tom stood by his ole massa all frough de wah. Aldo he was mighty pleased at de freedom comin', he nebber lef de side o' his massa, 'till one day de ole gemman was shot down in a fight. Den Tom struck an' run, and we nebber seed him eny more, till, wid the beatin' ob de drums de blue coats marched in de town, shoutin' ' You'se all free an' equal !' O, dat glorious day !''

In her excitement, the old woman had risen from her lowly seat on the door-step, and holding the baby to her breast, extended her other hand in the declamatory manner natural to the negro. Her face glowed with enthusiasm, her eyes caught some of youth's fire, the mellow old voice trembled with emotion.

Dennis, in surprise, studied this phase in what he had thought only a kindly creature, whose nature expended itself in dog-like faithfulness. At the remembrance of that dawn of hope, how excited she grew. Even yet, her poor old heart beat responsive to the wonderful word— Freedom !

While he watched Mammy, the light faded, and the wrinkled face came back to homeliness, as, shaking her head, and wiping away a tear or two that trickled down her cheeks, she said :

" But I ain't seed much ob de glory, since dat bright mornin'. I finds de folks speaks more ha'sh now den when I was a slabe. An' my ole man los' his life a castin' his first vote. But de Lord knows best."

She sat down on the door-step, shaking her head and looking on the ground, while Dennis, fallen into musing, did not disturb her. Softly through the open door came Julie's voice, and this voice brought Mammy back to her story.

" Listen ter her, massa. Many's de time dat woice had sung her old miss asleep. She was an orful good ole missus, lobed Julie jest like her own chile, edicated her, and taught her lots o' tings dat fine ladies know. An' when Julie an' Tom lobed each odder, old miss was mighty sad, fearin' Julie 'ud leabe her. But Julie didn't.

Shd worked hard, so de ole miss might hab de tings she was used ter afore de wah.   An' many's de time dat gal went hungry dat de ole miss might not want, Dems de days Tom showed his lob.   He had taken off de blue coat, an' gone to raisin' wegetables.   Lor' bless yer, massa, he was makin' a pile ob money, an' ef he did'nt hab de nicest lot o' green stuff !   Dar nebber was de equal ob Tom fer peas an' dem like."   The old woman smiled in memory of the good things.   " Wal, massa, de nicest ob de nicest was sabed fer de table ob de ole miss.   An' dough dere nebber was any money paid down, Tom used ter say he made most o' his fortin' from de ole miss. He used ter beg Julie ter marry him, an' say he would help take care ob de ole lady.   But Julie wouldn't.   An' one night, wen Julie had sung de ole lady ter sleep, she nebber woked up agen, 'cept in de heabenly Jerusalem. Den Julie an' Tom was married, an' went ter lib in dat little cabin down by de end o' Massa Eaton's place. My, my, but Julie looked fine in de noo silk ‘dress Tom had giben her !   I 'members de day an' all de cake spread out fer de colored ladies an gemmens.   Wal, Tom an' Julie was happier nor de day was long.   Julie was edica- tin' Tom.   ‘ He's goin ter be a great man some day, Mammy,' says she, an' dere she was a hangin' ober his shoulder a larfin' at de marks he was makin' in a book, an' tellin' him he'd hev to study a heap.   Lor, Lor, I ken jest see them now, so happy, jes' like two chillen !   An' so dey was till one day young Mars Eaton stopped afore de cabin, an' stood listenin' ter Julie's voice.   He's orful wild, young Mars Eaton, leastwise he ain't got no 'spect fer a nigger, an' so he went in de cabin and began ter chaff.   I doesn't know what he said, but I guesses he tried to kiss Julie.   But Tom was nearer 'n he thought, an' Tom comes in, an' he picks up de young gemman an' frows him in de road.   Den he goes off a cussin' all de niggers.   Julie told me dis one day.   But she said she hoped it was all ober, an' no harm 'ud come ter Tom, an' now de baby's cum, an' Tom's a conwict, an' dis is de end o' all."

Mammy's groans and tears were brought to a sudden stop, for a shriek, wilder and more agonized than any preceding it, brought both the old woman and Dennis to their feet.

" Not guilty, oh God, he is not guilty."

Poor Julie! While her wrongs did not cease, and her miseries were not lessened, the woman recovered. She came back to her life in a world of which her portion was suffering. As soon as she could be moved, Mammy took her to her own cabin, and once more Dennis was alone. But he had no more quiet. Impulsive, generous, and withal steadfast, his nature kept him true to any cause he had espoused. He wrote to the Governor, stating the case of O'Neal, and to the captain of the guards, asking him, in common humanity, to tell the convict that his wife was safely delivered of a boy, and that both were well, and well cared for. To neither letter came answer, although the one to the Governor was an eloquent appeal for mercy.

Day after day he went to the post-office, hoping for news for the woman, who, with pallid face and eager eyes, stood by the gate of Mammy's little garden, watching, waiting, as each day brought but the same result— disappointment, and the sickness of hope deferred. To Julie, it meant despair. But to her, Dennis was an authority. His great charity, his wisdom, seemed capable of revoking the decision against her husband. Although condemned by the law, she could not comprehend but that once the error of this condemnation were stated to the Governor, or even the Judge, law would do justice. The morning she left Dennis's house, she had fallen on her knees before him.

" Oh, Mars Dennis," she said, "you have helped me

—help Tom ! He's not guilty ! God, who made him, knows it. Oh, have pity on him ! Bring him back to his home !"

Dennis raised the trembling woman reverently, as if she were a queen. Thus, to noble hearts, does sorrow elevate. She was a piteous object as she stood before him, with her clasped hands, and pleading eyes, looking at him as if he held the gift of her husband's freedom. He hesitated to convince her how powerless he was, seeking for words to encourage a hope he did not feel, his eyes encountered those staring ones of the copper-faced baby. That mite of humanity seemed to be moralizing on the uselessness of things in general, and of this big fellow in particular. In all the world, could there be more inoffensive creatures than this woman and her baby, or a more helpless protector than himself? Poor, maimed, a carpet-bagger ! One last relic of those who, after shedding their blood to free a down-trodden race, had settled in the conquered land, and, waving the standard of liberty over a country at peace, vowed that their adopted State should no longer be without the broadening influence of opposing views, that those views should educate the growing youth, and protect the freed-men. But this army of ex-warriors found themselves in a bad plight. Threatened, overpowered, assassinated, without protection at home, or countenance from the party that owed them support, they were martyrs to the cause, and martyrs to those names to which the world delighted to link ignominy. They were in a battle, heroic as it was foolhardy, and worse than all, use-less. The blacks, in most instances, stood firmly by those who were striving to establish their republi-can principles in the South. But this faithfulness brought only added obloquy on the self-devoted band. Of this young party, only a few relics remained. And these, like this maimed soldier, were forgotten by the

North, and allowed to exist here, because they did not aspire to power, and were without influence. Yet, this man, forced by the nobleness of his own nature, was again about to wage an unequal battle, and without shield or armors, enter the lists for innocence and helplessness.

That unfortunate creature answering to the name of woman, was a woman to him, and entitled to protection, although a tainted blood filled her veins. Her sufferings seemed to him as real, as deserving of pity, as if she were the highest lady in the land. That man, whose cry of despair had pierced his heart, was a man to him, in spite of the ebony of his skin. So felt Dennis Day, descendant of a race of Puritans. He was helpless, yet he could not stand idly by and see these more helpless perish. A sea of difficulty, of danger, surrounded them, yet into that sea he would plunge for these, who to him represented principle.

"I am sorry for you, deeply sorry for you," he said, finding but poor aid in his own thoughts, and no help at all in the baby's grave eyes staring him out of countenance. "I am sorry that you have not a more powerful friend than I. But what I can I will do most willingly. It is useless to appeal to the law, for the law has condemned him, and even if it were possible to obtain a reversion of sentence, there would be required too much time and money, neither of which we have to spare. The mercy of the Governor is the first hope. I have written to him, but sometimes letters miscarry, and as I have had no answer I will write again. If, after a reasonable time I hear nothing from the second letter, I will try to see the Governor. But as a Republican and 'carpet-bagger,' I fear I shall have little influence on a politician. In the meantime I will go to the camp where your husband is. Perhaps I can manage to have a message reach him. If you can be assured of his safety and he of yours, you

could wait more patiently for action from the Governor.
No, don't thank me. This trip to the southern part of
Georgia is only hurried. I had intended to go there to
collect facts for some work I am engaged in. I beg you
not—"

But Julie was on her knees, sobbing out her gratitude,
and calling Mammy to quiet her, he left the room.

So he wrote again to the Governor, and to every one
likely to have influence in the matter, and day by day
went to the post-office, expecting answers to his petitions.
Each day, as he passed Mammy's cabin, Julie's pallid
face and sad eyes would watch for him. Dennis had
written down the story of this negro family, of Tom's
faithfulness to his master during the war—a faithfulness
unto death. He wrote of Tom's good character, and
then of the injustice of the trial to which he had himself
been a witness, enlarging upon the horror which such
injustice must awaken in the mind of every honest man.
In this Dennis greatly erred ; for here he touched a political question, and aroused politicial enmity. For
strange inconsistency ! While as man, one may feel, as
politician, the end generally justifies the means. The
only answer his letter received, was a short note from
the Governor's secretary.

"His Excellency, the Governor, after causing inquiries to be made into the trial of the convict, O'Neal,
and finding that it was fairly conducted, before a judge
of high standing, and that the negro was defended by a
competent lawyer ; must decline all interference in the
case. Whatever his private feelings may be, his office
obliges him to protect the people from crime, and justice
is the preservation of liberty."

This was all the comfort Dennis could give the woman
leaning on the gate holding her baby, and watching for
him, as, with letter crushed in his hand, and his side
throbbing painfully, he walked up the hot, dusty street,

Even the trees caught the dust, and with leaves more brown than green, formed a background for the frail figure of Julie, her pallid face and eager eyes.

"I asked for bread, and ye gave me a stone." Yes, a stone ; cold, hard, cruel, crushing hope from out a human heart. Dennis hardly knew that he had hoped, for surely the case seemed black enough, until this letter made it really hopeless. He tried to soften the blow to Julie. But where is the softening for such a blow? "Let me read it, sir, please," and holding out her hand, she took the letter. As she read, her face faded into a deadlier pallor, and a little moan came from her compressed lips. She staggered like one receiving a death-blow, and then was still.

Faint as it was, Mammy heard her cry, and hurried to the door. Seeing Dennis, and the letter in Julie's hand, she suspected what had happened, and tried to help the stricken woman.

"Lor, Lor, chile," she said, not noticing Julie's despair, and hiding her face, down which tears were pouring. "Lor, Lor, Julie, chile, 'tain't no use, 'tain't no use. Jest gimme de baby. He am de bes' chile. No more trouble dan nuffin." Then, taking the child from its mother's half conscious hold, she went into the cabin and putting the baby on the bed, talked to herself all the while her fingers were busily at work.

"Why wos yer borned, yer pore little nigger, why wos yer borned? Jes' ter suffer an' ter die. De Lord knows bes', only it seems mighty hard to dis chile." And she stopped her ironing to wipe away her tears. "Pore chile, pore chile ! When will Heaben open an' set de sinner free?"

Mammy went on ironing, singing, crying, and outside in the heat and glare, Dennis was striving to comfort a deadly sorrow.

"It is not for life, you know, Julie," and then, as she

raised to his face those eyes of despair, he could say no more. Falsehood, even merciful falsehood, did not come easily from his frank tongue. Not for life, when two years are considered a life sentence! Julie was still looking at him, searching his face, as one in the dark for a ray of light. There was no hope for pardon, the only comfort he could give would be to gain some personal information about O'Neal. He would wait no longer, but start for the convict camp. Already had two months passed since the day of the trial and conviction.

"Julie," he said, "don't despair! I will start to-morrow for Camp Osmerillo. You shall have some tidings from your husband. I may be away a month, as I shall walk part of the way, and have some business that will detain me. But I will write to you, so keep up your courage until I return. Good-by. I'll start in the morning."

He held out his hand, she clasped it with her thin fingers, she kissed it, and, kneeling in the dusty road, she blessed and prayed for him. Her eloquent words touched his heart, her tears wetted his hand. Embarrassed by her emotion, he turned away.

"Good-by, Julie," he said, and hurried to his home. Once more he was a soldier dedicated to a cause.

CHAPTER IV.

A HAPPY FAMILY.

HAVING made his simple preparations for the morrow's journey, Dennis walked up and down, out into the garden and back again, but everywhere he was haunted. It was useless to argue with himself. His daily life, and especially this cabin, were shadowed by the sorrows of that black man and his wife. Standing at the open door he bethought himself of Brown and his invitation, and with the thought came a smile at the peculiarities of the honest fellow.

During Court week, he had occasionally seen Brown standing at the Court House door, stolid as if cut in wood. It was not until he was just about to pass, that the man's face gave any sign of recognition, when suddenly it would be metamorphosed by a wink. It was but for a second, yet the second's change was irresistibly comic. It grew to be a disappointment when the bailiff was not in sight. After Court week he disappeared, and Dennis missed his round face and look of jolly good humor. But the days passed, and until now he had not thought of his promised visit.

"I will go to day," he said, and supplying himself with a huge package of candy with which to propitiate those ten youngsters, Dennis started.

Under the tall trees, Brown's house appeared so tiny that the query suggested itself, where all the children could be stored. But he forgot to question, as shouts of merriment reached him, and mingling with these a jolly fat laugh that made him laugh in sympathy, a laugh which he would anywhere have indentified as Brown's.

"Dad !" "Dad !" "Dad !" was being called in great variety of tones and voices. And Dennis, drawing near, caught bits of advice, suggestions offered in such quick succession as to be almost unintelligible.

"Put a knot in yer thread."

"Let me try."

And then a scream and a laughing "eff yer sticks me agen I'll kick," as a break in the trees showed Dennis the family group.

On his knees with a huge needle in his hand and a thread much longer than his arm, was Brown. His coat carefully hung on a branch, waved as a banner above his head. His hat was pushed back to allow of the expansion of brain consequent on his arduous task, upon which, interrupted by an occasional fat chuckle, his whole attention was concentrated. It was a great patch he was trying to secure to a greater hole in a small pair of trousers, the wearer, who was jumping and laughing, having evidently not yet recovered from the needle's recent attack.

At Brown's side, gravely holding the patch in place, stood a pale little girl, on whose face there was no trace of amusement. In great profusion all around "Dad," were tow-headed children, with round eyes and rosy cheeks. They were hanging over his shoulder, catching at his thread, climbing on his back, doing everything that childish mischief could suggest.

These children the grave little girl was trying to quiet, and to Dennis the most comical feature in the scene was the attempted protection of Brown by this embryo woman. She interposed herself between him and his tormentors, calling them to order with, "Now children, let Dad alone. Give him a chance, can't yer?"

But she had an unruly element to control, and Dennis' laughter nearly betrayed him; when seeming to recognize her difficulties, she called strategy to her aid. Suddenly looking over her shoulder, she whispered, "'Sh, mammy's comin'."

Instantly there was a change. Books hidden somewhere in leaves and grass were unearthed, and all that was heard was the busy hum of voices conning "ba-by, sto-ry."

Taking advantage of the lull, Brown stitched away with such hearty good will that the patch was nearly secured, when a girl, apparently the eldest of the family, peeping up, chanced to catch the wink with which he was answering his little daughter's demure smile.

"Meg's fooled us," shouted the tall girl, throwing away her studies, and springing to her feet—an example quickly followed by the other students, who, with shrieks of fun, began to pummel their father.

Shaking with laughter he rolled over on the ground, and lay full length under the attack of his progeny; while the boy in whose service he had labored, and from whose garment the needle still dangled, began to battle in his father's behalf.

It was at this moment that Dennis, feeling himself almost a child, opened the gate to go to the assistance of little Meg and her one ally. But the appearance of a stranger put the children to flight. Even Meg's champion with the dangling needle disappeared. The little girl alone remained, and helped her father to rise, while her brothers and sisters hiding behind Brown, their red faces and round wondering eyes peeping out in all conceivable places, transformed him into the appearance of a huge hen sheltering her young brood.

"Wal, wal, sir," said Brown, giving Dennis a hearty hand-shake. "Yer sees us in all our glory. Come out, Nell," and he tried to pull from her hiding-place the ringleader of the mob. But Nell, burrowing her face under his arm showed her disinclination to be disturbed by sundry kicks.

"Wal, stay thar," her father placidly replied to the young lady's vigorous reasoning, "stay thar, and the rest of us'll eat up all the candy."

Candy! The word acted like magic. Before its power the timidity of the young Browns utterly disappeared. Like a swarm of bees they surrounded Meg, who had received the package from Dennis with a little courtsey after acknowledging her father's presentation.

"Meg, Mr. Day. Meg, our captain."

Mr. Tim with the patch, being duly introduced, acknowledged Mr. Day's acquaintance by his best bow, assisted by a backward plunge of his left leg. Hands and mouth being filled with candy, he could in no more fitting manner show his appreciation of the gentleman's offering to the clan of Brown.

' Ha ! Ha !" laughed Brown. " Them's a reggiment. The Brown Guards we calls ourselves."

Mr. Tim pranced up and down, somewhat restrained from perfect freedom of motion by a certain tightness in the region of that patch. A game of ball was proposed, and enthusiastically carried, Dennis gaining the children's hearts by his dexterity as catcher.

While the fun was in the thickest a report was heard, and Tim's shout, "I'm a goner !" called all eyes to that treacherous patch. It had started from its place. To add to the affright a voice was heard calling : " Meg, bring them childer ter supper." It sobered the little captain and turned her father pale. " Meg, what are we to do ? I'm afraid mammy 'll lick Tim "; he turned in appeal to his diminutive daughter.

Meanwhile Meg rose to the occasion.

" Give this to mammy," she said, handing Tim the candy he had himself rescued for her from the rapacity of his sisters and brothers.

"Oh Meg !" remonstrated Tim.

But Meg was no longer listening. She was busy marshaling the crowd in a line of two and two.

Off they started to the creek and there were rubbing and scrubbing, a drying of rosy faces on the towel Meg produced from a bush, and a general hurry and scurry, until finally, as the voice from the house called : " Are you coming ?" Meg gave the order of march.

" Now," she said, and now it was. The little regiment made for the open door, at which, with a stout willow in her hand stood the formidable mother of this family.

Dennis had already portrayed to himself the shrew

who held in terror Brown and his progeny. He was totally unprepared for this dumpling type of woman, who was not much taller than Master Tim, and whose round eyes and rosy cheeks presented a new phase of domestic tyrant.

She looked young enough to be Brown's daughter, yet that elderly man stood in awe of her, and smiled deprecatingly, uncertain of what welcome would be accorded Dennis.

Meg had left his side and was now whispering in her mother's ear. Possibly some argument of the little girl's, or probably Dennis's own handsome face won the victory, for with several gracious courtesies Mrs. Brown held out her hand.

"How de do, Mr. Day?" she said. "I'm sure, sir, I'm pleased ter see yer, though we ain't got no right ter take pleasure in this world o' sin. But I'm that vexed with Brown fer not tellin' me, so I could ha' got suthin' better fer yer than bread an' butter."

But flattered by the deference of Dennis's manner, a deference natural from him toward all women, and delighted with his frank ways, Mrs. Brown stopped her apologies. She forgot to notice the rent in Tim's trousers and threw her rod behind her—that powerful instrument being quickly secured and hidden by Meg Tim was saved. Dennis shared in the triumph of the faithful little sister, and smiled as he caught her eye.

It was a marvel to see the piles of bread and butter disappear under the attack of the young Browns.

"Look at 'em," said Brown, nudging Dennis, "jes' look at 'em."

And Brown leaned back in his chair fairly shaking with laughter, while his face beamed with gratified pride.

"Don't be a fool, Brown," his wife said sharply, and then to Dennis : "He's such a fool about them children.

But he can't help it. He's proud o' them, an' they ain't bad childern as childern goes."

Exhausted with their labor several of the Browns were nodding with sleep. But called back to consciousness by their mother's sharp command : " Yer ken take them ter bed, Meg," they protested they were not sleepy, and begged to stay up just to " see Mr. Day off ;" in which prayer Dennis so ably seconded them, that Mrs. Brown graciously said : " Wal, ef yer wishes it."

So an hour was passed wherein some of the youngsters listened open-mouthed, while the elders talked, and the others, tumbled together in a warm heap, fell sound asleep. Tim leaned on " Dad's " shoulder and Meg nestled in his arms, putting her little face against his grizzly beard. Mrs. Brown was in the best of humors, but catching herself up in a hearty laugh with a sigh over its sin fulness she fell to work with redoubled energy at her knitting,

" Res' fer awhile little woman," said Brown, putting his hand on hers.

" Don't be a fool Brown," she answered sharply—but Dennis noticed that she let him hold her hand.

The red light of the open fire fell on the family around it, and the moon peeping through the window warned him it was time to go.

The Browns in full force—even the sleeping ones— walked to the gate with him. And with hearty " goodbyes " he disappeared in the shadows carrying with him the picture of these people who, in spite of poverty and differences, loved each other and were happy.

CHAPTER V.

A FREE BALLOT.

IN the gray of early dawn a man walked out of Ilanah, with head erect, quick martial step, and on his back his blanket strapped; a soldier, but with no comrades at his side, no cheering sound of fife and drum; a soldier, carrying an empty sleeve and painful bullet in his side, and thus disabled starting out on a campaign wherein lurked insult, danger, death. As he passed Mammy's gate he had seen a woman praying— praying for him and his cause. In that dim light she seemed rather the spirit of her unhappy race than an actual creature. And as he said "Good-by, Julie, keep up your courage," she had fallen face downward, pressing her lips to the dusty road where had touched the feet of the carpet-bagger.

A long journey was before the man, whose face and accent proclaimed him of Northern birth in a land where the name of "Yankee" awakened suspicion; whose empty sleeve told he had been one who had borne arms in a bitter struggle. The bitterness yet rankled in the conquered country—conquered in open battle. But who was victor now? The negro was he freed? A bitter laugh broke from Dennis, as, striding on, he remembered what this freedom meant. Innocent men in irons, voters maltreated, counted out, or, as he had seen at the polls, refused the right to put in their chosen ballot.

He stopped to rest under a tree and taking off his hat let the morning air refresh his hot head. But though that throbbing in his side began its heavy pain, it was not physical so much as mental fatigue, that affected him. There had come before him a scene at an election, when he had been arrested and fined, for disturbing the peace. It was at the polls and Mammy's husband Uncle Dan, had come to vote. Old and gray-haired, he had, despite his years of slavery, within his breast, that divine stuff of which heroes are made. There was a group of white men at the polls, and a few timid-looking negroes, and among them Uncle Dan with his weak, uncertain steps, came with his ticket in his hand, and a smile on his lips. At a little distance, a one-armed man whose painful side made him languid and ill, that rainy morning, turned to see his old neighbor out of the crowd. One of the men at the ballot-box knocked aside the feeble black hand, as the negro raised his ticket to drop it in.

"Uncle Dan," said the man, "you don't vote that ticket ; take this."

"No, massa, no, I tanks yer, but I has ter wote fer dem as freed de blacks. I ain't got long ter lib ter 'joy dis blessed freedom, but dere's little chillern comin' arter old Uncle Dan's gone dead. I wotes this ticket massa."

"I tell you, you dont !" said the other, glaring at him.

The one-armed man came a step nearer, forgetting his aching side, seeing only that old black face, still wearing its gentle smile.

"Now, massa, jes' don't say nuffin, but let de ole nigger put in his wote."

And the black hand, shaking with age and nervousness, raised to the box his ballot when,—there was an oath and the gleam of steel, and the old man, shot through the heart, lay on the ground.

Dennis Day sprang to the negro's side. He picked up the precious ballot, and succeeded in putting it into the box, before, bleeding himself from a dozen wounds, he was thrown unconscious beside the body of Uncle Dan.

Dennis's brows were frowning, his hand clinched,

his teeth set as if again he were in the midst of that scene, which, like a red hot iron, had seared his soul. With a half gasp, a half sigh, he came back to the fact that he was standing in a country road, his hand bleeding from the blow he had struck at a tree, as if once more face to face with the brute who had killed old Dan.

"Freedom! Justice! What a fool I've been all my life to believe in such impossibilities."

He replaced his hat, and strode on. But his mind was in the past.

Again he was the impetuous boy listening with suspended breath to the call for volunteers. He must go. Who was there to keep him back? An orphan—double reason for his helping those whose miseries and chains called to every freeborn American. A moment more and he was an enlisted soldier. Then a hurried parting from weeping and indignant guardians, and with beating of drums and sounding of trumpets, he marched bravely away to the war. And this was the result! He trudged along a dusty road under the beating sun of August, in the vain hope of helping in some faint degree one of that unhappy race for whose freedom he had flung away every chance of his life.

"Fool! fool!" he said to himself, but on he marched.

CHAPTER VI.

SHE WHOM HE PITIED.

WHEN Tom O'Neal, bleeding, overpowered, was dragged from the death-like figure of his wife, it was as if some goodly tree had been blasted by lightning. Put yourself in his place, you men who

walk abroad. He was innocent, yet condemned to the
blackest depths of guilt, a free man, yet worse than slave.
And against the mighty strength of his grand frame was
arrayed the mightier strength of the law, backed by the
people and armies of a great country. Despair had
crushed all sweetness from his soul, and in the clasp of
that fearful law, he had, a second Ajax, defied a god who
could direct the scorching lightning, the roaring thun-
ders of his rage, against the innocent. From the ·court-
room he was thrust into the contractor's wagon, which
sure as the grave of its prey, had been waiting outside
during the progress of the trial. A last blow from an
angry policeman cast the blank of unconciousness over
a woe immense as the universe. When he came back to
life and misery, he was at the bottom of the wagon, jolting along a country road, the dust pouring in through
the small iron openings, and the heat intense. He struggled to his feet, the two powerful hands with their iron
cuffs almost useless now. The iron was screwed so tight
that it pressed through the skin into the flesh, letting out
the blood.

Yes, under that despised black skin were blood,
nerves and sinews like those of other men. The blood
trickling down his hands, did not differ in its color from
the blood of the white. And no Caucasian could suffer
more intensely than this negro, from whose eyes were
rolling slow tears of despair, as, on his knees, holding
to the wagon's side he peered through those iron wires,
and saw the roofs of the town pass into the distance.
Perhaps in that swoon he had missed one last glimpse
of his Julie! Was she dead? Oh! if he could but
know !

After hours and hours of stifling heat and dust, the
wagon stopped. Horses were changed. A new driver
on the box, joked with the one on the ground about his
"precious freight." He was "clean tuckered out"

after his long drive, he declared, and went in "ter take a smile, an' suthin' ter eat."

Did neither of those men remember that other man, to whose cracked lips a drop of water would have been a boon?

After a little the door of the wagon was opened and a miserable group pushed in—a woman, a boy, and a man. Three more castaways! The woman was weeping bitterly. She was not like his Julie, for her face, though young, was without delicacy. But she was a woman, and unhappy, and O'Neal moved aside to give her his place near the door where an occasional breath of air came through the iron screen, in slight relief to the stifling heat. The woman was too miserable to thank him just then, for the guard was at the wagon, and she gave a last cry of "Oh, sah, doan' sen' me ter de camp," as he slammed the door and laughed a brutal laugh. The boy was a mulatto, and his face, drawn in a heavy frown, was lost in stolid misery. The man who had followed him into the wagon made the hot air heavy with his frightful oaths. All were handcuffed, and all were black. His people! O'Neal's heart had been bursting with his own woe, but he felt it grow heavier with the added misery of these others.

With tears and groans, and longing for sympathy, the woman told her story. . She was a mother, and could get no work, while her children cried for food. From door to door she went, beseeching help. At last despairing, with those little ones waiting for her at home, she had passed a baker's shop, and seeing a loaf of bread near the door, had seized it. While her children, yet ravenously tore at it, the witness of her guilt, she was arrested. Then came her trial, and then conviction.

"Oh, sah, what will my chillen do? What will my chillen do?" She wrung her iron-bound hands, she cried aloud and prayed, until the man sitting oppisite cursed her, for a howling fool "ter pray when de only answer am a cuss."

O'Neal's misery increased. Here was a case as pitiful as his. And now when the face of his Julie came before him, there crowded around, the faces of those lonely children, moaning and crying for their mother, "who was not." The boy did not speak to, or notice his companions. Strength and intelligence were his. Looking at his high brow and well-formed head, one might predict a bright future for him, as a helper of his race. And now he was "cast into that outer darkness, where shall be groaning and gnashing of teeth."

O'Neal could say nothing to comfort the mother whose moans kept pace with the curses of the man opposite.

The night was far advanced when the wagon stopped again. This time there were ten convicts added to the fated number, as again without a draught of water, without a morsel of food for the prisoners, the black wagon rolled on. With midnight came another stop. More wretches were pushed and crowded into that small space which, made to hold fourteen men, held thirty. The air was hot to suffocation, the dust strangling in its thickness. Groans, cries and curses fell continually from despairing lips.

The woman O'Neal pitied suddenly fell forward, in a swoon, overcome by the stifling air. He had protected her as best he could, with his iron-bound hands, fighting off a stout fellow who had tried to push her from her place. But as she whispered : " Tank yer, sah, I'se berry weak. I ain't had no heart ter eat," her body quivered and he felt her head drop, a dead weight, on his shoulder. He held her in her seat with his knees, defending her with his body, for once under the feet of those crowded, desperate beings, she would have been crushed and mutilated.

"But not killed, no, not killed. Death don't take such wretches as niggers," O'Neal said under his breath.

And still the wagon with its miserable freight rolled on.

The whistling of the driver mingled with the groans and curses of the creatures inside. The dust and heat increased; a moment's ease was impossible. Where in the conception of man could exist a more horrible hell? The morning shining through the iron bars revealed a dense crowd of creatures scarcely human. Some sat with tongues hanging out from thirst, some sucking in their blood from cracked and bleeding lips, to allay that burning of the throat.

One was dead!—The woman O'Neal had pitied and succored. And the first lifting of his black despair came as he looked on that calm face. "Thank God," he said.

When the wagon stopped they were at the railroad, where several other black wagons were waiting, each crowded to its uttermost. The guard opening the door and seeing the dead woman, pulled the body out of the wagon. And with curses for carrying " a useless nigger fer nuthin'," flung her, as one would a stone, on the roadside. There she lay in a piteous heap, something for crows to pick at, for beasts to devour. But no abuse could break the calm of that dead face, and O'Neal felt a thrill of triumph. She was past cruelty now.

The car used for the transportation of convicts was no more comfortable than the wagons which had brought them across the country. The guard in charge of these wretched beings brought in some coarse bread and meat, and distributed it as carelessly as if to dogs. With eager hands extended, clutching at it, fighting over it, the half-starved creatures ate hungrily as wolves, becoming less and less human as they sank lower and lower in the degradation of their lives.

Looking at them O'Neal sickened. In misery too great to admit of hunger, he had given to a young girl the portion of food which fell to him. Her face was worn, and the hollows around her eyes made its youth pathetic. He wondered what had brought a delicate child into such company. She ate greedily, casting around terrified looks, as if each moment she expected it would be taken from her.

"Of what did they accuse you?" O'Neal whispered.

"I killed a man," she answered, "I didn't mean to. But it was one day I was goin' home from Miss Jane, who was teachin' me. She's a lady, a born lady, and owned mammy before the freedom came. And Miss Jane was teachin' me to be her own maid an' to read and write."

The child began to cry in a quiet, gentle way, as if afraid to make a noise.

"I was walkin' along the street when I met the gentleman. He was stagg'rin' and caught me as I passed. I's so frightened I screamed. He swore and told me to be quiet. I screamed again and called 'Help! help!' But nobody came. Thar was nobody near only two or three more gentlemen who wor holdin' on to each other and laughin'. I got so frightened I didn't know what I was doin', but I struck at de man who was holdin' me. He let me go and as I ran off cryin' 'Help! help!' I saw him fall. Some people caught me and grabbed my hand. I had in it a little knife Miss Jane had gi'n me. I'd been playin' with it when I lef her house. I'd forgotten it was open, but when they called me a 'murderer,' I saw it was all covered with blood. They took me to jail. Miss Jane, she came to see me when my own mammy was afraid. Miss Jane tried to save me, but she couldn't. The judge said my youth recommended me to marcy and he didn't believe I meant to kill. I didn't, I didn't! Does you think I sent his soul to hell? I can't g't away from his face. Does you think God will forgive me? Miss Jane said He would, and that I should be pardoned. She kissed me here," and the slender hands with their iron cuffs went up until one finger reverently touched her forehead, and the tear-filled eyes were raised in prayer.

With a little sob she went on. " You don't think I'll die, do you, sir? I'm so young, on'y fifteen. I's so happy 'till that court day. But Miss Jane she sat near me so grand and quiet. Dear Miss Jane, I does love her."

The terrified look passed away, and the tears softly rolled down over her face, as half-smiling she thought of her friend. And thus, in smiles and tears, she fell asleep resting against O'Neal.

"Pity they'd not killed her," he thought. "It would have been far kinder to have ended her life than to cast into a den of wolves a child so young, so helpless."

He shuddered as he looked at the faces that filled the car. How little of humanity remained in them! Some were justly condemned, some were victims of chance or accident, some sacrifices to their race! But is it mercy to save even the worst of criminals from a quick death to throw them to lingering torture, to treatment so inhuman that it but lowers them to brutality? Most of the convicts had fallen asleep exhausted. The little girl, Nettie, whose head lay comfortably resting on O'Neal's arm, smiled in her dreams.

Neither sleep nor hunger were possible to O'Neal. There had been only one other who had not eaten—the mulatto boy. With a gesture of disdain he had pushed aside the food, a gesture for which he was repaid by a blow in the face from the guard. The blow brought blood, but he neither moved nor noticed the insult except by a red flush which showed plainly through his light skin.

"Oh, poor boy, poor boy?" groaned O'Neal, his heart burdened to bursting.

After midday the train stopped. The names of fifty convicts were shouted and they were huddled off the cars. Nettie had drawn closer to O'Neal. At each fresh name she trembled.

"I pray dat I may go with you," she whispered.

O'Neal saw the miserables of his race as each stepped from the car, grasped roughly by a guard and handed over to a group of men. There was a blacksmith ready, and on each leg was fastened a manacle. The engine whistled, but above the noise of the train as they moved away he heard the blow of the hammer welding the iron around flesh and blood.

At the next station O'Neal was called out. Nettie's face blanched as he rose to leave her.

"Good-by," she whispered.

He was dragged from the car; and though each stroke of the hammer, as the manacle was fastened, was a blow on his bursting heart, O'Neal stood quiet as if of stone.

His magnificent form and noble face impressed even these brutal guards. "He's a statyer in black marble," said one, and laughed at his own cleverness.

Following O'Neal came the mulatto boy, and treated as O'Neal had been, he tried to control his young blood, but nature was too strong. At the words, "Hurry up, you damned convict," he turned.

"I'm innercent," he said, and proudly raised his head. His answer was a cut from a heavy whip across the handsome young face, that raised a welt from which the blood oozed.

"Innercent, innercent; I never seed one 'o the damned lot, but he was innercent," sneered a guard.

Not a moan escaped the mulatto's lips. His pride stung anew, he suffered in silence.

Innocent! That word echoed in O'Neal's heart. Why did not the heavens fall, and blot out a world of such bitter wrong?

The blacksmith had manacled O'Neal and the mulatto, and the heavy chain, four feet in length, which was attached to the manacle they had been ordered to fasten at the waist. They were pushed roughly aside, and the smith, quick at his work, had added rapidly to the gang. The guards, with pistols in their belts and long whips in their hands, examined the convicts, to the accompaniment of the low, snarling growls of a pair of bloodhounds. Terror and despair were on each face, when suddenly there was an exclamation of joy from a young voice, and looking up, O'Neal saw Nettie. Pulled, cursed, insulted, she noticed nothing but the face of the man who had been kind to her. The delicate hands with their heavy cuffs were, for an instant, held toward him, and the childish face was bright with smiles.

"If lightning 'ud but strike her!" thought the black man, looking at this poor waif of his race. But there was no lightning in the clear sky, and the hot sunshine rested quietly on that group of unhappy wretches and their masters.

At last they were ready. The blacksmith whistled cheerily, keeping time to his hammer as he fastened the condemned to their slavery, and finished the last manacle. It was such a pretty little foot that he looked up to the face above and saw Nettie, pale and tearful, with her white teeth pressed into her lips. The whistling died away, the tune remained unfinished.

"A little gal," he said, under his breath. "That's the wust I ever seed."

With guards in front and at the rear, the sad procession moved on. Now and then the lash descended on some wretch less able than the others to keep up with that quick motion, and a cry of pain followed the sharp whiz of the whip. Noting each object, marking well the road, O'Neal led the convicts. He had resolved to escape. He would fulfill each requirement, give no cause for complaint, bend every energy to one end—escape. If Julie lived, he could not die, and if man could escape, he would. He was like one buried beneath a mountain. Beyond it there was light and air. Reach them he must or die in the attempt. His resolve, too desperate to be called hope, lifted the negro from the slough of despond, and gave motive to every breath and look.

The sun, in clouds of red and orange, was setting in the west. His glory falling on these black faces seemed to mock at their misery. O'Neal ground his teeth to keep from cursing the light that could calmly illumine such despair. They reached the camp as the convicts were coming out of the mine. There they stood, a long line chained together. A rod passed through their chains which now were lying on the ground. They were sooty creatures, who shivered even in this hot air! Looking at these new recruits, some of them laughed, as demons might in welcoming lost souls to hell.

Dripping with sweat, panting with exhaustion, they stood while a guard examined each link of their chains. Another guard, whip in hand, lashed with pitiless blows some who were pointed out as failing in their allotted work.

Sick unto death at sight of this terrible scene, O'Neal yet kept his eyes fixed on it. He was calculating all the fearful odds against escape. He marked the brutal face of the man with the whip, the relentless force with which he brought the lash down on the shrinking shoulders of his victims. Tom's blood ran cold and his hands were clenched as he saw the man approach a woman. Old and feeble she looked, but there was no mercy in that cruel face with its small, wicked eyes and heavy jaw, no pity in the strong arm as it raised the lash bringing it down upon the almost naked body of the trembling creature. Her clothes hung in rags upon her, and her black skin showed through her miserable apology for covering. Again and again the lash descended. Fainter and fainter came her shrieks of agony, until at the last blow the woman fell. Tom heard a piteous moan. Then there was stillness.

The guard kicked her with his heavy boot. No sound ! "Dead. Damn her ! Unfasten her chain." Then, turning to the terrified creatures who stood near, he growled :

"Do you see this nigger ? Whoever shirks work as she did shall be treated just the same."

If he had sought to subjugate the new-comers completely he could not have chosen a better method.

"March on," he shouted with the heir of authority which proclaimed him head of the guards. "March !"

Terror stricken, the convicts obeyed. They scarcely dared look at that still figure lest they should bring upon themselves the guard's anger. At a word the new convicts extended their hands to have their cuffs taken off, then they followed the others into the barracks.

As the first blow of the lash fell on the woman, O'Neal had started forward, when one of the guards— the one who had called him " a statyer "—moved a step nearer. He had a brutal face, yet the whisper, " Ye fool, yer can't help, ye'll only harm the pore devil," was not unkindly. Silent, with breath coming in quick gasps and quivering of flesh, the negro stood, until the last faint shriek of pain was followed by awful stillness. " Dead," the guard had said. O'Neal breathed freer. Another victim had passed beyond their reach.

Escaped ! The word seemed whispered in his ear. Would that be his escape? He looked at the gurads armed to the teeth, at the convicts, crushed and terrorized, at the dogs, only waiting the slipping of their chains to fasten their fangs in human flesh. Was any other escape but death possible? There came upon him an impulse to spring upon the guard whose whip had lashed to death the helpless woman, and here before her body to strangle him and thus seek his own eternal sleep. But Julie, his wife!

CHAPTER VII.

PLANNING FOR A FUTURE MOVE.

WITHOUT being allowed to wash off the dirt and dust of their long trip, the new convicts were marched into the den where meals were served. The place, already full to overflowing, was reeking with the hot air from bodies all day underground, whose rags were wet with sweat, and covered with coal dust. They were allowed neither knife, fork nor spoon. Tin cups and plates only were given to these creatures, who like ravenous beasts tore with hands and teeth the food that was given as it might have been to beasts.

Nettie, pale and trembling, her eyes full of tears, drew closer to her only friend.

"I'm so frightened," she whispered, looking around on the wild creatures about her. "Kill me, please kill me. I can't live in dis place. I'm so 'fraid."

Well might she be afraid, poor child. Her pretty face and delicate figure had attracted the notice of a large, heavy-looking negro sitting opposite. While devouring his food, his eyes were fixed on her with a look that terrified her.

At O'Neal's other side was the mulatto boy. The

angry welt from the whip was swollen and inflamed, his food was untouched, a heavy frown was on his face, and with it that look of misery which first had drawn the man's heart to him.

"Eat something," he whispered, when for a moment the guard looked away.

"If you only knew," the boy answered, raising his eyes.

"I know my own case, I'm innercent too," O'Neal said hurriedly. "Eat, or you may get whipped again." The boy's face worked convulsively and he gasped as one who would not cry aloud. This unexpected sympathy touched his young soul. As a stoic he had borne wrong, abuse, blows; but kindness softened the proud heart, and sent tears to the flashing eyes.

There was no further chance for a word. The boy ate a little of the repulsive food. Coarse, badly cooked, cold, unclean, there was nothing to invite appetite. Yet the hungry, overworked creature at his side, who had eaten every morsel of his own, begged for the boy's with eager looks, and ate it ravenously. The meal was soon over. Then came the order, "To the night cells."

O'Neal, the boy, and Nettie, with several more men and women of the newcomers, were marched to a long building that stood at the end of a row of similar ones. Without windows, its only ventilation was through the crevices between the logs of which it was built. As O'Neal entered he could have touched the ceiling of the room. It did not exceed nine feet in height, fifty in length and twenty in width, yet within this limited space were crowded one hundred and fifty human beings, with three tiers of bunks for their accommodation.

A number—fifty at least—were surrounding two tubs of water at the end of the room. These, without soap or, towels were striving to wash off some of the coal grime. Others stripped themselves of their rags and hung them up to dry, for this was one of the prison rules ; thus naked they jumped into their wretched bunks and covered themselves with the more wretched clothing.

The stench was terrible. Strong man that he was, O'Neal grew faint from it. And clinging to him, the poor little girl stood trembling and weeping. That difference of sex existed in convicts seemed forgotten, for in this den, indiscriminately huddled together, were both men and women.

The mulatto boy was a fellow prisoner with O'Neal.

"Them's yer bunks," the guard had said, pointing to three near the door. Then he gave them their numbers, O'Neal's 1,016, Nettie's 1,017, and the boy's 1,018. "An' don't yer forgit 'em," he had added with a threatening gesture. Closing the door with a bang, shutting the one avenue of air, he locked and bolted it, and they heard his step marching up and down.

Through the chinks between the logs there came enough light to faintly distinguish objects. When the crowd thinned, O'Neal and the two children who in their greater helplessness clung to him, went to the tubs. The one man there turned, and catching Nettie around the waist tried to kiss her, but a blow from O'Neal's fist made him recoil. With a whispered oath and a whispered threat, for no speaking was allowed, the negro went to his bunk. It was next to theirs. There seemed a fatality in it, O'Neal thought, as he watched to see where the man slept. He decided himself to take the lower bunk, then put Nettie on the next and the boy on the highest.

Then he turned to the tub. Nettie had dipped her hands in the water, but as she held them up, even in that dim light could be seen sticking to them the coal dust and grease that had been washed from the filthy bodies of the men. To wash in such water was impossible.

Nettie, passing the negro's bunk, was rudely grasped,

but was released at a sounding blow from O'Neal, and the trembling girl climbed to her place of rest. Rest! Great God in Heaven, could that be called rest? There was a space five feet in length, on: foot and a half wide, and a mattress hard as stone, and infested with vermin, so foul, so disgusting, that but for terror of that man even now leaning out of his bunk to look at her, she would, affrighted, have fled from her bed.

But those creeping creatures were less terrifying than that fearful man. The filthy rags called bedding she put at her feet, and weeping, praying, she wore the night away until, exhausted, she fell asleep. In the bunk beneath, O'Neal, full of his own misery, was still watchful of her. After some hours, when loud snoring told of the convicts' sleep, he heard a motion. It was perfectly dark, but instinct told him what it was, and putting out his hand, he caught fast hold of a man. Grasping him tighter, tighter, forcing him back to his bunk, and pinning him fast with his knee on the fellow's brawny chest, O'Neal plead with the brute for the poor little girl. If one spark of humanity had lingered in the negro, he might have elicited it. But all that was human in him was the outer form.

"Yer damned convict," he exclaimed, "d'ye think I'll mind yer? take yer blasted han's off o' me, take 'em off. That yaller gal's mine."

"I'll tell the guards," O'Neal answered as a last resort, determined to protect the defenceless child.

"Tell 'em, an' get lashed fer yer pains. Warn't thar twenty little nigs borned hyer? An' they'll soon be handy wukkin roun'. Take yer han's off, or I'll—"

His words were lost in a gasp as O'Neal grasped him tighter. Another struggle and then, overpowered, the fellow lay still. Clutching his throat until breath was almost impossible, O'Neal spoke: "I swear to you, if you touch that girl I'll strangle you!" A tighter grasp, the

3*

sound of strangulation, and then loosening his hold
O'Neal demanded : " Will you leave her alone ?   Do you
promise ?"

"Damn yer, I promises."

With this O'Neal had to be content, though in such
a promise he could put little faith.

Lying on his pallet, more than a foot too short and
much too narrow for his mighty frame, the horrors of
this convict life were upon him in full force.   The night
was hot, the stench of the rooms unbearable, the snoring, groaning of the sleepers hideous, those creeping
vermin worst of all.   This was the hour of sleep for a
Georgia chain gang, the preparation for the labors of
the day.   How fearful must be the day when this torture
was called rest !

CHAPTER VIII.

A DREAM REALIZED.

AT earliest dawn, the convicts were marched from a
cold and scanty breakfast to their work.   They
were chained together in gangs, and when they
reached the mine, their allotted tasks were given.
O'Neal, Nettie and the mulatto boy were to work in the
same division ; O'Neal was to pick down the coal, Nettie to fill the buckets, and the boy to wheel out the
loaded car.

"And if you don't work well you'll get this," said the
captain of the guards, shaking his heavy whip.   As if to
give ghastly point to his words, not far away, thrown as
carrion, lay the dead body of the woman, who, yesterday,
under that lash, had yielded up her life !

Coal dust flew everywhere, filling eyes, nose and

throat, even penetrating under their clothing and eating into the skin. O'Neal, working like a giant, with muscles and sinews that would have fitly imaged Hercules, was strained to his uttermost. How, then, was it with the boy and that delicate girl? He glanced at her. Black now as the coal itself, she was filling the heavy buckets one after another, and with hardly a moment to rest for breath, she seemed about to fall.

Catching his pitying look, she stopped. "I don't mind this," she said, in short whispers. "I don't mind this. But oh, that man! I'm so afraid." Then she quickly went on working, for the guard's step was heard in the tunnel, and speech was forbidden.

When evening came, they met the boy. The same look of despair was on his face. Wet with sweat, he was breathing heavily, and seemed hardly able to stand. Yet he had failed in the full requirement, upon him came the cruel lash of that cruel master. The small dull eyes brightened as the blows descended, the brutal face grew more brutal. But in spite of those cutting blows not a sound came from the boy's lips. When with a last blow the captain passed, Nettie saw the boy stagger. She put out her hand to steady him. That slight touch moved him, upon whose spirit the lash had had no power. One instant turning his face, he smiled at her. And through her tears of pity, she saw his mouth was bleeding where his teeth had pressed through the lips. O'Neal, in front of the boy, heard those fearful blows. His hands were clinched in unavailing rage. Again he felt that impulse to throw himself upon that brute and kill him, and again Julie's face came between him and death.

And there came with it the face of the little child they had hoped and looked for. "I trust it is dead, dead in its birth," cried out the bursting heart of this father.

When all the chains were examined, the order to march was given, and begrimed with coal dust they went to the crowed eating-room. Again food, repulsive in the extreme and scant in quantity, was given to these exhausted creatures. But repulsive as it was, O'Neal ate of it, and at his bidd'ng, the children ate also. They must keep up their strength. Escape he would, and doubly desperate as it rendered his chances, he would take these children with him.

In all its own despair, his aching heart had opened to these two, who, in youth's tenderness were already leaning upon him. Yes, he would take them when he went. Could he leave that little girl to a fate more horrible than any death ? And that boy, whose mouth was full of his own blood, drawn by his teeth when he held back the scream of pain as that frightful lash tore his flesh ?

O'Neal, looking at the proud young face, felt a choking in his throat as he thought of his own unborn child. He could not leave the boy. He could not desert these two. When he went, they, too, should go. Already he was beginning to plan how he would make the desperate effort. His eyes were ever seeking something to loosen these chains, these manacles.

Even here at their supper his thoughts were busy on that one theme. There was no noise in this den other than such as beasts make while eating. Nettie and the boy were forcing their food, while watching each mouthful with hungry, begging eyes their neighbors would have snatched their plates had they not been kept in awe by the stalwart O'Neal. And still slyly watching Nettie was that negro who so deeply terrified her. She moved a little closer to O'Neal. He could feel her trembling. Poor children ! Truly as if he were their father would he hold to them.

First to enter the sleeping cell, O'Neal protected Nettie and the boy while they washed. His immense frame and great strength compelled obedience from the miserable sufferers, already fallen to the level of brutes. What else but brutality could there be for them? What had they to expect in the future? What to look on in the past? And the present, who could endure it, and not become degraded? Days passed, each more horrible than the other. Hardly one slipped away to eternity, without some fresh cruelty, some wretch driven to madness and death.

During the miserable hours of the night, with the stench of the room sickening him, and his narrow bed giving no rest to his wearied body, O'Neal arranged his mode of flight. He had noticed that about midnight the guard was relieved, that the second guard rarely walked all around the building, and that on the side of the cell where their bunks were placed there was a marsh. It was covered by long grass which would hide footprints. Beyond this marsh was a shallow lake over which every night hung the mists of miasma. This lake was dangerous; he had heard the convicts whispering about its quicksand bottom. Yet this was the way he concluded to take for escape.

Once out of the building, he and the two children would make for this lake, and if pursued would hold themselves under water until the pursuers passed on. There were a great many reeds rising about the water where they could get an occasional breath. But if they strangled? Better that than to be retaken. O'Neal began to practice retaining his breath, filling his great lungs, and thus holding them. In one of the chances of exchanging a whisper with his young comrades, he directed them to do the same. The boy Frank gave a nod with a quick flash of intelligence in his eyes. He seemed to comprehend O'Neal's motive. And Nettie did it because her friend bade her. This prison life had greatly changed the girl. She was failing fast in strength, becoming thinner each day, the pretty little face taking on a wistful, plaintive expression. She worked very hard, making greater effort as her strength decreased. And yet even she, whose weakness and youth should have been her shield, fell under the blows of that terrible lash.

Months had passed in the horrors of the camp when one night an uproar was heard outside of the barracks. The yelping of dogs, trampling of horses and shouting of guards grew fainter and fainter. Trembling, the convicts sat up in their bunks. " Some nigger's 'scaped," they whispered.

" Dat's Sam Booll, I knows it," said one, not far from O'Neal. "He sed he was gwine ter cut. Lor, Lor, I hopes dey won't get him."

Nettie clasped her hands and prayed to the God Miss Jane had taught her to love, and O'Neal listened in agony. The escape of this man was a test of his own. A week ago he had been whipped in the most brutal manner. He was a man of great strength and endurance, had worked next O'Neal in the mine, and once or twice, when for a moment they had been alone, Booll cursing frightfully had whispered to O'Neal that he "wouldn't stan' this hell much longer. When I'se dead an' damned I 'spose I'll hev ter, but if I lives I'll 'scape from this hyer one. I'd rather die out yonder on de marsh dan rot by de roadside like old Mag. Dat ole woman was my aunt. Pore ole silly, she'd no right in dis place. An' I had ter stan' by an' see Cap Hilton kill her. I'd sell my soul ter de debbil ter be free one minit an' alone wid dat man."

Missionaries who go across the seas to preach Christ crucified, look nearer home for your field of labor. In your own land flowing with milk and honey, precious souls are daily perishing. Do they perish, these poor ignorant creatures, these human beings degraded below the brutes' level by their brutal treatment ? None but God can answer. That mysterious Creator before whom we all bow, and who holds in His hand the balance of justice—only He who permits this abortion of law can tell whether these men and women, more wretched, more suffering than Lazarus, shall lie in His bosom, while those whose gold is coined from human blood shall share with Dives.

While Nettie prayed for the escaped convict, Frank hoped, and O'Neal, lying in his wretched bunk, listened, with beads of sweat standing out over his body. The sounds of pursuit had died away in the distance, the negroes, quieted, had fallen asleep—only the tramp, tramp of the guard told of wakefulness and watching.

As dawn approached sleep came also to O'Neal. He dreamed he had escaped. He was free! Nettie, exhausted, was carried in his arms, and Frank manfully strode at his side. Once more the blessed air came to him without the intervention of prison bars : once more his limbs moved without that clank, clank of the heavy chain. And as the sun was rising over a free and beautiful world, " I believe in God," he said, and falling on his knees he adored his Maker. Then suddenly rushing on them from every side came the bloodhounds. Seizing Nettie, they tore her cruelly. Frank, fighting bravely, was thrown down and mangled, while two fierce dogs with yelping growls fastened their fangs in his own flesh. Then Captain Hilton, pinning his body to the ground with a bayonet, shouted : " Let him lie there, the damned nigger. He'll teach the others how to run !"

Starting up in bed, that brutal voice still ringing in his ears, O'Neal's dream became partly reality. There were groans and shrieks of human pain, making night hideous, but they were not the voices of Nettie and Frank. That was surely a man's shriek !

And was not that the growling of dogs busy in mangling something ?

Presently, above these blood-curdling sounds rose a voice each convict knew.

"Haul off the dogs! Don't let the damned nigger die too quick!"

The horror-stricken creatures within heard hideous snarling and struggling; and then rose moans and curses most horrible. O'Neal's blood ran cold from his heart of despair. The man was caught! His brave effort but opened the way to a frightful death. If, un-hampered and alone, he could not escape, how could O'Neal, with these two children clinging to him, dare to attempt it? And yet he must; if the children were will-ing to risk the danger, they should go with him. Even for them, better the most terrible death than a continu-ance of this life.

While his ears were still tortured by the moans of the man outside, O'Neal pressed his hands on a bit of steel that yesterday had rewarded his perpetual searching. Every instant since that one when the blacksmith had welded his manacle, he had kept his eyes always seeking something, anything, that could be utilized as an instru-ment to aid escape. And yesterday, picking away in the tunnel, he had seen, though covered with coal dust, some-thing unlike coal. Watching his chance, he had snatched and concealed it in his bosom. How it came there he could not tell. It looked like the end of a pick, but was beaten almost to the thinness of a knife. Now, lying in his bunk covered with the sweat of horror called forth by the agonies of the victim outside, O'Neal remembered how two weeks ago, during the blacksmith's ague fit, Sam Booll, who was a blacksmith by trade, had been ordered to the shop. Perhaps then he had fashioned this steel, for the beating he had afterward received had been for a broken pick. And perhaps after using it he had cast it in the tunnel that some other wretch might seek the freedom, to gain which his life had been sacrificed. There was something above the human in this touch of kindness from one who had long lived in this fearful camp, and a thrill of grateful prayer stirred the soul of O'Neal as these probabilities came before him.

Where could he conceal this treasure, bought at such a price? Doubtless in the morning each convict would be searched. He could not conceal it in his clothes, for between the exhausting sweat and the perpetual swinging of the pick, his clothes had become rags equalling those he had seen upon the convicts on the day of his arrival. The bed? No; it might be turned over and searched on the morrow, since the escape would make the guards doubly vigilant. O'Neal ran his fingers along the huge logs that formed the cell, testing with his nails the cracks in the wood. Finding one that fitted, he slipped the steel into it and softly scratching the wood he covered the crack. As the day dawned he examined the place: it looked like many other places in the log where the worms had been at work. There he must trust this precious key which was to open the way to freedom. In the morning when, swinging from her bunk Nettie whispered: "Do you think he is dead?" Her eyes seemed to hold the image of that body outside —a lifeless body, they both hoped, for the groans had ceased.

At the hour of exit for work O'Neal saw that which in spite of the probable lashing awaiting him for infringement of rules made him say to Nettie; "Look the other way"; and Nettie, faint with horror, obeyed.

In the damp mud of the marsh lay what had once been a man. There was yet life in those eyes, and the body, literally torn to pieces, still breathed. The dogs' teeth had mangled the face, and the bleeding arms lay helpless. There was left scarcely the semblance of a human being. Whip in hand, the captain of the guards stood unmoved before his work. Seeing the negroes file out, this bleeding flesh which yesterday had with them bore his burdens, seemed to gather strength, and out of that torn mouth words came.

"Pore devils," the voice thick with blood could hardly articulate. "I'd radder be in de hell whar I'm gwine dan lib like yer. Curse yer, Cap Hilton, curse yer. May yer own blood be de fire ter burn yer soul."

With an oath and upraised lash Hilton sprang to the man. There was nothing now to hurt—only a mass that on the morrow would be putrid. Life, that spark of the godhead, was gone.

Where? Answer it, ye whose laws put him in that den. And ye whose fine linen and purple are colored with his blood.

CHAPTER IX.

"THE YALLER GAL."

SINCE the day when Nettie's timid touch had comforted Frank, staggering under the lash, a tenderness for each other had sprung up in these desolate young hearts. Through all the filth and grime of this most hideous prison, the flower of love lifted its head.

From Frank it took the sullenness of dispair, and gave to Nettie added powers of endurance. That she might be spared the pain of seeing him beaten, the boy worked until from exhaustion blood spurted from his nose and eyes, and wiping it on his grimy rags he would cover the spots with fresh coal dust, that she might not see them. And Nettie, faint with fatigue, each day suffering worse than death from the constant overtaxing of her feebleness, worked on, though sometimes black mists rose before her, and falling to the ground she would recover consciousness to find O'Neal bending sympathetically over her. Knowing the risks he ran in thus leaving his post her first words would be :

"Go back, oh, please go back!" and then with a little
smile, "go back, I'm quite well now."

O'Neal saw the affection of the two children for each
other, and pitied them the more for it, believing that love
would only aggravate the woe of such outcasts. Some
one else saw it—the negro who had terrified poor Nettie,
watching her ever, like wild beast its prey. The growing
feebleness of the girl failed in any degree to soften this
wretch. Only the fear of O'Neal, only the remembrance
of that strangling clasp on his throat, kept him in check.
Yet this fear did not prevent him from constantly
frightening her. With a shudder she would escape from
his repulsive glances, turning her eyes for relief to the
face of Frank. He too watched her, full of a love that
cast a halo around this fearful life. There were stolen
whispers, a touch of hands as Frank climbed to his bunk
above hers. Not much to keep hearts alive; and yet
enough to transform a loathsome den.

The night after Sam Booll's recapture O'Neal had
gone to his bunk horrified at the thought of having lost
the bit of steel. All day he had been tormented with the
expectation of being called up and confronted with the
piece of steel. He pictured himself torn by the bloodhounds—and that girl left to an unspeakable fate. But
the day passed and nothing unusual happened. The convicts, each and all suffering for the escape of Sam Booll,
came under the lash. Those cruel little eyes, that
brutal nature of Hilton's, were not yet satiated with
blood. The sharp lash on his own back O'Neal bore
well enough. He was so harassed by the dread of
losing what he had so lately found that bodily pain
could not take his thoughts from it. But when, after
beating Frank, the lash with a sharp "whizz" came down
on poor Nettie, he clinched his teeth and only held
himself back by a supreme effort of his iron will.
Frank, too, started, as her faint moan followed that

cruel blow. He turned, and had the whip once more descended on those frail shoulders her lover would have sprung between it and her, and thus have laid his life at her feet.

But the lash uplifted, ready for its blow, was restrained. Something in that wan little face, those piteous pleading eyes, reminded Hilton of another young girl, and with a muttered curse he passed on. That morning the girl had had a more serious swoon than usual. Overpowered by the horror of an object she had not seen, she had been unable to eat, and had fallen to the ground after filling the second bucket. The same guard who had once whispered a warning to O'Neal, whom he always called "the black statyer," seeing the girl lying like one dead, and O'Neal vainly trying to revive her, had actually put in her mouth a few drops of whiskey from his own private bottle. And although O'Neal filled the buckets for her until she grew stronger, he failed to report him. For the first time since becoming a convict guard, this man had shown mercy, and the sensation was pleasant—partly from its novelty. He had cursed to himself when Hilton started to whip the sick girl, and then heaved a sigh of relief as the captain passed on without giving the second blow.

"There's suthin' 'bout the yaller gal as teches even him," he thought.

There was, indeed, something about this creature, so weak, yet so brave and patient, that must touch any heart not wholly stone. Was it that the angel of death was overshadowing her with his wings?

That night, after a moment's agony, for the steel had slipped a little, O'Neal found his treasure. Waiting only until the snoring of the negroes told of their heavy sleep, he began to cut one of the great logs that formed the side of the cell. First carefully removing the bark, so that he could readily replace it, he placed the steel upon the wood, with both hands pressing and drawing it across the log. Starting every instant in affright, the cold sweat breaking out upon him, he continued his task. It was slow work. Every time the step of the guard drew near he stopped, scarcely daring to breathe, until fainter and fainter sounded the heavy footfall, as the guard passed to the other side of the cells.

He would not have attempted to escape so soon after Sam Booll's death had not Nettie's face in her deathlike swoon nerved and hastened him. Her face was marked by death. Unless she escaped soon she could never escape save by the road that leads to that other world. O'Neal felt a tear on his sooty cheek as he vowed that at least she should die free.

So he worked on. Suddenly a hand was placed on his shoulder, and trembling, almost falling, he barely recovered as Nettie's voice breathed in his ear : " When ?"

" If possible in two days," he answered.

" Thank God, thank God !"

" Are you willing to risk everything ?"

" Everythin' !" and catching his hand, Nettie softly kissed it.

All the next day Nettie's heart was singing " Te Deum ;" and all through her work she felt an exaltation that lifted her above fatigue, and gave beauty to the delicate little face.

A moment's whisper and Frank shared her joy. In these young souls there was no hesitation to follow where their friend would lead. Even that fearful object lying out on the marsh did not daunt them. Beyond that marsh was freedom !

" And then you'll marry me," whispered Frank, and leaning out of his bunk he touched Nettie's face.

" Yes," she answered. Their happiness made them forget their loathsome surroundings, made them forget the horrors of the lash, the insults of that brutal negro who but an hour ago had frightened Nettie from the washtub ; made them forget everything but the story of their own hearts, and that stealthy scratch, scratch, of the man who was working for them.

Before the gray of dawn O'Neal had replaced the bark and then rested and planned escape. They would have to wear their chains and manacles. Nettie alone, whose emaciation was great, could slip her foot out of hers. These chains would retard their movements, but by wrapping them with rags, the clanking of the iron could be deadened. Since Booll's death the guard had become more careful in examining each link, so that there would be too great risk in tampering with the chains. Once out of the cell, they would strike for the lake. He dreaded hiding Nettie under water, but it must be done, even if it killed her. She would at least die in peace and freedom. On the other side of the lake was a wood. Of its extent he could not judge. It would be a better place for hiding than the open country, where every house was filled with enemies to runaway convicts. The water would interfere with the scent of the dogs, and as it was known to have a quicksand bottom, they might not be searched for in that direction.

How he would obtain food for them O'Neal did not now stop to question. Freedom was what he sought. And every pulse throbbed with excitement as he realized that his second night's work had cut through the great log, which now was held in place only by fibres. He could easily force it from its place so as to afford them room to escape.

Ah! He could feel the blessed air blowing on his breast. He could not wait through another entire day ; he could not see the sun again go down over those miserable black faces. He could not nerve himself to the whizz of the lash and the painful outcry of some stricken creature. Now was the hour of escape !

His heart beat almost to strangulation as he rose to his feet and looked into Nettie's face a moment before rousing her. How peacefully she slept! Poor child, it seemed almost a pity to disturb her. A pity? Great God, he was going mad! Was he not about to take her to freedom? He raised his hand and then he started back! Was not that light which shone on the girl's face dawn! Were not those rustlings the sound of waking convicts? He turned to see if any were yet awake. Yes, one—the negro who watched Nettie.

"Wot's yer doin'?" he muttered, starting up in his bunk.

"Back!" and O'Neal's heavy frown, his fist raised threateningly, enforced submission.

Nettie and Frank with the light of their own happiness shining in their faces, labored all the following day as if in a dream. "To-night," O'Neal had breathed in Nettie's ear. "To-night," Nettie's lips had formed the words for Frank. "To-night," every heart-beat was saying over and over again. Would the night never come? How slow was the sun in reaching the west. Down in their black hole Nettie and O'Neal could not reckon his progress. Neither blessed sunlight nor fresh air reached them in that stifling place. But to Frank above, pushing out the car, the sun seemed standing still. And Nettie counting her buckets, by which heretofore she had measured the day, had exceeded the usual number before the summons came to stop work.

"De last time," she whispered, and she kissed the bucket's rim. "I pray de nex' pore soul who works here won't have such a hard time." Then with a loving little look at O'Neal she hurried to her place, waiting with the other convicts to have her chain examined.

Clink, clink, went the hammer, sounding every link of each manacle. The wind blew so chill that wet with the sweat of her great fatigue, the delicate girl began to shiver and cough. She grew a little faint and sick. Something was rising in her throat, filling her mouth. What was it—blood? How much better she felt? It was a good thing to be bled; Miss Jane used to say so. Dear Miss Jane, how glad she'd be to see her little Nettie again.

The smile on her face, the red blood on her lips, caught the eyes of Hilton, the captain of the guards. He half turned as if to strike her for daring to smile here; but again that something which reminded him of another face stayed his anger, and he passed on.

Supper, then bed, and then—freedom? O God! freedom!

While the convicts were eating a rumbling sound was heard, followed by a loud explosion. Some of the convicts knew the meaning of these sounds and their consequences.

They meant an accident in the mines, and double duty; all night work for part of the gang, that the damages might be repaired and the mines ready for the morrow.

But even the unusual sounds did not disturb the peace of Nettie and Frank. Not until from the door Captain Hilton called, " 1,016," and O'Neal rose, did their happy hearts cease their glad throbs.

Other numbers were called, but the two listening children heard only that one; their eyes dilating saw only him. Their friend, their deliverer, must go. That meant another night in this prison, another day; perhaps he might never come back! To encounter the gas in the mine after an explosion was dangerous, often fatal. If he should die! Nettie's heart ached with pain as this fear took possession of it. O'Neal had the night before whispered his plans in Nettie's ear. He had told her if anything should happen to him to go with Frank. And now her eyes full of tears seemed already to see his dead body. No, she could not go away and leave even his lifeless form here. She pressed her hands tight on her heart as if to keep it from bursting with grief, and bit her lips that she might not sob aloud.

At the door as he passed out, O'Neal turned and smiled on her. Through her tears she saw him and tried to smile back, but it was only a pitiful quiver of the poor little mouth.

The wan young face full of sorrow made O'Neal involuntarily pause. It was but for a second, yet in that second he had seen another face, her tormentor's watching Nettie with such triumph, such brutality, as made him shiver.

"If there be a God, protect that child," he passionately prayed, as chained to a gang of about fifty convicts he was marched back to the mines. After an exhausting day's labor these men were again set at work, and if strength failed the lash forced them on.

CHAPTER X.

THREE MISSING.

WHEN supper was over, the convicts in their cells and the door locked, the negro with a growl like that of some savage beast, turned on Nettie. More terrified than if she were at the mercy of a tiger the girl sprang to her bunk; and Frank, small, slender, with flashing eyes and clinched hands, stood before her, facing the wretch.

"Git out, yer fool!" he growled, but Frank did not stir. There was a moment's tussle, and then glaring at the boy the negro dealt him a blow on the head that tore away the skin and knocked him senseless. Seizing Nettie in a grasp of iron, the monster dragged her from the bunk, to the wooden side of which she desperately clung, with weak hands, that in this struggle for more than life were endowed with superhuman force.

She dared not cry aloud for help, dared not summon the guard with that cruel whip ever ready to fall alike on the innocent and the guilty. Even in this moment of supreme horror the girl had pity on that crowd of debased and timid creatures cowering in the corner and afraid to help her.

"Mercy!" she gasped. But there was no trace of mercy in that brutal face with its bloodshot eyes. From the hideous mouth of her assailant came sounds half growl, half hiss. With her bleeding fingers she still clung to her bunk, her strength waning, a black mist rising before her eyes.

"Mercy! Help!" she shrieked in agony.

It was not a loud cry, but it pierced Frank's stupor, and brought him staggering to his feet. He wiped away the blood, which, pouring from his wounded head, had half blinded him. Nettie's agonized voice had called him. Where was she?

At the mercy of that brute!

Rage and love lent him strength. Like a wild-cat he sprang upon the creature's back, clutched the huge throat and dug his fingers into the flesh. Pain forced the wretch to loose Nettie and defend himself from this fierce attack. Clinging to him, tearing at his nose, mouth, eyes, the boy fought bravely. But the struggle was unequal. The blows from those great fists could not fail to reach him, and when they fell their force was terrible.

At last, catching Frank by the hair, the brute dragged him over his head and dashed him on the lowest bunk. There was a sharp sound, an agonizing shriek, a moment's loss of consciousness;—the boy's back was broken—he was dying.

Yet could those darkening eyes see Nettie struggling, gasping in the power of that wretch.

And in the corner, looking on, were men and women —if those exhausted, half starved, wholly terrified creatures could be called men and women. Why did they not help her! Already the cold sweat on his brow warned him that death was very near. He could not die and leave her thus.

Tramp, tramp, the guard's step drew near. God had sent him. "Help!" the dying boy cried—and then louder and shriller, "Help!" But no help came. Fainter, fainter grew the measured tread. His eyes were growing misty, a numbness was creeping over him. He heard again that choking sob: "Mercy, mercy!" Save her he must. "God, God! help me!" he moaned.

Putting his fast chilling arms around the negro's leg he drew himself nearer, and fastened his teeth in the flesh, as with a wrench the girl was pulled from her hold on the bunk. A pain, sharp as the cut of a knife, stayed the man. Looking down he saw the bleeding face, and with an oath he threw Nettie beside her lover and grasped the boy's head.

But those jaws were fast locked in death. As the girl's body touched him and he looked in her face, Frank's spirit fled from the world that had been so cruel to him.

Ignorant and superstitious, as are all degraded creatures, the negro screamed in fright. He called for the guard, but the sound of those regular footsteps came faintly from the distance. He pushed back the ghastly face, tried to force the jaws, but all his strength could not loose the hold faithful in death. Shaking and almost crazed with terror, his eyes starting from his head, his teeth chattering, he tore himself away.

With arms around her brave defender, with face

pressed close to his, Nettie's soul had followed Frank's. From her parted lips flowed the tide of her life. Slowly it ebbed, but the fearful red stream did not mar the peace of her wan face. Perhaps those two immortal spirits might have looked pityingly then on that poor wretch, who, by nature cast in lowest mould, was, by man's laws, forced deeper into vice and degradation.

In the black tunnel, facing danger and death, O'Neal was praying for them even as they died—praying that if the effort for freedom must result in failure for him, it might prove their salvation, might—

What was that? He stopped his work and listened. He thought he heard a sound as of soft spring leaves stirred by gentlest wind—strange sound in that place, so black, so noisome. Again he listened. Nothing now to be heard but the steady fall of the pick, and an occasional word of direction. It must have been his fancy.

Was it fancy, indeed? Or was it the rustling of snowy wings, wafting those upward for whom he was praying?

In the morning, when the guard opened the door and ordered out the convicts, there was a look of horror on each face; and, reluctant as was usually his exit from the night cell, now every convict was in such haste to get out that he fairly pushed those in advance. Counting, the guard found the number short by three. Could they have escaped? "Come out there!" he called roughly.

No answer.

One of the negroes turned with a tremulous "Massa" on his lips. But at a threatening gesture from the keeper, he stopped and said no more.

Once more the guard called: "Damn you, come out!" With another curse, he strode to the door and looked in.

Brutalized as he was, he involuntarily started. On

the lowest bunk, the girl's arms clasped around the boy's neck and both covered with blood, lay the bodies of Frank and Nettie : while, crouching on the floor, his knees drawn up to his chin, his eyes standing out from their sockets, was the negro. Twined around his neck, an end held in each extended hand, was a filthy rag that had once been part of a blanket.

He was stone dead. But those sightless eyes still seemed to hold the terrible picture before him.

The convicts were questioned. They all united in the story that the boy had called for help as the guard passed, and that when darkness fell the negro was alive. Only the morning had revealed his corpse.

The report was made to Hilton, who came, whip in hand, terrifying anew the wretches drawn up in line outside that cell of horror. When the captain saw the ghastly group, he made no further comment than " Fool ! damn him ; he was one of the best workers. Here !" he called to several convicts, "take these things away. More room for fresh niggers." Then he scowled at the dead. But they no longer trembled at his wrath, nor feared his tyranny.

Waiting in the eating room for the convicts from his cell, O'Neal watched for Nettie and Frank. They were missing. And the negro ? What had happened ? Sickened at the possibilities which rushed through his brain, he could barely taste the food before him. He impatiently waited for the moment when again at work he could, in the guard's absence, question a convict near him. At last in the tunnel he heard how those children died. " Released," he said, and turning away his face, he wept.

CHAPTER XI.

THROUGH YOUR OWN BLOOD.

EVENING had come, the day's work was over, and drawn up in line the convicts were waiting to be examined, when a carriage driven rapidly entered the camp grounds. Amazed, the negroes gazed at the strange apparition—all but O'Neal. He was absorbed in a desperate purpose. In the tunnel, just preceding the moment of exit, he had taken his pick and so loosened the last link of his chain that a slight effort could twist it off. He had noticed that the guard, tired perhaps when he reached the end of the line, was not careful in sounding each link ; and though exhausted by thirty-six hours' labor, he had resolved that to-night should see his death or set him free. He dared not leave the severed log to the chance of discovery, nor could he rest in the bunk where Nettie and Frank had been killed.

Wearied as he was, the weight of the chain became a consideration, and feeling somewhat secure of its not being discovered, he decided to wrench the link. But this evening a new guard was on duty, and with the ardor of a novice gave full attention to his work. O'Neal saw him carefully sound each link of his neighbor's chain and then with undiminished zeal approach his own. He had risked too much. Here at the very outset of his undertaking he was to be tortured and killed. He vowed to himself that he would sell his life dear. Waiting as for the executioner, O'Neal stood ready as the last link was reached to spring on Hilton and kill him before he could be overpowered. One more link, just one, and—Thank God ! The link unsounded, the guard rose to his feet. O'Neal unclinched his teeth and drew a long breath ; he was saved ! How ? He raised his eyes and saw the carriage. It had stopped, a footman opened the door, and a woman came forth.

It was a lady, and a most haughty one. The tall and majestic figure advanced, and with a gloved hand waved aside Hilton, who, surprised at this unexpected visitor, stepped a little too near. As he moved back she saw the convicts and started in horror at the sight. Were those human beings, chained together like beasts of prey, and gazing at her with wide opened eyes from sooty faces? They were half naked and shivering under rags! She threw aside her own costly wrap, ashamed to be protected by its warmth in the presence of these wretched creatures, some of whom seemed in the last stages of emaciation. For the first time in her life she was brought face to face with the effect of laws, which in the abstract she had thought just. For the first time she felt horror at the Government of Georgia, her native State.

Had little Nettie been sent to this place? Was she subjected to like rigor, and as illy protected as these poor creatures?

Not noticing the guards, who stood staring at her, she glanced about searching for one gentle little face among those other faces.

"What's your business, ma'am?" Hilton's voice, much softened from its usual tone, was gruff enough to make the lady lift her head yet more proudly and look at him with redoubled haughtiness.

"I mean, ma'am," Captain Hilton explained, "this is a private camp, and no strangers are allowed to enter without permission."

Not deigning to speak the lady held out to him a large envelope. It contained an official document— the Governor's pardon for the convict, Nettie Green— and a letter from the owners of the mine directing that all courtesies be extended to Miss Jane Dawson.

The light of the setting sun shone full on the lady as she proudly turned from the guard.　To O'Neal she had been an angel of deliverance.　The very air seemed laden with sweet odor from her garments.　Who she was he knew not—only that for him she had opened the gate to freedom.　It was not until he heard Captain Hilton's order, "Bring Convict 1,017," that the peace of O'Neal's soul changed to agony.

This was Nettie's protectress—here was her deliverance!　"Too late, too late," cried his heart.　He longed to speak one word to that noble lady, longed to throw himself on his knees before her and tell her of Nettie's love and reverence for her teacher, and how even in this den, her soul had clung to the thought of her and she had died martyr as she had lived an innocent child.　If he might but touch his lips to those flowing garments, that swept the ground as the lady turned expectantly. But he was black!

A life's education could not in an instant be forgotten.　And the lady, true woman that she was and filled with softest pity, would have recoiled in horror if at her feet that sooty figure had fallen.　How could she know that beneath his opaque skin was hidden warm blood and a great heart?　A blow, a convulsion of nature was needed to tear away the contracting force of established institutions.

The blow was coming!　Bearing in his arms something covered with a cloth, the guard approached.　That something was the slender body of a young girl.

"Nettie," said the lady, speaking gently as if to a sick child.　The guard came nearer, but there was no motion in the body.　Hilton's face, cold as usual, had a look of grim humor mingling with its cruelty.　"Are you ill, Nettie"? said the lady whose proud face was very pale.

Nearer came the guard.　Looking at the motionless figure the lady began to tremble.　She turned yet paler, but compressing her lips walked up to the guard. She put her hand on the girl's shoulder and recoiled in horror. And then in a whisper so intense that it reached each ear, vibrated in each heart :

"Dead !" she said.

She stood a moment, as if transfixed, while the colored footman who had been waiting at the horses heads approached with a robe on his arm. He whispered to his mistress, and at her unspoken acquiescence wrapped the robe about the dead girl and laid her gently in the carriage.

His action roused the lady. She turned as if to follow him, when her eyes fell on Hilton, whose face was yet full of something like amusement.

"Cruel man," she said, "you are the murderer of this poor child. I see it in your face, the terrified looks of these poor creatures, the emaciation of that body Man's law may permit these cruelties, but surely as there is a God, your sin will find you out. You will be punished through your own flesh and blood. Stand aside !"

For Hilton, ghastly with rage, stepped nearer. But the lady drew up her head in proud defiance, and entering her carriage was driven away as rapidly as she had come.

CHAPTER XII.

SHE BELIEVED IN HIM.

WITHOUT a scowl, without a blow of the lash, the convicts were ordered to supper. Calling to him the nearest guard, Hilton said hurriedly :

"Keep careful watch to-night. I shall be away for a few hours. I'll return at dawn."

4*

Softly as they were spoken, O'Neal heard the words, and saw the speaker walk rapidly toward the lake. Then taking a little plank road which led to the extreme southern point of the marsh, Hilton pulled a boat from the shelter of some willows and pushed out from shore. O'Neal had noticed the flush on Hilton's face, the twitching of his cruel mouth, and as he followed the convicts to supper he wondered if such a man could feel remorse.

But it was not remorse that agitated Hilton. Twice had he heard the curse that through his own blood misery would come to him. And this man, crueller than beast, yet had one tender spot in his heart. There was one for whom he felt love, intense and protecting; from whom he concealed his daily life; for whom his cold hard voice took tenderest tone; and to whom he seemed all goodness. The fair face pressed to his own stirred his heart as angel the muddy pool.

For her he labored, for her he lived. His hope was, that having saved enough of the wages of his cruelty, he could take her away from this place to some land where never again would he be forced to leave her. To lose her reverence, her trust, would be worse than death. And yet would this tender creature, this bone of his bone, this flesh of his flesh, his own child, honor him if she knew his occupation?

She who had flown weeping to his breast caressing in her hand a dying mouse, what would she do if she could see those black faces? To him they were " only niggers," things without souls, things made for man's use, and to this use to be forced by fear and by punishment. Their feelings were possibilities that never entered into his calculations. If they possessed them, they were of the same order as the beasts, to which class they themselves belonged, and like beasts they existed only because of their services to man. But could he make her think thus?

He stopped rowing and wiped away the moisture, which at this thought started out over head and face. What would she think, his tender flower, his one ewe lamb, could she know the words spoken by that proud lady?

"But she will never know. I keep her too well guarded. And she is happier thus, contented perfectly with my love. I wish I had not taught her to read."

And, he thought how of late her mind had matured, how, though only possessing such books as he selected; she was forming independent opinions. Yet how sweetly did she yield them to his will! Though not convinced, she could not lie, but with her tender eyes fixed on his, as she nestled at his feet she would say : "I cannot think so, father, but I know you must be right."

No, no, the curse would fall to the ground! She was too true, too loving, to be any thing but a blessing—she could not betray. "And for the rest of the world, I defy them."

He scowled as he spoke, and with a few vigorous strokes soon reached the shore. There, having secured the boat to some bushes he entered a small building and soon came out leading a horse.

The man was transformed. A suit of fine dark cloth replaced his guard's uniform, his hair and beard were carefully brushed, and on his lips there was a smile that hid the cruelty of his mouth. A felt hat pulled down over his eyes to shield them from the bright rays of the setting sun, covered his receding forehead. Aud his voice —was it possible that the voice calling cheerily, "Up, Stamford," was the same the faintest sound of which made human flesh quiver?

On he rode through the thick wood, the trees meeting overhead and brushing his shoulders as he passed. The sunlight faded, and the young moon shining through leafy boughs, made fantastic shadows on the path that gradually widened until he reached an open glade where stood a cottage. It was a pretty little nest covered with rose vines and surrounded by a garden ; the air was sweet with the perfume of its flowers. Hilton smiled as he reined in his horse and the door opened.

"Father ! Father !" called a soft voice, and down the path—not rapidly, for while not lame her steps were not quick or brisk—came a young girl with outstretched, loving arms. She was so delicate and fair she seemed a creation of the moonlight that covered her. Her large eyes and pale gold hair, her slender figure and flowing drapery, all seemed part of the beautiful night. Her motion, half swaying, wholly graceful, was like the shimmering of the silver moonlight when the evening winds lightly stir the leaves.

" Father," she said, as, clasping to his heart this fair creature, he held back even the force of his love, lest it should crush her. " Father, how I have wished for you !" Her arms were around his neck in softest embrace, her face was pressed to his bosom, and her voice had music, sweetest in the world to his ear.

Hilton caressed her face and hair before replying : "Have you been lonely, child ?"

"I am always lonely when you are away. Yet not sad," she added, hearing him sigh. " Not sad, for I'm always thinking of you. How good you have been to me, father ! I can't be sad while you're alive and love me."

He listened to the tender voice and looked into those earnest eyes gazing at him with love unutterable ; he felt that he was her world, and he was happy.

" How beautiful the night is ;" she uttered, her thoughts like one who lived much alone. "And yet, when you are away, I fear to come out after the sun goes down. When there are no birds to keep me company I tremble. The stillness of evening is too great for an atom like me. Sometimes I think I hear a voice calling to me : 'Give up your useless, self-indulgent life. Seek out the sick Lazarus lying at Dives' door. Wash thou his sores, and when he rests in my bosom, he will stretch down his hand and lift you to bliss.' But, father, I can find no sick to nurse, no sinful to pray with. I ask Janet if she knows of any that are ill and suffering, that I may go and help them. But she tells me there are no sick."

Hilton did not speak. He was watching the lights and shades of her lovely face, and from its purity there shone on him such a reflection as even hardest stone wins from soft moonlight. As he was still silent the girl went on.

"If it were not right, you would not make me live idle as one of the roses on that bush, would you, father ?"

She looked into his face with questioning eyes, but as he shook his head she was content, and nestling once more on his breast, her eyes sought the moon that shone down in silent blessing. Her uttered thoughts, so sweet and pure, seemed fitter confidence to the stars than that listening man.

"Christ, the Teacher, bids us work and pray. I do pray, but I can't find any work to do. I like the book of Christ better than all the rest, yet it makes me troubled."

She ceased, and Hilton, understanding little of her meaning, yet felt his heart stir with tenderness for the secluded dreamer. To hold her thus, to know she was all his own, his pleasure her happiness, his wish her law —that was what he lived for. She was so true a creature ! Never from the first lisping word had she uttered less than perfect truth. Even now, these inner thoughts and yearnings, while they disquieted, delighted him, proving, as they did, that from him she concealed nothing ; that with the trust of childhood, she held up to him the pure transparency of her soul.

She believed in him! That was his inspiration, and even as he felt this, he started, for to his mind arose the form and words of the proud woman who had warned him. He would no longer trifle with his happiness. He had some money laid aside; after this year he would leave the camp, and taking Mary, put behind him all associations, that, coming to her knowledge, might change her love for him. This child had been given him by the death of its mother, a young girl whom Hilton had married through one of those strange chances which ally porcelain with iron. She faded rapidly, and in dying begged for her child a little of the love that was never given to her. Perhaps the man felt remorse at the early death of his young wife, perhaps there was a strange power in the baby eyes looking into his. Whatever the cause, Mary Hilton became the idol of her father. Cruel to all else, to this child no mother could have been tenderer. The loss of his slaves during the war reduced him to the necessity of self-support, so that he not only could not forgive the results of the contest but felt malignity against the "nigger." One of a family of hard masters and accustomed to seeing the negro beaten and overworked, he believed these to be the natural consequences of possessing a black skin, and despised all who affected sympathy with them. As for the Yankee, he hated him with a hatred that he would if he could have transmitted to the third and fourth generation. Narrow-minded, bigoted, troubled with no reproach of conscience, like most similar characters, he always justified himself in all he did.

Such men are found in every country, in every party. They were among the Roundheads of Cromwell, among the Pilgrims who, fleeing from the religious persecution of their mother country, inflicted in a free land torture and death on old and friendless women. They abound in Europe, Asia, America. It is against these that laws are needed to protect the weak, and cruel are the consequences when law gives to them a power over life and limb.

Before his appointment as convict guard, Hilton had found it difficult to earn a living. He was badly educated and full of that vulgar pride which forbids manual labor. Now clothed with the authority of the chain-gang, having under his command a class he not only despised but against whom he felt personally aggrieved, the place suited him perfectly. Equally well did he suit those whose desire was to make money with as little expense and delay as possible, and who had no scruples about the manner. In truth, the owners of this mine rarely came personally to inspect their property. And as the State Government did not trouble itself concerning the treatment of its hired convicts, Hilton, whose honesty was irreproachable and whose politics were of the most Bourbon type, was the subject of no complaints. His employers were more than content with his management and the yield of the mines. No thought of the sufferings of the human beings working in their service disturbed the comfort of these gentlemen. Their speech was as full of noble sentiment as if they had no share in the responsibility of degrading souls to their own destruction. Can they so easily shirk this responsibility when the Judgment comes?

In poverty, as in prosperity, Hilton had managed to keep his daughter strangely apart from all associates. At her mother's death he had given her as nurse a connection of his own, an old Scotchwoman who, under a stiff, cold manner, hid a warm heart. It was this stiff manner together with her trustiness that induced Hilton to employ Janet Wilson. Had she been tender in her ways he would not have placed his daughter in her care ; for even in her babyhood he would have no rivals in the love of his child. Extreme in this as in everything, he was

jealous of her very smiles.   It was this jealousy that held
her apart from every associate other than himself and
the old nurse.   Mary had grown to womanhood, while
about her lingered still the perfect innocence of the child.
And thus a nature full of poetry and love, having no
other outlet, lavished all on her father.   Sweet fancies,
secret thoughts, were uttered to him as freely as a flower
yields its perfume.   So jealous was this father that he
did not wish his child to read, yet when one day he found
her puzzling over so me queer characters Janet had
made for her, he taught her himself, that thus through
him she might receive every blessing.   Not sickly, and
yet most delicate, this very delicacy made her all the
more treasured by a man whose sinews were of iron.
It made him ever fearful that an early frost might blight
his blossom.

Living always in quiet country nooks, never having
seen the distant roofs of towns or cities, Janet and her
father formed the girl's whole world.   Her only other
friends were the birds, flowers, insects and smaller
animals.   These alone she knew.   These alone were
allowed her by the strange jealousy of this strange
father.   Janet taught her a little religion, so far as,
that there was a God above all.   Janet's Bible, from
which, to mark the Sundays, the elder woman would
puzzle out a few verses, soon became Mary's delight.
The Old Testament, with its atonements and human sacrifices, terrified her.

" Don't let us think they ever lived, those poor, unhappy people, Janet.   Brothers against sisters, friends
against friends !"

" But we maun do it, my bairn," Janet would answer,
stroking the girl's soft hair.

Still, she made no objection when Mary, turning
away from the fire and brimstone which formed Janet's
idea of religion, would find the life of Christ, and, with

eyes and heart full of the tender teachings of the Master, would read the Sermon on the Mount, until the noble words, thus interpreted, would bring tears to Janet's cold eyes. When, at one of his visits, she told her father of the beautiful story of Christ, and then added : " I like the Bible, for I believe Christ is God," Hilton said she should have a Bible of her own, and was seemingly pleased at her delight. But a few moments later, chancing to meet Janet in the hall, he frowned on her until the woman trembled, wondering in what she had displeased him.

She had been very poor when Hilton, in giving her the care of his child, lifted her into comfort. He paid her liberally for that care, and Janet, having supped on the dregs of poverty, loved, with a miser's fondness, her little hoard. So, between her fear of losing her place and her genuine affection for Mary, Hilton was well served. This bower of his darling was fresh and dainty as any lady's, and if not costly, everything was pretty and homelike. His visits were frequent but never long, and generally the girl was so full of her love for him and his for her, that she rarely asked questions. Perhaps with the intuition of a sensitive nature she felt that her father did not like to be questioned. Yet he always answered her, and never showed even a trace of impatience when sometimes, with wistful eyes, she would seek some knowledge on unknown matters. Once, in answer to a query as to the " business " that kept him from her, he had told her that he was mining. She had asked what mining meant, and when he told her how men dug down into the bowels of the earth for gold, stone and coal, and how this was necessary that houses might be built, and fires burn, she had shuddered and pitied those who labored thus.

" Do they not fear to go into black pits and leave the beautiful sky and fresh air ?" she asked.

Those clear gray eyes raised to his own, those delicate dark brows drawn into a trembling frown, awakened no pity for his victims, no regret at his own cruelty. But a sudden fear smote him lest she should know the truth.

Patting her soft cheek he had described an ideal life, wherein song and laugh accompanied the ringing of the pick. Won to smiles, she had leaned on his knee, and asked that she might see the mine. He had hesitated for a moment and then said: "Darling, I'd rather not." She never questioned further. Her law had been given. She trusted him perfectly, she obeyed him perfectly.

Mary's reading had been limited to a few hymns. Janet's treasures, and some histories of the dryest type. But to these the poetic fancies of her own mind added charm and interest ; and now in the Bible she had wider scope for her imagination. Christ with His never-failing love, His divine forgiveness, won her pure soul to adoration. The woman forgiven, and Magdalen's penitence were to her outlines for romances as beautiful as mind ever conceived. Sometimes she would ask Janet about the places she had seen, the people she had met, for to her the world meant only valleys, mountains, trees, flowers, streams. She would coax her nurse to make an outline of some tall buildings, and then gaze in delight at the rough sketch. For the pictures on her walls were only repetitions of the subjects familiar to her. And even while she loved these she felt a desire to know and to see those wonderful places called cities, where crowds filled the roads or streets, where soldiers marched and music sounded. There were cities now, she knew, as in the days of ancient Rome. But her desire to see these cities did not mar her peace. She was happy as a flower, and her only tears were of pity for historic cruelty or for the pain of some injured creature. Eighteen years old, she was as innocent as an infant : ignorant, too, of

many thing that infants know, yet gifted with quick intelligence and warm heart.

Such was the child that Hilton pressed to his bosom,
exulting in her ignorance as in her beauty.

Were sin and crime frequent? She hoped not, prayed
not. But even while she longed to help the sinful and
sorrowing she believed the teaching of the Bible, that for
the sufferers forgiveness and peace were close at hand.
Above those dark pictures, there ever smiled for her the
divine face of the Christ in whom, though untaught, she
yet believed. He counselled obedience. Therefore
without disquieting thought she was content to obey and
be happy in her father's love. Without guile, without
one sin to mar her nature or disturb her peace, she was
like a fount of sweet waters where weary travellers
might be refreshed, and, listening to its music, dream
Heaven had come to earth.

The hours that Hilton passed with his daughter
brought her her chief happiness. Listening to her, ready
with his sympathy and seeking to divine her every wish,
he was the *sun* of all her light, the source of every blessing. And he, glorified by this fair creature, was king
where alone he desired to reign.

In the little sitting-room, where the wood fire and
shaded lamp illumined his many gifts, she clung to him,
holding his hand with her tender fingers.

She uttered her every thought, bringing him her folio
of written fancies, and showing him the flowers she had
gathered. She led him to her own room, a snowy nest
fit for this white dove, and bade him look from the window where, day by day, she sat watching the road he
traveled.

Swiftly flew the hours, and at midnight he left her.
"It is for your sake, Mary," he said, as she held him in
her tender arms, loth to have him go. "It is for your
sake that I leave you. But I promise by the new year to
give up all work that keeps me from you."

She was so frail a creature he could with one touch have disabled her. Yet how strong were those soft arms! He had said he would return to the camp before dawn, and must not delay. Never before had his daughter evinced wilfulness, but now he could not tear away her arms. And there were tears in her eyes; like dew upon a white rose they glistened on her cheek. Why was this? Again before him rose the lady and her curse. Again a strange fear chilled his heart; and again the thought of the impossibility of any ill that might come through his child put to flight the folly of such a fear. She pressed her tear-wet cheek to his as he bent over her. "Father, I don't know why, but to-night, even with you, my heart is not at rest. The Bible tells of visions; none has come to me, yet somehow I feel as if you would never take me in your arms again. You'll always love me, father?"

"Always," he answered: and kissing her he walked down the little pathway. He had gone but a few paces when hearing a soft rustling he turned at the gate. She had followed him.

"Kiss me once more, dear father," the sweet voice murmured. He kissed her and then mounted his horse.

He had overstayed his time and rode quickly away. At the wood he turned for another look. Mary still stood at the gate. Her arms were held out toward him, her light drapery floated around her. She looked more angel than woman, beautiful and unreal.

"Keep her safe!" He spoke aloud. But to whom? This man did not believe in God or future state. And in the hours past, while his daughter spoke of Christ, His love and His forgiveness, he had felt a throb of jealousy. In that heart, all his own, he desired to admit nor man, nor God!

CHAPTER XIII.

A FREE MAN.

BEFORE O'Neal reached the night cells, the bodies of Frank and the negro had been removed. Never more would he look upon that proud-faced boy, that gentle little girl!

His turn came, and he entered the building.

His bunk was spattered with blood, the old blanket was stiff with it. It thrilled him with horror and with grief. Bowing his head he reverently kissed the filthy rags hallowed by that sacred baptism. Lying down he seemed to sleep, and waited. The moon was so bright that not until midnight could he start on his desperate undertaking. Every nerve was throbbing with excitement. He pictured himself free, and then recaptured, tortured, killed, like Sam Booll.

"Better even that than this life," he muttered within closed teeth. How slowly the night wore away! How the convicts gasped and murmured in their sleep! Poor wretches—he wished that he might take them all away to freedom with him.

Tramp, tramp! The guard came nearer and nearer. He was walking completely around the building to-night, obeying Hilton's injunction of extra care. The prisoner would have time to break through the log, replace it and crawl to the marsh before the guard came round again. He had calculated the distance many a time, together with the moments that elapsed between the one when the cell door was passed, and that when the step of the guard would once more approach, in his progress around the barracks. But to-night the guard seemed to be walking more rapidly. O'Neal must count again. Great Heavens! there were two minutes less! And every instant was needed if the lake was to be reached. Was he, after all, to lose his chance? He could not. He resolved to wait till midnight, and then when the moon sank, he would break through the log, spring on the guard as he passed, and strangle him. What sin was the killing of one of these brutes? And O'Neal's eyes grew fierce as they looked from his haggard face, even as a voice spoke in his soul, "Thou shalt not kill." Julie and his child, his little child! Frank and Nettie, too—all seemed near him, gazing through the blackness of his meditated crime. A sob died in his throat; he clinched his hands. Should he give it up? Should he let the morrow come, let his jailers find his broken chain and kill him? He had never injured a human being—should he let these brutes torture him? Yet above all the wrestlings of his spirit came that voice, "Thou shalt not kill." Why should he not kill? Had not these men killed all the usefulness of his life? He fixed his eyes on the moonlight shining through the cracks between the logs. Over and over again he counted the steps of the guard—always two minutes short! There was nothing else for it—either he must kill or be killed. Julie, Frank, Net— He slept. Thirty-six hours of work, no rest, and little food, were enough to weary a giant.

With a start and shudder O'Neal awoke. It was perfectly still. What! Had he slept at such a moment! To trifle thus with his liberty! He was only fit to be thrown to the dogs! He was lost through his own fault—this was bitterest of all. Good-by, Julie! Hot tears stood in his eyes, cold despair clutched his heart. He raised himself on his arm, with dulled sight looking at the light glimmering through the opening. It was dawn. No! No! No! He dashed the tears from his eyes, he pressed his hand to his mouth to keep back a shout of joy. It was the moon! There was a God of mercy somewhere!

Hush! There were voices whispering!

O'Neal crept to the door, and softly pressed his ear to a large crack.

"Oh, come! We can't play without you. Hilton 'll never know. He'll not be back till dawn. And we'll stop the game at 2."

"I can't," said another voice; "suppose some of the nigs should escape?"

"Escape! don't be a damn fool. Are they likely to do it, so soon after Sam's death? A pack of fools, they've no pluck. Oh, come, I say! Don't stand fooling here; you're wasting time."

Would he go? Tremblingly O'Neal awaited his answer. After a moment's quiet and a few more urgings the guard replied:

"Well, I'll tell you what I'll do. I'll go for two hours. Nothing much can happen, but to make sure I'll just tie Brown Cæsar to keep watch for me."

The brown hound was the fiercest in the pack; O'Neal knew it well. Yet had it been to walk into a lion's den, out of that cell would he go to-night to freedom or to death!

He heard the men bring the dog, heard the growls and snarls of the huge beast, heard the men's retreating footsteps, and then—waited.

Slowly paled the moonlight, chiller grew the air. The silence was broken only by an occasional clank of the dog's chain and the snoring of the sleepers.

How his heart throbbed! Every pulse in his body was beating a wild tattoo. It grew darker. The hour had come!

One wrench and the chain was off. He moved his feet. For the first time in months he had no fear of jangling iron. Pulling the bark from the log, he slipped his fingers around it. With one vigorous pressure it yielded. Another, and into his arms came the wood, lying on his breast, as for one instant he breathed the clear air. Cautiously he crept out, carefully he replaced the log, and then stood erect, a free man !

How fresh the air ! How glorious the sky !

In that faint light, the moon's lingering ray, the convict read hope.

He had no time to lose. Crawling on his hands and knees, gratefully realizing that the wind blew with him, and hoping the dog would not catch the scent, he hurried on for his life. A growl from the dog and a straining at the chain turned the man's blood to ice. Controlling the mad impulse to rise and run, keeping close to the ground and aching in every muscle and nerve, he sped on to the lake. Oh, for that welcome water ! Oh, for the shadow of the trees ! How heavy the marsh, how scant his breath ! More fiercely came the growls from the angry beast as he tugged at his chain. "Death, death, come quick !" Controlling with iron will his failing nerves and weakening sinews, the negro crawled close to the ground, not daring to rise. In this position the place looked strangely unfamiliar. Was he going in the right direction, or had the mad whirl of his blood turned his brain ? For a second he stopped, looking back to where lights marked the camp. Yes, he had chosen the right path and had made good progress ; the lake was not far off. But—God have mercy, they had discovered his flight ! There were lights moving hither and thither, and noises borne on the wind told of an awakening camp. Crouching on the ground, he listened.

Horses' hoofs were approaching. He must run. He rose to his feet, but his stiffened muscles did not, on the instant respond, and he fell. "Julie ! Oh, God !" he gasped in despair. But his outstretched hand touched

something which put new vigor in his veins. Reeds!
He had neared the water, and had yet a chance!

With wild strides he dashed on. He heard shouts,
and then the ground gave way beneath him, the water
lapped his feet; desperately catching the reeds, he
dragged himself under, as there came to the water's
edge a horseman holding the chain of a huge dog.

"Cæsar, you fool, he's not here. Damn you! I've
lost time by you."

The dog was fiercely tearing up the ground, now and
again touching with his nose the tall reeds to whose roots
while almost strangling, O'Neal clung fast. A moment
longer, and he must die. Consciousness did not leave
him; he heard the voice above, felt the stirring of the
reeds and divined its cause. The dog was seeking for
the lost scent! He was safe from those fangs beneath
the water, which would perhaps be his grave. The
agonies of suffocation were dulled, a languor was creeping over him, and fearing that his dead hands might relax
their hold he twisted them in the reeds. He would soon
be gone—No! He saw his Julie—he could not die! He
must battle for his life.

Loosing his hold he rose to the surface. There was
no sign of man or dog. All was silent, and the only
living thing was his dark face breaking the smooth
waters.

Half floating, half swimming he made small headway
in his exhausted state. The moon had set, and Hilton,
making up for lost time, came galloping through the
wood, as a dripping figure reached the lake shore near
the little stable, and sank helpless to the ground. Opening his eyes after a moment's semi-unconsciousness,
O'Neal saw the building, and with the instinct of a
hunted animal fled from what seemed man's habitation.
With wet rags clinging to him, cold, aching, shivering,
he hurried along the very road in which Hilton was has-

5

tening back to the camp. Faint for want of food, his head grew light, the road began to swim round and round before his eyes, while the roaring in his ears kept out other sounds. Stones tore the black feet that left their tracks in blood, but in this race he had no time to stop for quivering flesh.

A sound arose above the roaring—a voice calling, "Up, Stamford." That voice! The shivering creature stood erect. His breast swelled, his eyes gleamed. At last man to man he would face this wretch. But sharply as a knife a pain ran through him, and over his eyes came a blackness that was not in the air. He leaned against a tree, all strength seemed gone, and a bitter tear fell upon his cheek.

"Up, Stamford!" The voice, almost in his ear, forced him to action. Down in the bushes O'Neal watched and waited as with bended head, thinking of his daughter, Hilton rode by. He did not see the dark figure that, crouched on the ground, with hands clenched and teeth set, was ready for a deadly spring.

O'Neal rose to his feet. He was strong now : fire, not blood, ran in his veins. He stood looking after the receding horseman. Should he follow and repay him for his foul deeds? He started irresolutely, then staggered a little, his head turning dizzy. He pressed his hand to it—it seemed ice against flame. Yet would not the hand warm or the head cool.

"Another time," he muttered, shaking his fist at the empty road ; then turning he staggered on. He was hungry, that's what it was. That's what gave him such strange feelings. He broke off twigs and leaves, crammed them in his mouth, and then unconsciously let them fall again. How curious this wood was! It seemed alive with people. There was Sam Booll grinning at him ; he knew he was dead, yet there he was ! And there were hosts of strange faces he had never seen before. Ah, well, it was no matter ; they would not in-jure him, and he must get ahead.

Running now, once in a while putting out his hand to some face that looked at him, and then starting a little as he touched only tree or shrub, the negro hurried on. He was still toiling painfully along the road when day-light, kissed into brightness by the sun-god, shone through overhanging branches on the wild black figure. He longed to lie down by the wayside. A stupor was com-ing over him. But he must reach the edge of the wood, see what was before him, and then he could rest—rest until night's charity made his rags less hideous. On he staggered like one blind or drunk. His throat and mouth were parched. Oh, for a drop of water ! He tore a rag off his clothes, but it was stiff and dry. What cramps, what pains beset him ! Grovelling in the dust, he seemed about to yield up the pitiful thing called life.

"Julie !" he murmured. There was magic in that name. His wife, he *must* see her again. He rose to his feet once more, steadying himself by the bushes that fringed the road.

Strange, strange ! The trees were spinning past him —running to the camp ! They would tell ! "Stop !" he shouted, but they heeded not. Perhaps he had gone astray—perhaps they were friends showing him the right road

His limbs were shaking under him, from his mouth dropped mingled froth and blood. And now round and round the trees were closing as if to hold and keep him until the dogs came up. He groaned and, almost breath-less now, ran on a few steps. Suddenly Heaven seemed to open ; its light shone on his blinded vision, its sweet-est perfume filled the air. An angel in glistening white, singing strains of seraphic music, floated toward him, and, covered with roses, the celestial throne seemed to gleam before him. He reeled and fell just at the con-fines of the wood.

A black heap he lay unnoticed under the dark bushes, while among her roses Mary Hilton sang softly, and, walking rapidly down the road, came a man of her own race.

———◆———

CHAPTER XIV.

A PURE MAID.

TRAVEL-STAINED and worn, with a look of fatigue on his handsome face, Dennis Day walked quickly toward Mary's cottage, and in wonder saw this fair creature, this rose blossoming in the wilderness. The convict camp was not far off; his long walk was nearly over. He had walked out of Milton, and in looking for some quiet cottage where he might obtain something to eat, had turned off from the main road into one that seemed little used. Through the trees he had seen this house in the distance. Its position pleased him, and as he approached, its neatness, the clustering rose vines and the beauty of the little garden made him congratulate himself on the lucky chance that had led him thither. He heard a voice singing—very sweetly it sounded, mingling with the roses' perfume. The place was in better condition than the generality of country cottages, but was not too pretentious for him to doubt that its inmates would permit him to pay for his meal. How sweet was that voice!—and now he caught a word or two of the song. Dennis walked a little faster, his face growing brighter with its smile of expectation, when, rising from behind the rose-bush where she had been fastening up a branch, that, weakened by its wealth of beauty, trailed on the ground, Mary Hilton stood before him. "The loveliest rose of all," he thought.

She did not turn to retreat, as he half dreaded she would. Looking at her he forgot the long weary walk of these hot days, when he had felt himself a second Quixote charging a wind-mill. Useless as it might be, disastrous to himself as it probably would be, yet he felt that he must do it. His nature forced him to it, his principles held him fast. A human being perishing had called for help, and help he must give, whether the skin be black or white. His was the broad religion that without doctrinal tenets yet embraces Christianity's teachings. For a guiltless convict, his sick wife and helpless child, this man had slept under hedges, fared meagerly, endured fatigue, and now was ready to face danger.

He had resolved, following his war experience, to make a careful survey of the convict camp, and, if there was a possibility of success, aid the prisoner to escape. To Dennis, the negro was a political prisoner, for indeed the laws that made this free man a slave, were the outgrowth of the war, that, claiming to have suppressed slavery, established this new bondage : wherein, being no longer a marketable article, the slave's physical condition was of no consequence. He was the borrowed animal whose indifferent owner questioned not what treatment he received. So Dennis, in his own person, fighting the battles against this cruel system, husbanded his purse, to use it, if possible, in buying an ally among the convict guards.

He had decided that his first approach to the camp should be at night, when, relying upon the chance of meeting a single guard on duty, he would see what strategy could accomplish. He was already feeling the excitement of this " campaign," as he had named his trip to the convict camp, when he turned out of the main road in search of some quiet house where he could rest until the afternoon was further advanced. He had almost concluded to return to the road, for there was not a house visible for many miles, and as he advanced the country grew wilder. But again his natural obstinacy kept him on the path he had chosen, and to his surprise, as he made his way through a thick grove of trees, this little cottage came in view. A nearer approach disclosed the lovely girl, and he forgot everything else in pleasure at the sight of her face.

"Good morning." As he raised his hat she clapped her hands in glee.

"You speak English. Oh, how glad I am, how glad I am !" And her laughter like rippling waters trilled on the air.

A human being had come to her from that other country, that outer world of which she had dreamed. An impulse to call Janet had been unheeded. She had feared that in her absence he might pass and disappear. Did he speak her tongue? Or was his language one of those that to her would be only sound ?

With the sunlight lighting into brightness the pale gold of her hair, with her gray eyes in their clear radiance fixed on his face, and her fair hands held toward him, she scarcely breathed until his "good-morning" filled her with delight.

"Come in, pray come in," and she opened the gate, and taking his hand, gently drew him into the garden.

"Tell me," she said, "is the world great where you come from ? Are you from the cities where men fill the streets ? Or is it country like this?" Eagerly she questioned, with eyes as well as voice, still holding his left hand in her two soft ones as she looked up in his face.

What sweetness of voice—what grace of motion ! And what strange questions for a woman ! Had it not been for the intelligence of her face, the rapid changes, in those beautiful eyes, Dennis would have believed himself in the presence of one of those called in Ireland "innocents."

But there was no wandering reason in the face before him. Amazed he looked at her, as now with clasped hands and fast-filling eyes she gazed in pity at his empty sleeve.

"How did you lose it?" She spoke in softly uttered whisper as if that empty sleeve had taken her breath away. "Was it in war? I know of no war later than 1847. Surely you were not then a soldier. Does it pain you? Poor man, poor man!"

She put her hands before her face, and Dennis saw tears trickling through the slender fingers. Were those tears for him? He felt in fairyland. He feared to speak lest a word might startle and drive her away.

"My bairn, my bairn!" A harsh voice calling from the house brought him back into life's realities, as a tall, raw-boned woman, with sleeves rolled up, appeared in the doorway.

The amazed Janet started back at the sight of Mary Hilton, her face hidden in her hands, standing close to a stranger. And then, all possible doubts and fears assailing her, she rushed down the steps, from the little porch, and put herself between·Mary and Dennis.

"How dare ye come in that gate? How dare ye speak to the young leddy?" she said angrily.

Before Dennis could reply, Mary had interposed: "'Twas I spoke to him, Janet. Ah, look at him, poor, poor man; he has lost his arm, he has lost his arm!"

"Lost his arm! 'Tis pity he hadna lost his life. 'Twad be better for the world ef mony a livin' mon was lyin' stiff in his grave," Janet answered, glaring at Dennis as if there was nothing she would so like as to send him to his grave on the instant.

"Ah, Janet, you shouldn't speak so. Those who live are doing the will of God, just as those who die! And I am glad you live," Mary said, turning to Dennis. A smile broke over her face, beautifying it as the sunshine the fair earth after spring's gentlest shower.

Still smiling, "Come into the house;" she said, as she took his hot hand in her cold fingers.

"Miss Mary," Janet screamed, her face changing to an expression of horror. "Dinna take the hand o' a strange mon," and tearing away her mistress's soft clasp she clutched her as if to save her from some deadly contamination.

But Mary released her hand, and put it again in that of Dennis. "Janet, it isn't wrong, for I read in the Bible when strangers came, they took them by the hand and led them in. How do you know but this man may be an angel in disguise?"

So calmly she spoke, so innocent she looked, that Dennis, to whom the whole scene had seemed funny enough, lost amusement in admiration of the perfect guilelessness of this beautiful girl. He was ready to follow her any and everywhere, as with another joyous smile she turned to him from Janet and said: "I'm glad you've come. You look tired; you shall rest in our cool little parlor while Janet gets lunch."

Janet stood before them. With homely, excited face and bony, upraised arm, she did not look like the typical angel. Yet she was resolute as the one whose flaming sword had sent the first man and woman homeless into an empty world. And no paradise could be more desired than that little parlor where Dennis hoped he might for a time feast ear and sight on the charms of this perfect creature. It seemed an unattainable paradise, however, for Janet still interposed herself between it and him.

"What would your feyther think, Miss Mary, what would your feyther say, should he know? To tak a stranger into yer ain house! It isna decent!" she cried.

"My father would have me do right," Mary answered calmly. "Isn't it right to welcome the stranger guest? Hospitality is a sacred virtue, and even the heathen nations practice it. Would you who believe in Christ have me do less? Come," and she once more turned to

Dennis, „do not think Janet unkind. Move aside," she said to her nurse in gentlest authority.

Stepping back as Mary moved on nodding to Dennis to follow her, the woman caught his sleeve and whispered in his ear :

"Sir, sir. dinna wrang the child. In all her life she hasna luked upon the face o' mon. Only her feyther an' me has ever spoke to her."

Mary heard these words, and turning, raised her head with the pride an angel might feel.

"Wrong me, Janet? Who could wrong me while God protects me? And you would not, sir ; you feel kindly to me ; I know it because of what I feel to you. Don't be cross, my dear old nursey," and she patted Janet's sunburned cheek.

But Janet could not be soothed even by Mary's caresses. Her anxiety increased a second later, as going very close to Dennis and resting her cheek on her clasped hands, Mary looked full and long in the man's eyes.

"Ah !" she sighed, and then smiled. "You would not wrong any one. You could not look so true, so frank, if ever you had done wrong."

At these words a flush came to Dennis's honest face. Sins and errors long forgotten rose from the ashes of memory as he replied :

"Lady, I have done many things I would not show to your pure eyes. But believe me, once having seen you will make me better for all future time."

"Gallanteries, gallanteries !" groaned Janet, looking at the pair, who, gazing into each other's eyes, had forgotten her. "What has come over the world? My bairn is lost, my bairn is lost. Gude God protect her !"

"Come, Janet, dear Janet, and get the lunch," Mary called from the open door as she entered.

"I'll come," Janet answered, wringing her hands as she talked to herself: "Fule, fule, not to hae told her o' the wickedness o' mon. Yet I darena ! How dare I when her feyther said he'd tech her a' she should know. But I'll watch o'er her, and deil catch that mon ef he dares breathe a word to hurt her."

She shook her fist at the unconscious Dennis, who at the moment was innocent of all thought except one of wonder at Mary's loveliness.

" I'll watch ye, I'll watch ye, wi' your bonny face an' leein' tongue !" Janet muttered, feeling greater reliance on her watching to keep harm from Mary than the power of the " Gude God " she so often invoked.

With another threatening gesture at Dennis the Scotchwoman entered the house, deciding that the sooner the luncheon was made ready the sooner she could be rid of the unwelcome guest.

Mary was in her room pouring water into the crystal basin " for the stranger," she said, looking smilingly at Dennis, who in the hall stood watching her. Something in his face pleased even Janet. Her hard look softened, and unperceived by Mary, she whispered :

" Sir, sir, will ye gang as soon as ye hae eaten ? The bairn's as innocent as a new-born babe. She knaws na sin, na guile ; she hae lived her whole life far frae the haunts o' men. Her feyther's a cruel mon. He loes her noo, but wad he loo her did he knaw she hae done what he wadna hae her do ?"

The woman's eyes had tears in them. Her large mouth and unattractive face, twitching nervously, told of her sincerity, and touched Dennis's heart.

Should this fair girl suffer through him ? No, that must not be.

" I will go now," he said to Janet.

" Na, na, not noo ; the mischief's done, an' the bairn hae set her heart on the lunch ; but after—will ye ?"

" Yes." He had just time to say it as Mary turned. " The water is ready. Go in and refresh yourself."

She gave a gracious wave of her hands, and then a smile parting her lips and a pink flush coming to her cheeks, she said in much the same coaxing manner she had used to Janet: "Don't be long. You may wish soon to go away, and I have so much to say."

She moved across the hall, standing in the doorway of the sitting-room as sunshine against shadow. She turned, looking over her shoulder at Dennis, while, as from every place she stood, there came the perfume of roses.

"What is your name?" she asked with a soft laugh.

"Dennis Day."

"And mine is Mary Hilton."

Then bending her head, she vanished in the darkness. Mary Hilton! This then was the daughter of that cruel man who guarded and ruled convicts! No wonder tears came to Janet's eyes. Dennis's brain reeled as he thought from what vile mud had sprung this spotless lily. He stood a moment just as she had left him, gazing after her. Then entering the bedroom, closed the door, and looking around her snowy chamber, adored the purity of a pure maid.

———◆———

CHAPTER XV.

A WORLD OF DELIGHT.

HE was only a few moments in washing away the traces of his dusty journey, yet, as he rejoined Mary she held up her hand in playful reproach.

"How long you have been! Janet came twice to see if you were ready. And now I fear you will be gone be-

fore I ask half I long to know. Shall I call Janet and
bid her hasten ? Or will you sit and talk with me ?"

She motioned him to an easy chair opposite her own,
and near to which she had drawn a little table holding a
bouquet of white roses.   Their fragrance filled the room
and seemed the essence of her own fair spirit.

It was not in the nature of man to refuse the entreaty
of that sweet face smiling in the security of not being
refused. The cruel father, Janet's tears, hunger, fatigue,
all were forgotten.

" I'm in no hurry, and am only too glad to do anything you wish," Dennis answered, as he seated himself,
his handsome face in a glow of pleasure.

She clapped her hands gleefully, and then with a
glance at the door as if fearing Janet's summons to lunch
—"Quick ! quick !" she said, "tell me how you lost
your arm."

He started. She had asked the very thing of all he
would have kept from her. Was he to tell this white
soul of man's inhumanity to man ? Was he to brush
from her nature the dew of perfect innocence, letting fall
on it the blight of the knowledge of evil ?

She saw his hesitation. "Oh, tell me." Her clasped
hands were extended on her lap and her eyes raised in
pleading.   Could he do less than grant her wish ?

" It will sadden you," he answered. "Not the loss
of my arm. My whole body, is worth one of those bright
tears you shed at the sight of this empty sleeve," he
quickly went on, flushing as he spoke. "But the cause
was a great cause, and the war a grievous one."

" It was truth, wasn't it ?" she questioned ; "History ?"
And as he bowed his head she said. "I must know all
truth whose knowledge is not evil. If I suffer perhaps
it will be taken as part atonement for some wrong. Do
not delay ; we waste time. Janet has told me pressing
business awaits you, and I must not keep you long."

Thus adjured, Dennis in as few words as possible, and softening its horrors, told the story of the war. Without mention of party, without display of feeling, but as one afar looks down on some terrible struggle and describes its cause, continuance and results to an innocent child. Mary, her hands pressed together, her eyes fixed on his face and tears falling down her white cheeks, listened in rapt attention.

"I never knew of this," she murmured. "And in this war you lost your arm. God bless you!" Her hand rested on his empty sleeve, her eyes were raised in solemn prayer. The man's heart thrilled as he looked at her. He felt himself in the presence of an angel and would not break the silence she made so beautiful.

A moment more and her eyes came to his face. "Is it not strange, living as you say, in the land where the negroes are in great numbers, I have never seen one. Poor souls! To be born black!" And then, with sudden motion, rising and bringing her Bible open at the story of Ishmael, "See, he must have been the founder of their race."

Then she put the book from her, giving him her full attention as she asked:

"Did you know these negroes? Had you friends among them?" He shook his head. "No! And you periled your life for them? You lost your arm to free from bondage a suffering people! You are a noble man!"

Dennis's face turned scarlet.

"Why do you turn so red? Are you angry?" She looked at him, her brows drawn in a trembling form of query that only made her lovelier.

"Angry! Could a man be angry with an angel?" he said impetuously. "No, Miss Mary, I am not angry, but embarrassed at being over-praised. I did nothing more than duty. Thousands of other men did the same. Thousands of them suffered, died and even lived martyrs for the cause of freedom."

"Does the number of those who do it lower a noble deed?" Mary asked.

He did not answer and she went on : "Do you not suffer? Is it no pain to have lost your right arm?"

He could not answer. At that moment he was suffering pain, exquisite pain. For he looked at this lovely creature and remembered bitterly his own maimed body. Perfect as she was, her very womanhood made love a necessity to her, and some man might win her, some man who—he bit his lip. He could not think of such a possibility while he could look upon her face, flushed by excitement, and those eyes suffused with pity and tenderness. Yes, tenderness, but not for him ! What was he, to waken one throb of personal feeling other than the divine tenderness a seraph feels for suffering humanity?

"Why do you not speak?" she asked, her face growing more wistful. "Is it not noble to offer one's life for principle? And though whole armies do it, does not each man suffer as an individual, die as one? Ah, don't be hurt because I call you noble !"

She rested her hand on his. He longed to kiss its fairness, but he would not startle her, and looked away from the pretty temptation resting confidingly on his own strong hand. Meeting her wistful eyes, he smiled whereat she laughed with pleasure, and then asked, as if confident of his answer : "Tell me what brings you here so far from your home, and why you walk across the country ?"

Again he hesitated, dreading to show her too much of the crime and sin of the world. And again her pleading forced him to it.

He told her of the hot morning, the crowded court-room, of the conviction of an innocent man, the grief of an unfortunate woman. and making light of his own part in the sad picture he finished by asking :

"Could a man do less ?"

He saw the reverence in her eyes and felt abashed even to the earth. Her face turned from white to rosy red, her eyes brightened.

"Hero!" she said. "A hero!" and with a swift graceful bend of her head pressed her soft lips to his hand.

The touch of those lips opened to this man a world of delight. That hand became his dearest possession. "O'Neal! Julie!" she murmured. "And the baby, what is it's name?" she asked, laughing when Dennis gave a quaint description of that little copper-faced philosopher. She was silent for a moment, and then said—

"Now tell me something more of the great world. Tell me of some happiness. Surely in a place so large there must be many who are happy?"

"Happy! yes, surely!" answered Dennis, searching in memory's storehouse for some happy lives to show to the girl. But he was at a loss. Sorrow, disappointment and too often despair—these were the pictures of life that rose before him, all teaching the one great lesson "endurance."

"Hurry," she cried with pretty impatience. Smiles on her lips and entreaty in her eyes. "Janet will soon come, and then you must go. I dread the sound of her step."

Tempted thus by an angel, Dennis was about to supply fact with fiction, when there came to his rescue the jolly face of Brown and his comfortable enjoyment of his ten children. So he drew the picture of this happy man with young ones climbing all over him, and Mary clapping her hands laughed in delight.

"I shall think of them all, the robin-eyed children, the little copper baby, Julie and O'Neal. Ah, that is a wonderful world you tell of. If it has sorrow it has happiness too. For all the sufferings of Julie and O'Neal, think of the delight of their love!"

Her eyes in dreamy reverie were gazing at him, and

love with its madness was busy in his brain. But with scorn of his maimed body, his miserable condition, he drove out the bright spirit and called cold reason to his aid. But Love, that naughty elf, even while sobbing at this cruel treatment, sank deep his darts into the man's heart, and thence, laughing through his tears, sought shelter in the maiden's snowy breast.

While Janet in the kitchen was nearly strangled by smoke as she blew the fire, and in her nervous haste retarded matters, just so long those two in the little parlor wandered in a world of delight. Thought followed thought, as leaf by leaf the lovely flower of her mind unfolded to his ravished vision. Thus perfect, might Eve have been before she knew sin. But to find a like pearl now atop of this hard world was a marvel exceeding great.

"Will you please come to lunch?" Janet at the door let in the prosaic on the pretty poem.

"Come," Mary said with a sigh and a smile. She preceded Dennis into the bright little dining-room, where on a snowy table garnished with white roses was served a simple, dainty meal.

Janet, tall and straight, her gray hair covered by a white cotton cap, guarded her mistress, watching Dennis's every look. At last, taking an opportunity when pouring water into his glass and while Mary at the window holding back the curtain was showing him some favorite trees, Janet whispered:

"I pray ye gang, sir!"

Not knowing what the results of further delay would be to this fair creature, Dennis rose.

"Are you going so soon?" Mary asked. She had turned on hearing his chair moved, and as she spoke two bright tears sprang to her lovely eyes, more potent than Niagara's flood to him who looked upon her.

"I must go," Dennis answered, while Janet hastily interposed with: "Why, Miss Mary, it isna reet to ask the mon to stay. Gin ye wad keep him alway?"

"I wish I could," she murmured.

Words trembled on Dennis's lips, words that would have driven Janet into insanity, but he did not speak them. He only took the girl's hand, and bowing over it said more to himself than to her:

"I must go." He would not listen to his own madness, could not let her guilelessness entrap her.

As he spoke she smiled through her tears, remembering his mission, and that in telling her he had cautioned secrecy. "Forgive me," she said; "go, and God speed you!"

She followed him to the door, and despite Janet's protest, to the gate. Dennis tried to slip money in Janet's hand. But the old woman drew her hand away.

"Nay, I dinna want your goold," she whispered. "An ye harm my bairn, I wad die afore I teched aught. frae ye. An ye wish her weel, I'm paid enoo."

Mary did not hear the words or see the gesture. She was plucking a blossom from her rose-bush.

"Take it," she said, offering it to Dennis. "May it remind you of a friend. I am your friend and you are mine, are you not?"

"Forever," he answered. Taking the flower and pressing her hand he hastily closed the gate, not trusting himself to look again at her. Quickly he walked on. He dreaded lest she should see his agitation.

"Dennis!" her voice calling, made him turn. She was on the road standing outside the gate. As he walked back to her she hurried to meet him, while Janet followed wringing her hands.

"Good-by! good-by!" Mary held his one hand in both of hers. "I could not let you go without another word. You will come back some time, some time? I shall miss you. Ah, how I shall miss you!"

Her eyes were full of tears, her innocent heart was on her lips! He might have kissed it off and carried it

in his breast.   But he only bowed his head until, reaching the white hands holding his, he touched his lips to
them reverently, as one might the holy of holies.

"I will come again," he said, and with another
"good-by" turned away.

----◆----

CHAPTER XVI.

ON TO THE RESCUE.

LIFE had changed for Dennis.   Was it possible that
only two hours had passed since he left the road
and walked toward the cottage?   He turned
once more to look at it, that he might carry in his heart
the perfect picture of that bower where lived the woman
he loved.   Yes, the woman he loved ;—he proclaimed it
to the warm, soft air, with glad triumph in his eyes.
Beautiful and fresh was the rose he held when she gave
it to him, and now in his hot hand already it drooped its
head.   He kissed it and put it near his heart.

He dared no longer linger, dared not steal away this
white dove and take her to poverty and privation.   His
maimed body, his empty purse and the bare little house
called his, passed before him.   His abilities, what were
they? He could write.   And now, with the great motive
power of making a home for her, he would write as
never before.   No more time-destroying reveries, no
more useless repinings, but work, work, work, and success!   He would succeed.   This hope, this new-born star,
illumined the whole firmament.

"I will come back. Mary, I will come back."

He took the crushed rose from his breast, kissed it,
and then walked on, leaving the small road and gaining
the highway.   He did not heed the dust and heat.   His

heart was strong with hope and that diviner something which men ridicule and yet in whose power each living man becomes as wax.

On he walked until in the distance he saw the camp. It was made up of a number of low buildings. As he drew nearer he saw lines of black—negroes chained together, he thought, and there came to him all that he had heard of the sufferings of this wretched class. During his long walk, whenever he had chanced to meet any of the country people who knew of the matter, he would question them about these convict camps, and their stories were all similar. Several of these camps existed in this and the neighboring States, and all alike were foul dens wherein flourished crime, brutality and cruelty in their direst forms. Of Hilton's barbarity numberless incidents were told—he heard of escaping convicts torn to pieces by bloodhounds loosened on them by his orders ; of dying negroes left to rot in the marshes. And when in a burst of honest wrath Dennis asked how they could permit such wrongs to exist, he was answered by shrugs and " We are not responsible for the sins of others ;" or, " Can the poor break down laws made by tho rich and powerful?" Some of those to whom he talked would deplore the cruel management of these camps and call them crying evils, but evils which they were powerless to remedy. Beyond the facts of Hilton's acknowledged cruelty and strength, he learned little, except that his reputation for honesty was good, that he was believed to be without family, and that he was a secretive man who made few friends. This was all Dennis knew of the head of the camp wherein O'Neal was confined, until fate led him to Mary's bower. As each step brought him nearer the camp, and the black lines took the shape of human beings, more and more incomprehensible appeared the character of one with life so repulsive who had yet carefully nurtured and con-

cealed this lovely child. "What would be the consequences to her if she finds out the truth?" This thought
sent a chill to his heart. "She must never know it! I
will make a home for her and keep her forever ignorant
of her father's sin." He held his head higher, his step grew
prouder as this determination mingled with his hopes.

The sun had set, and all the convicts were locked
in their night cells before he entered the camp. In the
moonlight the scene looked peaceful enough. Only the
guards pacing up and down made it unlike other coal
mines he had visited. Relieved at finding matters so
much better than he had anticipated, Dennis stood quietly
gazing about, when the wind rising brought to his nos-
trils a sickening stench. He had known too much of
that odor in war times not to recognize it—a decaying
human body was near!

Standing in the shadow of some old timbers and
looking over a wide expanse of what seemed marshy
ground, he saw lying in the grass—what? Could it be
a dead body? In his involuntary movement of disgust
he touched the timbers and one rolling off fell to the
ground with a loud noise, that roused from his sleep a
dog chained on the other side of the wood. With sharp
bark he sprang up, peering around the timbers, and striving to reach Dennis, who with his finger on the trigger
and pistol leveled, was ready to protect himself.

The great dog snarled at him, its fierce eyes and
gleaming teeth were distinct in the moonlight. It was
a bloodhound that had been trained to hunt down human
beings. What cruelty is possible to man!

The snarling of the dog had attracted attention.
Quick steps approached and some one called aloud:

"What is it, Nero?"

"Not an unpleasant voice," Dennis thought, and then
stepping suddenly into the moonlight he saw a young
fellow in a rough costume that he took for a uniform.

The man sprang back on seeing a stranger and drew his revolver. In an instant that of Dennis was gleaming in the light.

"Young man," he said, "I don't want any fighting, but unless you put your pistol away I'll try to get the first shot. I'm a stranger in these parts, and seeing houses concluded I'd stop for the night, when that snarling beast made me wonder into what hole I'd fallen."

"Wal, stranger," the guard replied, putting his pistol in his belt, "yer've jest got ter the wrong place. We ain't keepin' lodgers jest now, 'cept those that don't like ter stay. An' I don't blame 'em, pore devils," he added under his breath.

Dennis, following the guard's example, put away his weapon, and then he held out some cigars, saying as he produced a canteen : "At any rate, you're not a bad fellow. Let's have a smoke and a mouthful of whiskey. Then after I've rested you will perhaps be good enough to show me the road to the nearest town."

Accepting the invitation, and following up the first drink by several others, the guard grew communicative and confidential. He cursed the dull life of a convict keeper, and having enumerated its hardships he ended by pitying the convicts.

"Wal, it's tarnel hard ter see the pore devils whipped, anyway. An', I ain't sorry I was lef' ter night when the most on 'em is away on a hunt."

"A hunt?" interrogated Dennis.

"Yes, a hunt for a runaway."

"Has a convict escaped?"

"Yes, an' a likely-lookin' man ef he warn't a nig. I ain't quite used ter this place. Ain't been here long, an' allus had a kinder pity fer that nigger. Almos' hopes they won't cotch him. But it's no use. He'll be cotched sure. They do treat the niggers orful mean. But I can't help it. An' we gets tollerably well paid. Thar ain't

no questions axed ef a niggar dies. Ain't thar plenty
more ter fill his place ? But ef a convict gets away it's
another thing. We're obliged ter cotch him or the other
fellers 'ud get demoralized. Can't see how this tarnel
fool got off nohow. Hilton hed gone on a secret biz-
ness o' his own. A tight mouth that Hilton has—never
jokin' with any feller. Only we have our guesses o' his
secret trips acrost the lake. How did the nig escape?
Wal, while we was havin' a little game, Cæsar, the boss
dog o' the pack, was keepin' guard an' we was a bettin'
high. It was as pretty a hand as ever yer seed ter be
beat. I had four queens, another feller had a flush
straight. Sir, I hev made it an onfailin' rule never ter
slight the women. So I jest put up my queens fer all
they wos wuth. Just then some one sed, ' What's that?"
' Nothin,' sez I, an' raises it two. 'Air yer a fool,' Dick,
he shouts, ' ter keep on playin' when Cæsar's a yelpin'
like that !' Yet fer all Dick's talkin' he called me, an'
I'm blest ef he didn't put in his pocket every cent I've
saved. I wos jest swearin' I'd never set no more care
fer a woman, when in rushes a feller who had gone out
ter see. ' Fools,' he yells, ' ter be gamblin' when a nigger's cut and run !' Wal, we wosn't long gittin' out.
But Dick hed ter divide fearin' we'd peach, as he wos on
watch. So arter all, the women warn't so expensive.
But I'm darned ef I'll bet on 'em so sure next time."

"Did you find out which convict had escaped?"
Dennis asked, his sympathies excited for the runaway.

"Did we find out ? Wal, I should say so ! Cæsar
didn't give us a chance to look at any but the right cell.
Ef that dog ain't got a nose fer the niggers ! He was
pullin' like mad at his chain, an' tearing up the groun'
so I couldn't help a pityin' the pore devil ef Cæsar gets
hold on him. An' it was 'bout the only one o' the nigs
I had a soft feelin' for. He was sech a big, fine-made
nigger I called him a statyer the fust time I laid eyes on

him. We opened the night cell nearest Brown Cæsar and seen his empty bunk. Wal, sir, he warn't no statyer but jest a devil an' nuthin' else. That nigger had been kep' at work fer nigh on ter thirty-six hours, an' no more vittals than a good sized boy'd put away in one dinner. Ef some on the men who come about here axin' questions, talks 'bout 'overworkin' the convicts, I tells yer arter this nigger's escapin' I'll never believe they works enough. Jest ter think o' the devil's havin' pluck ter run away in the face o' that."

And the guard pointed to the marsh where a dark object lay.

"That's all that's left of one o' the runaways; an' afore he was sech a fool as ter try ter 'scape he wuz a reg'lar smart nigger. We're bound ter catch 'em. Yer see, the dogs rarely fails ter find the scent, an' nobody'd dar give a convict shelter. That nigger was cotched the very night he skipped the camp. How them dogs enjoyed the fight!"

"Poor wretches!" Dennis shuddered at the horrible thought. "Do you know the name of this last escaped convict?" he asked, feeling an interest in one who would dare make an effort for liberty. The guard with the canteen to his mouth drank leisurely, smacking his lips, and wiping them on the back of his hand before he answered:

"Convicts don't have none. They has numbers. But this was sech a fine nigger that I axed him once how he called hissef. He told me Tom O'Nief or O'Neal, suthin like that."

Tom O'Neal! Dennis was on his feet and the guard looked up with sleepy, drunken eyes.

"You're goin'?"

"Yes, I'll start. But it's just as well not to meet the guards with the captured convict. Tell me which road they took."

Dennis had to repeat his question and shake the guard a little, as the latter had just about reached the reflective stage of drunkenness, and with canteen in hand sat gazing at vacancy.

"Which road? Ha ! ha !" and he gave a thick laugh. "Most every road, I should say. The last road they took was thar," and he pointed in a vague sort of way across the lake. Although the moon was shining there was so much mist on the lake that Dennis could not see the opposite shore. He had noticed some boats moored at the side of the coal dumps and started in that direction, when hearing the guard speak he stopped for a moment, thinking perhaps that he might hear some further direction.

"Ha, ha ! you should ha' seen Hilton's face when they comed back and sed the dogs could find no scent ! An' no one had seen the nig. An' then ter see Brown Cæsar tear down across the marsh an' snarl an' bark, jest as ef he seen the nigger in the water. Hilton didn't want ter go that way ; he always takes that fer his secret rides. I'll be darned, tho', ef I'd like ter be the one ter tell him so, ha, ha !" Holding the canteen he was talking to it in maundering confidence, and was perfectly unconscious that Dennis had unfastened a boat and had pushed out from the camp.

Hugging the shore Dennis made a detour of part of the lake, seeking anything that looked like a road which might have been taken by the guards in pursuit of the convict. But the trees growing close together overhung the waters, and the thick undergrowth showed no signs of being trodden by the foot of man. The dark shade of the heavy branches, the ghostly effect of the moonlight shining upon the mist-covered waters, made the lake seem a wierd enchanted prison from which there was no outlet, no escape.

Dennis had just declared himself a fool to be misled

by a drunken guard, when his boat grated on a shelving bank near a small frame building that stood like a sentinel guarding the stillness.

The earth looked as if it had been recently trodden upon. Some boats were fastened to the bushes. He was convinced that this was the place he was in search of, and springing to the shore he gazed about him.

Great holes were dug into the soft loam, as if animals had there been seeking some hidden prey, "Brutes, brutes!" Dennis spoke aloud, as his heart thrilled at the thought of all O'Neal must have suffered and dared. He regarded him no longer as negro, but as a fellow-man fighting against cruel odds. He would help him if he possibly could. Dennis was thoroughly aroused—just as he had been during the war when he had started in some desperate undertaking ; and with head erect, with eyes and ears on the alert, he walked at double-quick on to the rescue.

CHAPTER XVII.

HER SNOWY NEST.

HILTON returning to the camp after his visit to his child, was met by the news of O'Neal's fight. How it was managed seemed a mystery, for the guards supported each other's testimony that every man was at his post. Even after the sawn log was discovered the mystery was not solved. The long grass faithfully hid all tracks, and the lake had never yet been tried by escaping convicts. So despite of Brown Cæsar's determination to go that way, Hilton ordered the search in other directions. He did not intend that curious guards should know of the lonely cottage where he had hidden his treasure, nor would he have Mary's peace broken by the tumult of this strange hunt. It was not until the evening of the first day, after the convicts were in their night cells and the guards around the table were joking about Hilton's refusing for the first time in his life to follow　lead of Brown Cæsar, that he appeared unexpectedly at the open door. The men instantly became silent, and the one who spoke last turned very red. "I'll lay two to one the Captain's hiding a sweetheart in that wood, an' he don't want us fellers to find her!" he had said, just before Hilton appeared. Had he heard? they could not tell. Stern, Hilton's lieutenant, stood beside him. His was a smooth, pleasing face, a cold cruel nature. The guards knew him and feared him too, suspecting that he sometimes acted as a spy upon them. "Hurry with your supper. We start across the lake as soon as possible." Hilton spoke to all, but the guard who had last spoken felt that the Captain's stern looks were for him.

The sun had set, and the moon was just rising as the hunters started—hunters of human game. Brown Cæsar, fiercely snarling, was impatient to be off. Leading their horses, the men in small boats crossed the waters. As they approached the narrow road near the little stable, Brown Cæsar tearing loose from his keeper, gave a spring, lighting by instinct on the very spot where O'Neal exhausted had fallen for a moment's rest.

Tearing savagely at the earth, the dog kept on growling and snarling, and then, after a moment, with his nose near the ground, started off. Following his lead the other dogs in a group kept close at his heels, and immediately after them came the guards, with Hilton at their head.

"Silence," the Captain ordered. And so with no other noise than the deadened sounds of horses' hoofs, and an occasional yelp from a dog, the party advanced upon the fugitive who, burning and shivering, lay in the bushes.

Burning with fever, shaking with chills, alternating between delirium and stupor, O'Neal passed the day that saw Mary and Dennis talking in the shaded parlor, and Captain Hilton with guards and dogs scouring the country for miles around for the missing convict. Julie far away, well nigh despairing, was praying for her husband, who lay by the roadside, perishing.

Coldly shone the moon on his face, calmly looked down the stars from Heaven upon him. Angels of God, where are ye? Unweeping and unpitying can ye survey such scenes? Perhaps some angel did minister to him as a result of Mary's tender prayers for the Julie and O'Neal of Dennis's story. For suddenly starting from a stupor, O'Neal raised his head to listen. What sounds were those? Growlings, snarlings, yelps! The dogs were out! And nearer, nearer came the sound of galloping horses. No fever now, no wandering fancies—this was stern reality. He sprang to his feet and rushed through the undergrowth.

He falls to the ground, but instantly he is up again and running for his life! A light shines ahead. Nearer, nearer come those fearful sounds of pursuit! No shelter but in that house where the light gleams. Reach it he must. Enter he will. Even devils would give him shelter.

At the gate he fell again, but again the air heavy with horrible sounds forced him up and on. He reached the window and saw with despairing eyes a figure with long hair kneeling in adoration. So had Julie prayed! He pulled up the sash and as the girl rose and faced him, her expression changing from sudden terror to heavenly pity, he fell prostrate before her.

"Save me!" he cried. "I'm a convict, but innocent. Save me! If you shut me out I shall be torn to pieces by the dogs. Hear them!"

Yes, curdling her blood with terror came the wild
yelps of dogs, the voices of men urging them on. Before her in filthy rags, with torn and bleeding flesh, knelt
a miserable black man. God had sent Lazarus to her!
Cast him out? Never! Poor unhappy brother! Turn
aside from him whom God had sent? No! Far easier
to die than do this great wrong.

"Hide me, hide me," cried the distracted creature,
feeling his senses leaving him.

She hurriedly looked around, seeking some place of
safety. Where in that snowy chamber could she hide
him? All was fair and open as her own pure life. At
her garden gate there were savage dogs. Hear their
fierce growls, hear them tearing up the ground. They
would find him. They would kill him! She would die
with him. No, no, she must save this life intrusted to
her! Her hand in sweet protection rested on his head.
Her eyes in supplication were raised to God, her body
was quivering in an agony of nervousness.

"Where, where, show me! O God, show me!"

Again came that awful tearing at the gate. With a
crash it fell.

"Quick, under the bed," she whispered, stooping to
arrange the white drapery that in graceful folds hung
around it.

For an instant the negro's hand rested on her shoulder. "God bless you," he said.

She dropped the drapery and running closed the
open window, starting back in affright. There against
the glass, glaring at her, was pressed the fierce head of
some wild beast. The gaping red mouth, the gleaming
white teeth, the glittering eyes seemed to belong to a
fiend about to tear from her the victim hidden in her
snowy nest. Paralyzed by terror she hardly breathed,
and then clasping her hands: "Save him, O God, save
him!" she cried.

As if in answer to her prayer the savage head disappeared. But an instant later at the outer door she heard the tearing of those fearful fangs,—and then men's voices raised in loud discussion. Suddenly the door was thrown violently open, and as a voice shouted, " Hold him !" a huge dog bounded in. He stopped, with forepaw uplifted and nose extended sniffing the air ; then with a fierce growl he sprang upon Mary as she barred his path in the doorway, and fastening his teeth in her shoulder, bore her to the ground. A hoarse shriek, a loosening of those sharp teeth, a face she knew !

" Father !" she cried, and, smiling, fainted.

CHAPTER XVIII.

A TERRIBLE COMBAT.

WITH a growl that made the men in the hall crowd nearer the door, the dog turned on his assailant. His sinews stood out under the brown skin, his eyes glittered like balls of fire, and the huge mouth, gaping from ear to ear, showed to this father the white fangs dripping with his daughter's blood. As he kept his iron grip on the huge throat Hilton looked hardly more human than the beast.

For a second the combatants glared at each other ; a second, and then began a feaful struggle. Over and over rolled the man and brute, grappling, tearing, growling ; so close were they in this terrible contest that none dared fire with the hope of killing the beast. And over all—that still white figure, that horrible struggling group—streamed the bright light from Mary's chamber. In silent terror the guards looked on, some with pistols

ready, but none advanced.   Who would bring upon himself the rage of that fierce animal, infuriated by the taste
of blood?

The dog was uppermost, and with his fangs fastened
in Hilton's throat, with muttering growls he seemed
about to rend him to pieces, when in a supreme effort
the man rose above the animal.   Tearing himself loose
he pressed his knees upon the huge writhing body, with
bloody hands holding down that terrible head.

"Fire, cowards!" he gasped.

A shot, and Brown Cæsar lay dead.

Janet, who in sleep had heard the noise and confusion, waked at the shot.   Starting out of bed she listened.
"What did it mean?"   Throwing on a shawl, she rushed
to the hall.   On the floor in a pool of blood lay an
immense dog, while with bleeding hands and throat,
with agonized face bending over something white, knelt
her master.   At that moment, like a blast from a furnace,
there came to him the memory of that curse.   By his
own blood should he taste despair.   Taste it!   He was
draining it to the very dregs in this instant's agony.

Janet gazed at Hilton's face in affright.   "What was
it a'?   What made the master look sae strange?"   Then
she saw the white body in his arms, and rushed, toward
him, "My bairn, oh my bairn!" she sobbed, not noticing
that the hall was full of men, seeing only Mary and her
bleeding shoulder.   She caught the limp white hand,
felt for the pulse, and then wailed, "She's dead, she's
dead!   My ain, ain bairn!"

She had no care for Hilton now.   What mattered to
her his commands or wishes?   She had lost the only
thing she had ever loved, and tears poured down the
hard face.

"Hush your screeching!   Don't you see she has only
fainted?"   Hilton's voice was hard and dry.   His lips
were trembling.   He could barely speak.

Roughly he pushed Janet away, for the old woman had striven to take the girl. "Move aside," he said hoarsely, then as tenderly as a mother with her sick babe placed his daughter on her bed, bandaged the wound to stop its bleeding, bathed her brow and moistened her lips. For an instant he hung over her, listening to her faintly coming breath, apparently relieved, and regardless of his own torn hands and wounded throat, he went out into the hall to the waiting guards. With a heavy frown he walked up to the one who had dared suggest that in this house the convict was hidden. "Come," he said between his teeth, "you who are the cause of this; come, search the house."

In vain the man protested: "No, no," he said, "I am satisfied."

"Satisfied!" Hilton started as if he would spring at his throat, but he restrained himself. "D'ye hear me? Come!" he grasped the man's wrist, dragging him to the door of Mary's chamber. White and still lay the girl. At her side sat the weeping, anxious Janet. Surely there was nothing there but sorrow, sweetness and purity.

"What do you see?" asked Hilton, shaking with fury. His words sounded like a threat, his face was distorted by rage; but he said nothing more and stood awaiting the guard's answer.

"I—I see nothing," stammered the man, trying to release his arm.

Into every room of the little house, opening each closet, forcing him to look into each corner, Hilton dragged the guard. Out into the garden torn by the dogs' claws they went; no other tracks were visible, yet down near the earth Hilton pushed the man's head. Then once more at the door he stopped, still grasping the guard's arm.

"What have you seen?" sneered Hilton.

"Nothing," answered the man.

"Nothing!" With a bitter laugh Hilton held the guard close to him as he hissed in his face: "If she dies, I'll tear you limb from limb!" and then threw him back so violently that he fell to the ground.

Without looking at the fallen man he strode into the house. "Back to the camp," he said to the men whispering in the hall. "The damned nigger has escaped."

Glad to get away, the guards soon untied the dogs fastened outside the gate, and mounting their horses returned whence they came.

For an instant Hilton stood in the garden looking after their rapidly disappearing figures, then glanced around. Disorder and confusion where beauty had been. Trampled even unto the earth lay the bush of white roses. Her flowers! With a groan he went into the house and into his daughter's room. She was stirring, she would soon be conscious.

"My darling," he murmered, touching her brow with his lips. Then snatching from Janet a towel she had brought to him, he bound it around his throat, concealing the wound.

"I am going for a doctor," he said hastily, turning away. At the door he stopped, looked at Janet and frowned heavily. "Don't let her know I've been here to-night," he whispered, and left the room.

CHAPTER XIX.

STEPPING HEAVENWARD.

SPRINGING on his horse and putting him into a run, Hilton turned toward the city of Milton. Hardly had the sounds of his horse's feet died in the distance when Mary opened her eyes and looked at Janet.

"My bairn, my bonny, bonny bairn," cried the old woman, tears of sorrow changed to joy.

"Where is he, Janet?" Mary asked, as she glanced around searchingly, and not noticing Janet's agitation.

"Where is he?" Janet repeated Mary's words, and then said to herself: "Now comes the lee!" She cleared her throat, giving herself time to explain away as a delusion Captain Hilton's presence. "Where is who, my Mary?" For, not quick at invention, she could think of no other answer than this question, which would give her time to form the lie she must tell.

"Who?" Mary's eyes came back to her face. "Who?" and then there crept a something like horror as there sprang into her mind the fear that the one she would have died to save had been carried away. "O Janet, have you not seen him? He was here in this room. The convict, the negro—Lazarus, whom God sent to me."

"Gude God, save my bairn! Her's mind's ganged, her mind's ganged. She's mad, she's mad!" Janet thought as she tried to soothe the girl, who with her hand pressed to her head was striving to remember what had happened.

"Janet, a poor, unhappy black man came through that window. I tried to save him. I—quick, quick, —look under the bed."

"Under the bed! Oh, my bairn, my bairn's daft!" Believing Mary mad, Janet to soothe her did as she desired, but started back in horror as she raised the drapery.

"Lord save us!" she screamed, springing to the other side of the room, "a naiger, naiger!" Then remembering Mary she ran to the bed to take the girl in her arms and carry her from the room tainted by that black thing. But her shoulder, that awful wound she had seen Hilton bind! She dared not stir the girl or it might bleed afresh.

"My bairn, my bairn, there's a mon hidin' under the bed! A naiger! a black naiger!" she whispered.

Mary's fervent "Thank God," bewildered the woman. Her amazement and horror increased, as Mary hurriedly told her that while praying God to let her be of comfort to the needy, she heard the window raised, and, turning saw the negro. "He is a convict, Janet, but he is innocent."

"An who told ye that, Mary ?"

"He did," she answered solemnly, while Janet, shaking her head and wringing her hands, cried out :

"Gude God, protect my innocent bairn !"

"Ah, Janet, if father will only come to-night he will take this innocent man and keep him safe and well until the danger is over."

"Your feyther !" Janet started to her feet as there flashed through her mind the scene in the hall. Mary in saving the negro, had rushed into the jaws of death, and Hilton had killed the dog ! Again Janet heard his words to the guard with whom he had searched the house : "Is there anything in this room ?" "Gude God ! an' a' the time that black mon was under her bed !" The woman's teeth fairly chattered as she thought what Hilton might do, if he ever knew the truth. "He will kill her ! I must save my bairn !"

Her strong Scotch prejudice against the negro was forgotten in fear for Mary. Janet knew Hilton's occupation. In her yearly visits to the city, where she went to make purchases for Mary, she had heard frequent mention of the convict camp ; sometimes she had been told tales of the cruelties practiced on the convicts. But having no particular sympathy with anything down-trodden, and feeling an antipathy for the negro, she had dismissed the subject with, "It's nane o' my matters." and had attended to the business in hand. Now that Mary had taken into the house one of those "naigers," now that she had periled her life for him, and thus arrayed herself in battle against her father, Janet was appalled.

What could she do? Where could she hide? How could she get him to the door? She raised her white curtain and looking at the negro she saw that he was either ill or drunk. In spite of prejudice she did not think him drunk. She put the end of one finger on his head, quickly withdrawing it. The head was scorching hot, and even at that slight touch the man moaned, opened eyes that held no vision, and then moaning again, closed them.

"Gude God! if only he'd dee!" Janet said fervently, But even his dead body must not be found under Mary's bed. Perhaps Captain Hilton might take a fancy to lift that drapery? She must get the creature away. She'd take him to her own room rather than harm should come to Mary. But how could she get him to the door. And then—Mary's innocence might reveal the secret!

"Miss Mary!" At her name the girl unclosed her eyes. The pain in her shoulder was great, and her whole body was throbbing, yet now that the convict was safe she felt only thankfulness. "Don't worry, Janet, dear;" and she tried to smile on the anxious face. "I'll soon be well. And oh! I feel so blessed now the negro is all right."

"A' reet!' Janet groaned, "yes, yes, he'll be a' reet. An' ye'll listen to me, the mon's safe. The law o' the lan' wud mak' us gie him back e'en tho' he be innocent."

"Give him back! Never, Janet." Mary had sprung up in bed, her eyes wide opened in horror; but turning faint with pain she fell back white as her pillows. Janet wrung her hands. She thought Mary had swooned. But after a few moments the girl spoke again, and though the voice was low there was no yielding in it.

"I will never give up the innocent! Cruelty may be the law of the land, but there is a higher law—justice, the law of God."

Mary's face was flushing with fever, so although

Janet felt the utmost repugnance to the negro and in her own mind was fully convicted of his guilt, she would have bitten off her tongue rather than say it.

"God knows I'd a'most let in the de'il if it wud serve Mary," she said to herself, and added aloud : "Weel, my bairn, to please ye I will na' gie up the naiger. I'll tak' him in my ain room, nurse him 'til he's weel, an' gie him a bit o' siller to help him when he gangs."

"God bless you, Janet," Mary murmured.

"But God's blessing wudna do ony gude, an' ye tell your feyther."

"Ah, Janet, you forget how true and kind my father is. He would not shut the door to the homeless nor give up the innocent to punishment."

"Weel, weel, bairn, he may be a' that : but he's a mon. An' a man maun obey the law o' the lan' e'en if we women dinna. An' ye tell your feyther ye hae taken in a convict, that for his life ye hae held your ain life as nought, sure as God lives, your feyther'll gie up the mon to the law. Ye see, my bairn, he maun do it, else the law makes a convict o' him. Ye wudna like that, Mary? An' ye keep it frae him, the mon'll be a' reet; the law shall na' know, an' yer feyther is the fair guid man he olways was. Can ye, for God's love, can ye keep the secret?"

Full of terror lest Hilton should return before the negro was hidden, Janet could not give Mary time for thought. And Mary would not answer at once. For the first time in her pure life there came two diverging paths. Which was right? Must she deceive her father? Must she betray the convict? The delicate brows in their trembling frown, the earnest eyes full of doubt, looked at Janet's offered alternative.

"But, Janet," she said, with a puzzled look still on her face, "when the dog sprang upon me, and the horrible fear that he would rush into my room and find the negro made me ill, it was my father who pulled him off, my father who smiled at me. His face was full of love, he seemed to say : 'Well done, my child.'"

"Yes, yes, Mary, but nae feyther o' thine wud do it. Or any feyther for that matter. But it was only fancy that ye saw your feyther's face"—for Janet suddenly remembered Hilton's orders. "An' mind me, Mary, sure as your feyther knows the mon is here, he will gie him back to his prison. Keep the secret, Mary. Keep the secret, my bairn. Ye needna lee. Ye wrang nae person. Your feyther will never ask ye. Keep the secret and the mon is safe. Tell it, an' the naiger ye believe innocent maun gang back to prison."

Still Mary hesitated. To bind herself to a secret from her father seemed a wrong done to him.

"Promise quick, my bairn, an' I'll tak' the mon to my room an' mak' him easy. He is sick—like to dee. Promise quick ! An' sure as God hears me I'll be good to him as to my ain brither."

A groan from O'Neal in support of Janet's words hurried Mary's decision, and still with her trembling frown and unsatisfied eyes she said :

"I promise."

"Thank God," Janet ejaculated. Being of the practical order she only returned gratitude for those affairs that terminated according to her desires.

Knowing there was no time to lose she ran to her room, took a mattress from her bed, and opening the door of a large closet whose only outlet was through her chamber, made a comfortable pallet on the floor.

Then arranging her own bed, and making the room orderly, she ran back to Mary's couch to meet the apparently insurmountable difficulty of moving the sick man.

"How can I move that big naiger ?" she asked herself as she raised the drapery and looked at him. Then summoning all her strength, for there were not many moments to spare, she took his hand expecting to drag him out.

"Come !" she said, giving a little shake to rouse him. To her surprise the man crawled from under the bed, and holding to her hand, rose to his feet.

His bleeding body, his filthy rags and eyes wild with fever, filled Janet with disgust. Her antipathy was so great she could hardly bear the touch of his hot hand on her arm, by which he steadied his uncertain steps.

But Mary seeing him only felt tender pity. "Poor Lazarus," she murmured. "God will help you."

The man stopped, looked at her with bloodshot eyes, tried to say something, but his speech was thick.

"Come ! come !" urged Janet. She helped him to the closet, bathed his torn flesh, covered him warmly, and then having bound his head with wet towels, put a little sweet milk between the hard, dry lips. He muttered something, and then seemed to sleep.

"Poor deevil," Janet said, scrubbing her hands, "I hae sed I'd never tech one o' them naigers, but nae soul knows how low he may fa'."

Had she fallen, or was she stepping heavenward ?

———————◆———————

CHAPTER XX.

MARY.

SOFTLY turning her key and putting it in her pocket, Janet hurried back to Mary. When passing along the hall she noticed for the first time that not only was the dog's body gone, but the blood was washed away and a rug covered the stains—a rug that had been stored away in the large closet.

"That Hilton's a de'il," she said ; steppin' sae leet o' foot. God grant he will nae want to get aught out o' that closet again."

But when she saw Mary sitting up in bed, her face scarlet with fever, while through the bandages on her shoulder oozed that fearful blood, she lost thought or fear for anything except the girl.

In her delirium Mary was thinking of the convict. "Protect him, O God ! Take my life, but spare his who has suffered so much."

"Gude God! the bairn will tell her secret in her ravin's," cried the distracted Janet as each moment she expected the arrival of Hilton with the doctor.

Then, as soothed into quiet, Mary's eyes, upturned, covered their gray with half-closed lids, and her breathing, hot with fever, came in short gasps, Janet hung over her in fear, "She will dee, she will dee. Oh, my bairn ! Will they never come, or is it the world they're stoppin' to mak," she said, as moments sped on and Mary's life seemed hanging by a thread.

After what was an age to the anxious woman she heard a carriage. "Thank God !" she cried. Then with a last look at Mary she ran to her room, listened at the closet door—all was quiet. She locked it, put key in her pocket, locked also the door of her room, and then ran down the hall as the carriage stopped before the gate.

Night had fled. The sky was lightened by dawn, with here and there a fleck of crimson telling of the splendor of the coming day, when Janet opened the front door as the doctor walked up the path.

The tall, spare figure of Janet, with nose and eyes reddened by weeping, appeared more than usually unattractive.

"Not an ideal Goddess of morn," thought the doctor. Then bowing with old-school elegance, he said :

"Mrs. Janet Wilson, I presume."

Janet answering with a curtsey, he added : "I received your note. It is not my custom to attend patients out of the city. But your carriage being at the door and the summons urgent, I have come."

"Yes, yes," answered Janet, unable longer to control her impatience. "It's all reet. But I pray ye'll come to my bairn—my young leddy !" she corrected herself.

"Doctor Colton," said the old gentleman, "allow me to introduce myself."

He had been wondering how this woman, evidently a servant, had been able to command money and a carriage to send for him, the physician who stood at the head of the profession in Milton, and who now rarely took outside practice, delegating to his assistants all but those intricate cases, whose treatment would redound greatly to his credit and reputation.

When the summons came he had at first declined to go ; but the mysterious " young lady " referred to in the note, and a certain sleeplessness which had been annoying the doctor, decided him favorably.

The considerable sum of money accompanying the letter, while of itself no temptation to a very rich man, indicated that the "young lady" must be a person of some importance. And as Dr. Colton knew all the families in and around Milton, and had not heard of any important late arrivals, the visit to the injured young lady acquired the flavor of adventure. This simple cottage, this ugly old Scotchwoman, seemed to give a very commonplace conclusion to the adventure. The disordered garden was doubtless the consequence of some brawl, and the lovely injured woman a creature of his imagination ; he thought in disgust, for the Doctor was an aristocrat, from his wellset head to the tips of his fingers. And in spite of the facts that his age shaded sixty, and his skin was sallowed by time, he was accounted a "fine man," and one of the most eligible bachelors in the State. He had passed the enthusiastic age. His profession now was only attractive to him when it brought him some unfamiliar phase of disease. But now he was here and would do his duty however commonplace the patient.

"I pray ye, come." Janet tried to hasten the methodical movements of the old gentleman, who was removing his gloves with care and precision. Her face grew more unlovely in her nervousness as she looked up and down the road expecting to see Hilton.

"Where *is* the mon ?" she asked herself ; and then the doctor's preparations, even to rubbing his hands, being over, he signified his readiness with :

"Mrs. Wilson, I am at your service."

She preceded him into Mary's room, drawing aside the curtain and letting in the light of the morning on a picture that surprised him. The soft pink of the sky tinted with its flush the snowy chamber, resting on the beautiful girl whose long fair hair lay over the pillow partly covering the white throat. Her eyes were closed, but the dark lashes resting on the fair cheeks, the perfect shape of face and head, left nothing to be desired.

Gently, not disturbing her quiet, Doctor Colton removed the bandages, examined the wound, and then whispered to Janet :

"You wrote me the lady had been injured by a pet dog : had you any reason to believe the dog was mad ?"

"Na, na," Janet answered, not knowing what to say, and fearing in some way to displease Captain Hilton, who might be within hearing.

"It is a deep wound," the doctor went on, examining it critically and probing gently with his fingers, while Mary, still unconscious, moaned with pain. "A very deep wound. The animal must have been of unusual size. Where is it ? I must examine it."

"An' it's dead ; killed," Janet answered, using as few

words as possible, and still nervously afraid of the invisible Hilton.

"Dead! The idiocy of killing a dog under these circumstances,"—the doctor was talking to himself—"and necessitating severe treatment of such a wound, and such a patient! Leaving her imagination to conjure up the possible horrors of hydrophobia! Fools, knaves and victims make up the world!"

Meanwhile he prepared a solution to syringe the wound. "Poor child," he said, applying the acid to the bleeding flesh while Mary gave a cry of pain. She opened her eyes, looking steadily at him, and then said softly :

"Who are you that smiles so kindly on me? Your face is unlike my father's, unlike Dennis's? Oh," and she sprang up in bed with uplifted hands in horror. "I know you now. You are a minister of the law. You have come for that poor creature, Lazarus! Lazarus sent by God for me to protect. You shall not have him, not if I die first! It is a sacred charge, and God's law is mightier than yours. You may have armies, but He has legions of angels! Oh, save the miserable, and unhappy!"

She opened wide her arms, invoking heavenly aid. Her terror changed to sublime confidence ; and if at her words Heaven's angels had appeared, not one in the radiant band could have been lovelier than the girl who at this moment delighted Dr. Colton's artistic taste as much as she aroused his curiosity. There was more hidden here than the bite of a pet dog, the doctor thought, while administering medicine to break the fever and soothe her into quiet. Then, as gradually she sank to sleep, he used the physician's privilege of questioning the attendant.

"What agitated the young lady at the time of the accident ?"

"I wasna wi' her," Janet answered, looking at the

doctor with her small shrewd eyes, and then back at Mary resting quietly.

"Who was with her?" the doctor persisted, determined to force the canny Scotswoman to give a satisfactory answer.

Not seeming to understand, and with an expression of thorough stupidity, Janet replied : "Yes, yes, I went to my young leddy the minit I heard the noise, and found her lyin' fainted."

"Who killed the dog?" The doctor thought he would change his base of action.

"I dinna ken." Janet closed her lips as if she never intended to open them.

"What is the lady's name?"

"Mary." She opened her mouth only wide enough to emit the single word.

"Has she no other name?" The doctor was beginning to be vexed at this obstinacy. He who found himself sometimes bored by the confidences of his patients, was thus defied by a serving woman. The eccentric man considered himself particularly aggrieved, and had it not been for the rare and delicate loveliness of the patient, it is probable that his first visit would have been his last. Janet made no answer to his question, and he turned angrily away ; but his eyes falling on Mary his anger was softened.

"Mary," he said gently, "a fitting name for so fair a creature."

"What is her other name?" he asked suddenly.

"Was it na in the note?" Janet spoke, with such an increase of stupidity that Dr. Colton saw that she was playing a part.

He shook his head angrily.

"Na?" Janet said with the utmost innocence. "Weel, then, doctor, I canna' gie ye ither. An' it please ye, ca' her Mary 'til ye see her nae mair."

Dr. Colton looked at Janet haughtily, but the woman seemed unconscious of having given any but satisfactory answers. For a second he debated upon the folly of exposing himself to her impertinence, but another glance at Mary's face, and the Scotchwoman was forgotten. He gave minute directions as to the treatment of the wound and added: "I will call this evening about seven. Unless some unfavorable change should occur an earlier visit is not necessary."

"Ye dinna think the bairn is verra ill?" All Janet's stupidity had vanished, her face was working nervously as she asked the question.

For a moment the doctor was tempted to repay her in her own coin; but her anxiety was too real. "The wound is not necessarily dangerous. Her fever is a rather unfavorable symptom, but not sufficiently so to awaken alarm. She must be kept as quiet as possible. Conversation is forbidden. She does not look robust," he said, with a parting glance at the lovely sleeper, and left the room.

The sun was shining in full splendor as he opened the hall door, and the air was laden with the odor of flowers. "Ah!" The doctor was astonished. The fallen rose-bush now stood erect, fastened firmly to little stakes. The drooping plants no longer hung their heads, but smiled up into the face of their God who bathed them with His light. The gate, rehung, swung open to permit his egress. Not a trace remained of the late disorder in the carefully raked paths. No one was in sight except the coachman sleeping on the box. It was a hired carriage, he now saw, and the driver one of the laziest negroes about town. "He couldn't have done it," the doctor thought, stopping and looking around as Janet passed him quickly.

"Mon," she said, waking the darkey, "ye will ca' for Dr. Colton at five this evenin'." She moved gravely aside and courtesied as the doctor entered the carriage and drove away.

The mystery enwrapping the fair girl wakened an interest apart from her beauty. Dr. Colton was pleased with the beginning of his adventure, full of curiosity about the family and connections of this sweetest Mary, and surprised that in his various rides through the country he had never noticed the little cottage. But as he looked from the carriage window he saw that the cottage was almost hidden by a small grove of trees, and was unlikely to attract attention. "Like a violet, it grew too near the earth," he said, and smiled in high delight at his own poetical fancy, and then began to wonder who the girl was, and who directed the coachman to the cottage.

Hilton himself stood at the horses' heads while the driver, stimulated by a piece of silver, presented his note to Dr. Colton, with the words :

"Massa, dis yer note was sent by a lady."

When the doctor entered the carriage Hilton on horseback led the way to the cottage. Arriving there he left his horse in the grove and while the driver slept on the box and the doctor tended his patient, repaired the damages done to the garden.

He would return to the camp, he determined, as soon as he could learn the doctor's opinion of Mary. Under no consideration would he have Mary see him in his guard's uniform. She might connect him with the scene of last night. Even in the horror of that moment when Mary fell under the great bloodhound, her look of love, her smile, had pierced him like a knife. What if she should trust him less ? The curse of that proud lady—for as a curse seemed those words—still haunted him. He could not banish the superstitious dread it had awakened.

When the doctor left the cottage Hilton entered by a side door, sending Janet with the message to the coachman. Then hearing from Janet every particular of the interview with the doctor, he said : " I will be here to-night," and rode away.

The morning in its fresh beauty, the dew that in showers of brightness was dashed from the shrub and flower as he galloped on, the birds thrilling their songs of gladness, gave no pleasure to him. He neither felt nor saw the lavish gifts of the Creator. Chancing, however, to raise his eyes, he started at sight of one of the works of the Master—started so sharply and suddenly that the check on the reins pulled his horse back on his haunches. Walking along the road in the early morning with long, easy strides, and giving with his tall well-knit figure and handsome face the bit of life needed in the landscape, was a young man.

Hilton noticed the strength and grace of manhood that men acknowledge and admire. He frowned, feeling anger and not pleasure in the perfection of his kind. The proud bearing of this stranger aroused his suspicion. Why was he walking across the country on this lonely road ?

Half decided to utter a challenge, Hilton kept his eyes on him. But even as he debated the point the other came near, looked at him with a bright, fearless glance, and passed on. He turned, and as the man paused at Mary's gate, he dashed his spurs into the horse's side. His hand was on his pistol ; another step towards that cottage and a bullet would be his greeting. With his hand still on the garden gate the stranger faced Hilton, stood thus a second, then without glancing at the cottage, walked on up to the road.

Hilton watched him out of sight, then once more, but more slowly, rode away to the lake.

CHAPTER XXI.

TWO MEN.

TO Dennis that bright morning had been nature's answer to his new-born hope.

After reaching the bank he had walked only a short distance when approaching voices warned him of the guards' return. He had barely time to conceal himself when they came in sight. He saw at a glance they were disappointed, that they at least knew nothing of the escaped prisoner. Dennis was trying to decide which of the party was Hilton, when an order about "fastening Hilton's boat," and a muttered expression of wonder as to "which road now," informed him that Hilton himself was yet to come, and the chase was not over. He watched the men as they moved away in their little canoes, and when they had disappeared in the mist, rolled himself in his blanket and dozed and waited. It might be that Hilton had gone with a party in another direction. But since the boat was left for him he would return this way, and as the woods made good camping ground Dennis concluded he had here the best chance to assist the convict. Waking at dawn he found the boat still moored and was convinced that Hilton had not passed. After a cold plunge into the lake he had started out with the glad heart of youth once more beating in his breast. Life was joyous surely. He had been a stupid misanthrope not to have known it. That empty sleeve had won her pity, that lonely left hand, her kiss. For every loss he had received compensation, for every pain blessing. Under the trees he strode on, following the one road leading due east. Anxious as he was to get about his work, he would remain in and around Milton for a few days. Perhaps there might be a chance of

learning something about the convict. But should Hilton not have discovered him, it was possible he might
have escaped not only from the prison itself but the vig-
ilance of the hunters.   And again Dennis's heart thrilled
at the negro's daring.   Julie's mind could be relieved by
a letter, and then he would devote some days, perhaps a
week, to personal inspection of the mineral districts
about which, having attracted favorable notice by some
strong articles, he was now engaged in writing.   He had
been writing in a desultory fashion.   But with this new
motive—Mary—he would bring both ardor and industry
to labor ; he would win success.

He marched rapidly to the tune of happy thoughts,
and passing out of the woods he saw Mary's cottage.
His eyes were on it, the central spot in the lonely country.
The man galloping toward him was not of the slightest
importance to him, until on nearer approach he saw
something in the heavy figure, the strong coarse face and
the guard's uniform that convinced him that the rider
was Hilton, the convict ruler and Mary's father. He
looked intently at him, seeking to find in those features
a trace of the fair girl. But there was not one. They
were as different as the snowy lily and the mud wherein
rest its roots.   The horseman passed, and as Dennis
neared the cottage he saw a curtain flutter, then a hand
held up in warning. Was it Mary? No, only Janet,
with a scared look on her face. She made a little gesture of entreaty for him to pass on. It was hard ! The
words of a song he had once liked came back to him
with a force he had not believed them capable of.
" Thou art so near and yet so far." He spoke them aloud,
and then with the cunning of self-deceit his reason began
to upbraid him for being thus near her and not seeing
her. Gentle creature ! Should he be the one to cause
her a moment's annoyance? Might she not be disappointed if he passed without a word ?

His hand was stretched out for the latch as he scanned the windows hoping for a glimpse of Mary. With a sudden impulse he turned to assure himself that Hilton was out of sight. No! he was dashing toward him at full gallop. Dennis stood perfectly still. Hilton reined in his horse, and through all the intervening space each felt by the current of personal magnetism the other was an enemy.

In Dennis's impetuous soul there arose a longing to rush on that man in mortal combat. But between them came a woman's form and the sweetest voice he had ever heard spoke to his heart : "He is my father." With a whispered "right about face" and another glance at Mary's window he left the white cottage amid its roses and marched on to the city.

CHAPTER XXII.

"CAUSE O' SUSPICION."

THINKING of Mary and of all the happiness the future might hold for her and for him, Dennis walked on, his face growing so bright as his heart filled with hope, that the occasional traveller on the highroad which he had now reached, looked, smiled and wondered who that fine fellow was. Is there a beautifier equal to happiness? And could there be a thing equally delicate, equally destructible? Just now Dennis's happiness was trembling in the balance with Mary's life. Burning with fever, wandering in delirium, calling now on Dennis, now her father, and then with clasped hands and pleading tones praying for Lazarus, the white dove of Dennis's love seemed winging its flight to God.

Every night Hilton rode to the cottage to see his child. He generally found her under the influence of

7

opiates, and therefore remained unconscious of her wanderings and without suspicion of their cause. But the doctor's curiosity kept pace with his growing interest in his patient.

"Who is this 'Dennis' she calls for?" he asked of Janet. "If he would come it might calm her."

"Come, who come?" Janet answered quickly. Then she added, "I'll swear to ye, in a' her life till the day she was hurt, my young leddy has never set eyes on ony young mon."

The woman seemed speaking the truth, so the doctor's curiosity increased, keeping alive his interest in the fair young creature who seemed wounded unto death.

"Doctor, do ye think Miss Mary'll get weel?" Janet asked anxiously each day, as despite nursing and medicine Mary gave few signs of improvement.

"Who can tell the future?" the doctor would say testily. "I see nothing that leads me to think she is near death." For Dr. Colton was in a chronic state of vexation thus to be kept ignorant of even the name of his patient. Had she been a little less charming he would certainly have delegated one of his assistants to attend her.

At each visit he would growl to himself on the folly of rattling his old bones over the stony road and sacrificing his leisure honrs in order to see this stranger. Not once during the eight days of his attendance had Mary uttered a conscious word. Yet her ravings were all full of the piety and beauty of an innocent heart, and her voice was melody itself. So the doctor sat listening to her, looking at her, until gradually curiosity took the secondary place, and Mary's charms had gained a sincere admirer in a most fastidous gentleman. He suddenly became even more careful as to his appearance, choosing costumes as varying as they were elegant, until at last Janet, in all her anxiety about Mary, her fears that

Hilton might discover the convict, noticed the doctor's dandified appearance. "The auld fule," she said to herself, "d'ye think my bairn wud look at ye? Better the one-armed mon." And then as she would look at Mary's white face, she would forget all but the girl she so dearly loved, and falling on her knees pray as never before had been possible to her.

_____

In the closet still lay the negro. Faithfully did Janet keep her promise to Mary, tending the convict as if he were truly her brother. He had recovered consciousness after his sleep on the night of his arrival, but was so exhausted by fatigue and exposure and lack of proper nourishment that he too, to Janet's inexperience, seemed going to that other world.

But death was not for O'Neil; he had not yet sufficiently suffered, not yet sufficiently paid the penalty of birth. In his weakness dependent on her, receiving each service with humble gratitude, Janet found her repugnance to his color gradually lessening. Little by little he told her his piteous tale—of the log-cabin his wife had kept so neat, the field they owned wherein he toiled, and of their aim in life—to raise and brighten the sad fortunes of their race. He told of the evenings passed in study, which had seemed to them the stepping-stone to a higher place; and of his ambition when educated sufficiently to devote his life to the cause of protection and representation for the negro—not so much desiring political spoils as by representation to modify and extend laws that would keep his people from being the victim of class and color. Thus would he talk while Janet, listening and feeling the justice of it all, would respond

"It seems a 'richt, but I dinna ken. The warld's ganged wrang."

And then O'Neal, pointing to his manacle would exclaim: "But for me the hope is gone. A convict, a fugitive, hunted by man and beast, hiding forever and afraid to show my face. And yet innocent, before God, innocent!" With hands locked together, with dry and stony eyes, he gazed on his blasted hopes. He had forgotten Janet, everything but his ruined future. And she, crying as bitterly as she had done beside Mary's sick bed, no longer called him, even in thought, "a black naiger."

"Puir mon, puir mon," she said, shaking her head and rubbing away at her very red eyes and redder nose. Plain, prim and "canny" as she was, there was a woman's heart hidden within Janet's bony breast—a heart that had soft turns in spite of the angles of her physique.

O'Neal's first act when able to sit up had been to send a few lines to Julie, lines which without signature he knew she would recognize and from which she would gain hope and patience. This letter, with many cautions, Janet had intrusted to the coachman who daily drove the carriage ordered by Hilton for the doctor's visits.

"Noo, ye'll tak' this wi' mighty care," Janet had told the man, "for 'tis to my ain sister an' when the answer comes I'll gie ye a bit."

"Yes'm, yes'm," the darkey had said, grinning at the prospective present and promising everything Janet required.

"An' here's anither ; put it in the ither pocket, an' tak' it to Mrs. Jones. Ye ken the place ? Weel, she'll gie ye a wee token an' when ye'll bring the answer I'll have something fer ye," for Janet by no means belonged to that prodigal class who pay without value received in full.

Janet's letter to Mrs. Jones was soon answered by a parcel containing a suit of rough clothes suitable for a laboring man, and a few lines to Mrs. Wilson wherein Mrs. Jones "hoped as how the clothes would suit." She had done the best she could and made the storekeeper take off a percentage, telling him they were for Mrs. Wilson, who owed them to a man who was working for her—this being Janet's explanation to Mrs. Jones in her letter, and Mrs. Jones, having a pretty thorough acquaintance with Janet's manner of buying goods during the shopping expeditions of the Scotchwoman who always lodged with her while in town, knew nothing grieved her so much as to pay full price for anything. A penny saved is a pound gained, or at least seemed so to Janet, 'who sighed with content as she said :

"Mistress Jones is na sae bad."

But Janet's great triumph came when showing the clothes to O'Neal and shaking the pockets to make the silver jingle. "Do ye hear it? It's siller to keep ye on the way when ye're able to gang," and O'Neal with tears shining in his eyes had gratefully and respectfully kissed the rough hand of his benefactress. It was a strange sensation for Janet to receive gratitude. Except from Mary, who loved her nurse, no one she could remember had ever spoken to her words of interest or affection. Somehow O'Neal's simple act made her feel more like a gentlewoman than ever before.

"It's naething, it's naething," she had said, and absolutely forgot the little struggle she had had with herself before she would part with enough of her savings to make the purchase.

"But he looks bonny i' them," she thought when bringing O'Neal his dinner she first saw him in the new suit. The manacle, removed by a file which he had used while confined to the bed, lay in the corner of the closet, a rusty token of past pain. And now weaker and thinner than he had ever seemed to himself, O'Neal took little walks around the house in order to gain strength for the journey upon which he was to start as soon as possible. Both he and Janet felt the danger of his remaining in the cottage—danger which threatened even the fair girl lying so faint and ill. After nightfall O'Neal walking about would look at the window which had so mercifully opened to the fugitive, and feel afresh the marvellous charity of Mary. Each symptom of the injured girl was of vital interest to him. And while she lay under the shadow of death he could not think of his future. He dreaded to go away until she was better, dreaded to remain, for he might be a cause of injury to her.

There came no answer from Julie. But this did not occasion much anxiety. He had told her that a letter might be a dangerous messenger even though it were sent under cover to Mrs. Janet Wilson.

Mary had been ill for ten days—days of anxious nursing, more anxious watching and waiting, for to Janet the hardest feature of the illness was that she could do so little for the girl. "Quiet, quiet ; don't move or disturb the young lady," were the doctor's orders delivered each day, as each day he came and Mary lay either in stupor, or moaned aloud her feverish fancies.

Janet, quite reconciled now to the negro's presence, and feeling the need of human sympathy, would tell him of the minutest changes in her dear "young leddy." It was Janet who, hearing O'Neal's story, finished it for him with the picture of Mary lying wounded in her father's arms, and the great dog dead on the floor.

This tender maiden had for an outcast faced the most frightful death ! His life became a something loaned and consecrated by her sacrifice. Janet had not told him who was Mary's father. She had only said he "was a hard mon," and it would "gae hard wi' the bairn if her feyther knew she had saved ony mon's life." And then she cautioned O'Neal never to move out of the room nor even the closet until she was sure there was no danger of his being seen.

On the eleventh day of Mary's illness there came a

change. Janet, bending over her, saw upon the white brow that dew so welcome to anxious eyes, that blessed dew which tells of lessening fever.

"Tom, Tom, the bairn will live, the bairn will live!" She ran to the closet to tell him, and then hearing the approach of a carriage hastened to open the door for the doctor. "She's gettin' weel, she's gettin' weel," she exclaimed, and though her feeling was genuine and strong she looked so unlovely to the doctor that his only answer was a frown. This woman seemed always interfering with him. Here she was foretelling the progress of his patient, and infringing on his rights.

It was a lovely morning in September. Decay had not yet touched shrub or flower, and the air was filled with a soft golden haze, with the lazy hum of insect and with the delicious sense of the "sweet doing of nothing." The wind, laden with sweet odors, coming through the open windows had brought dreams to the heart of sixty-five. As the doctor entered the little gate and from Mary's rose-bush plucked a blossom, he put it in his button-hole with the air of a conqueror. It was the last of summer's beauties, and as he jarred the branch in taking it, her white sisters mourning such peerless lovliness slowly fell to the ground. A younger or more imaginative man might have felt regret that he had robbed the tree of its sole ornament, and hastened to premature death the fading blossoms; but the doctor only smiled at his own cleverness in selecting the one perfect flower. Perhaps he was thinking of another white rose as he looked at this; perhaps he was smiling as he pictured its fair beauty thriving on his breast. But the smile changed to a frown at sight of Janet's homely but delighted face, and with something as near a growl as so elegant a gentleman permitted himself, he told the woman that noise was to be avoided and that if Miss Mary was approaching the crisis of her disease, he would himself

watch beside her for an hour and summon her nurse
when needed. Meekly enough in seeming, but calling
him "a big fule" in her thoughts, Janet accepting her
dismissal went to the kitchen, coming to the door once
in a while to listen for Mary's voice.

Mary was sweetly sleeping, and Dr. Colton watched
beside her. He knew that when she awoke it would be
to consciousness, and that he would soon lose his patient
unless—

"How lovely she is!" he thought, as she smiled in
her sleep—and now she was talking in her dreams.
"Dennis! Dennis!" The doctor did not find this name
so charming. He started back, and as he moved Mary
awoke. Her large grey eyes were fixed in extreme bewilderment on this unknown face.

"Who are you?" she asked; and then, before he
could answer, she leaned out of bed, raising the drapery
as if seeking something. "Not there!" she said, and
called "Janet!"

The sweet voice rang out, startling Janet at her work.
"My bairn!" she cried, running to Mary's room where
she found the doctor quietly talking to her. When Janet
appeared Mary held out her arms as a child to its nurse.

"Ye've come back, ye've come back!" the woman sobbed, pressing to her heart this dear child of her love,
while the doctor, annoyed at the familiarity of a servant,
walked away from the bed. Left thus to themselves,
Mary, putting her lips to Janet's ear, whispered: "Where
is Lazarus?

"Safe an' weel, bairn. But dinna ye tell the doctor.
When the puir mon's ganged it willna be sae much.
But noo, ye mauna breathe his name."

Doctor Colton waited a moment by the window,
but finding the young lady and her servant were
very comfortable in each other's arms, returned as
abruptly as he had turned away. "Place the young
lady on her pillows," he said to Janet, and then to Mary

in his gentlest manner : " My dear young lady, you have been very ill and must be most careful. No excitement, if you please, Mrs. Wilson. Absolute quiet is my command ;" and with a courteous bow to Mary he left the room.

In the carriage, riding home through the peaceful country, Mary's loveliness filled his thoughts. " Why not ?" he said to himself, as the carriage stopped before his door and he looked up at the stately mansion that called him master. He saw not only its imposing front, but the long line of ancestors dating back to one who carried in his veins noble blood. He saw the wealth that waited at his command, and then the flower-wreathed cottage with its hidden beauty came before him. Fair as was that rose, yet it was after all only a simple flower, without surroundings of wealth and prominence. Why were not position and gold a fitting match for youth and loveliness? All day he thought of the pros and cons of that course which with the magic of Mary's voice had taken definite shape. In his office while patients came and went, while hearts sank or rose as his fiat was pronounced, his thoughts were following the same subject. He thought of it at dinner, which was served in solitary state with glittering glass and massive silver. He thought of it before the bright fire gleaming on the hearth whose flames aided the shaded lamps to bring out the rare adornments of the great library. The more he thought of it, the more proper it seemed to him. " A fair exchange," he said to himself, feeling generous and beneficent as he acknowledged this. And then he pictured how that white maiden would lighten the gloom of the grand old house. He dreamed of the fashion in which that sweet voice would waken echoes in the silent rooms and in his equally silent heart. With partly closed eyes he mused, and as the smoke from his cigar

7*

was wafted upward, through the clouds he saw the face that had smiled up at him from the white pillow.

While Dr. Colton smoked and dreamed, on the road through the woods wildly galloped a father to his child's bedside—a father whose despair changed to joy as he saw love and consciousness in Mary's eyes and felt once more the gentle clasp of her arms. In the moment's rapture he forgot all else—forgot the telegrams of the morning with information of the fruitless search for the escaped convict; forgot his curses and his oath that the man should yet be found and thrown to the dogs; forgot that that very day a helpless convict had fallen beneath his pitiless lash, and, dying, had called down curses upon his destroyers. Was justice dead, that wealth gave its powers to these destroyers, and that this brutal man, their tool and servant, should be wrapped in the embrace of purity and love?

"You will soon be well, my darling," Hilton said to his daughter, "you will be well, and dearer than ever to your father's heart. In the new year we will leave this place. I will give up business and we will be always together."

She looked into his face with loving smile, but with none of her eager pleasure at this often-discussed plan of their future life. A strange jealousy fired his soul What had changed her? Who had come between them? Some one had stolen part of her thoughts; there was something in her mind unrevealed to him! He felt it, he knew it, even now as she rested her head on his breast. Her face was not raised in rapture to his own, and those dreamy eyes held some vision other than that of their future life.

"What do you see, my darling?" he asked. If she but answered that she was dreaming of the happiness of being always with him, then the demon raging in his breast would take flight. All truth as she was, she could not lie. Breathlessly he waited the words which should exorcise this torture that destroyed his peace. He saw her momentary hesitation. A certain shyness came upon her face ; and the white lids drooped over her eyes. Why should she be shy, this frankest of creatures? He set his teeth lest he might say a word to startle her, and gently laid her on her pillows, that his arms might not contract and crush her to death. He would not injure her. She was true to him, even now, smiling at him. He had been a fool to doubt for an instant, and he smiled down on her in response.

"Father !" She stopped and then went on : " There is something you do not know." On its mate, lying on her breast, he placed the hand he held, and with his own clinched behind him listened to his child. " Wait until I grow a little stronger and I will tell you. It is something that has made me happy, and you will be happy with me."

He was afraid to trust himself to speak. He was afraid lest the curses in his thoughts would spring out if he but opened his mouth—curses against any other than himself who could so interest her as to make her happy He walked to the window, glaring out into the darkness at the impossible suggestions of his thoughts. And then he smiled at his utter folly. It was perhaps some dream of her delirium, or a fresh flower Janet had found, and she was fostering it as she had done the rose-bush she had reared from a slip he had given her. One day in triumph she had shown it to him covered with blossoms. And then they had planted it in the garden and had called it Mary's bush. He could remember her delight at his surprise. Yes, yes, she was a child, an innocent child. Beides, who was there for her to see ? Janet, the patriarch of a doctor, and himself. That old fogy could not have given her any pleasure. And there was no one else ! Even as he thus reassured himself there came to

his mind the stranger walking along the road the morning after Mary's accident. "But I watched him out of
sight," he said to himself, "and even if he came back
Mary had not seen him." Quieted by the certainty of
these facts and yet determined to question Janet before
leaving the cottage, he went back to Mary's bedside.
She was drowsy with the soft sleep of returning health.
Looking up dreamily to her father as he bent over her,
she seemed to see near him the other man who on that
bright morning had walked out of the unknown world
and entered the paradise of her heart.

"I love you," she said, and putting up her arms to
enfold both, fell into dreamland.

For a few moments Hilton watched his sleeping
child, and then went into the hall, seeking Janet.

She was near at hand, standing at a side door, and
advanced as she saw him about to enter her room. To
his suspicious nature she seemed waiting for something.
Why of late did she always keep near or around the hall.
Was this all due to Mary's illness? Could there be any
other motive than attention to her mistress? These new
thoughts acted as a check on the questions he had determined to put to her. Without speaking he looked at her
sharply. But there was no embarrassment in her face,
and the small shrewd eyes frankly returned his glance.
Stiff and prim as the stiff white cap that nearly covered
her hair, her face told as little of her thoughts, if thoughts
she had. Waiting a moment for him to speak, she asked:
"Did ye want me, Captain Hilton?" Her manner had the
same quiet respect from which she had never varied
during her eighteen years of service.

"Who has been in this house?" he asked abruptly,
still keeping his eyes fixed on her.

"Wha? Ye ken, Captain, better than I. Savin' yer-
sel' an' the doctor, I'm ignorant o' the others, an' didna
even notice the faces o' a' the men the night Mary—"

" I don't care about them," he interrupted her rudely, frowning as he did so. But Janet appeared not to see the darkening of his face as she alluded to the accident which had so nearly killed Mary. She was looking on the floor after a manner of hers that hitherto had rather pleased her master, as being suited to her station. But now he found fault with it. Was there something she knew ?

Again she waited for him to speak, and finding he did not, she looked up and met his eyes : "Hae ye cause o' suspicion ?" Her voice and expression were perfectly natural, and she added in the same painstaking way that had always been hers : "It's lonesome here for thieves, but if ye thinks anything has happened to fright the bairn I'll watch at night."

He did not answer her question, did not notice her remark, but still looking as if he suspected something unfavorable to her, asked : " Has my daughter spoken of recognizing me ?"

Janet knew what he meant. " Yes, she hae told me you smiled on her, and saved her frae the dog." The woman bore his look better than he her words, for now Hilton winced. Apparently, not noticing this, Janet went on : " But since I told her it was a dream, and that to say aught to ye might gie ye pain, she hasna spoken mair o' it. She is that innocent, she kens nae lee, sae she believed me."

Hilton felt so out of sorts that Janet's nasal voice and slow speech irritated him. However, he said nothing more to her. Just now she was too useful to Mary to be sent away. But he swore within himself that when he took his daughter from this place he would take her to strangers. For a moment longer he stood frowning, and then turned, and without another word left the house, mounted his horse and rode slowly away.

Mary's recovery had brought to him no return of comfort. Even her last words, " I love you," had not exorcised the demons raised by his doubt. He did not now, as had been his custom, turn to look at the house. He had turned each day during her illness for a parting look, in memory of her who always watched him out of sight. But to-day he rode away in moody thought, muttering to himself.

There was, however, a woman who watched him, but there was no love in her eyes, and the voice bore as little resemblance to Mary's as did her words to the girl's softly uttered blessings on her father.

"Ye are the hardest mon alive," said Janet, shaking her clinched hand at her master. " Ye are the de'il hissel' fer cruelty, an ye're sae ful' o' evil that ye'd suspect an angel. But ye hae met ane wha'll fule ye, an' lee till her soul's clean ganged, afore ye hurt my bairn or tak' the naiger."

CHAPTER XXIII.

ON GUARD.

THE next morning Dr. Colton made another early visit. Inspired by his own dreams and appreciating to the full the advantages he had to offer, he was not insecure of success, and felt like a youtful gallant come a-wooing.

But Janet was on guard. Like the dragon in the fairy tale she watched beside the enchanted princess Probably the doctor felt particularly benign : probably he was not averse to have some counter influence to Mary's charms, giving him a little more time to consider the subject before compromising himself. Probably he wanted to know something of the mysterious father to whom the maiden had given her first conscious word, and on whom she had so often called during her delirium. The girl was quite fair enough for the Colton family to open its arms and take her to its aristocratic bosom. But the father? He would be too near a relation to ignore. And the wise old gentleman who had waited and weighed so many times the probability of married blessedness, did not care to be too quickly hurried out of his caution.

So after he had greeted his patient and thought anew how very lovely she was, he walked over to Janet, actually smiling at her while regaling himself with a pinch of snuff.

Janet, knitting away as if life depended on her labor, did not raise her head. He made an affable remark about industry, and Janet's " Thank ye, sir," sounded most respectful. But if her thoughts had been visible the doctor might not have been so pleased nor have found a certain quaintness in the prim old-fashioned figure with the dark dress relieved by a white handkerchief crossed on her breast, and a long white apron. "The auld fule," Janet was saying in her secret thoughts, "the auld fule. He'll hae nae chance to be speerin' roun' my bairn wi' his questions. Na, na, though the de'il catch me, nae ane shall spot her soul wi a lee."

True to her resolution Dr. Colton had little chance of a word with Mary that Janet did not hear. Always at work, sewing or knitting, always perfectly neat from her white cap to the black shoes and gray stockings that showed under her dress, the dragon guarded her princess. Although the old gentleman felt inconvenienced by the presence of a silent, unsympathetic listener, he occasionally favored Mary with a most elegantly turned compliment whose composition had occupied the time while he drove from the town to the cottage.

These old-fashioned gallantries Mary received as expressions of good will, and would thank him in the sweetest manner for them.   The doctor was pleased with his success and felt that the fruit was ripening ready for the plucking.

Mary gained rapidly.   But a few days had passed since the fever was conquered when she coaxed the doctor to let her sit up.   Janet had promised that when that day arrived her "Lazarus" should see her, for between these two, O'Neal had never been called by other name.   "But he's nae mair Lazarus, my bairn. Wi' his new clothes, an' clean shirt he's a likely mon, in spite o' the black skin—which to me seems a strange fancy o' the gude God.   Ha' mercy on us," Janet added, fearing lest she had brought down the wrath of heaven and heated for herself the fiery brimstone by this expression of her opinion.   "His black skin."   Mary had not heard the other words.   "That is God's will, Janet.   We must not question if we believe."

"Ye're reet, my bairn, ye're reet," Janet had hurriedly agreed with her, dreading the effect of any discussion, and so the conversation ended.

By the window, dressed in a soft white wrapper and filled with excitement that was beautifying as it was extreme, Mary was receiving the doctor.

He remarked her fluttering breath, the trembling of her taper fingers as for an instant he held them, and appropriated to himself these evidences of agitation.   It would have been a lesson on man's egotism could he have known that Mary's paramount thought was the expected visit of a negro and a felon.

"Quick, Janet," she cried as the carriage rolled away with the delighted doctor.

"Yes, yes," Janet answered, hastening to do her bidding.

Although not yet strong, O'Neal was anxious to star on his jouney,   He longed for his wife and the little one

they had expected—the baby, who since his escape had
been often in his thoughts.

"He'll take up my life," he had said to Janet, and
each day this new hope had grown stronger.

Since the hour when Hilton's suspicions had been so
strangely aroused, he had not visited his daughter.
Janet, dreading what might result if those suspicions
continued, had not opposed the convict's departure ; she
had rather hastened it, in fact, with hints that his remaining might endanger Mary.

"Her feyther's a hard mon. There's nae telling what
he would do if he should find you," she had said while
hurrying to complete the necessaries for Tom's journey.

Everything was ready to speed the traveller on his
way, even to a disguise prepared by Janet of a gray wig,
to make which she had cut her own hair.

"La, Tom, your ain wife willna ken ye," she had
said to him when she had fitted the wig to his head and
stood off admiring her work.

A small basketful of food had been prepared and
hidden in the kitchen, for O'Neal had thought that it
would be his only plan so to travel as to avoid speech or
meeting with every one. Everything had gone so
smoothly, Mary's sudden improvement having been remarkable, that Janet, whose faith was eminently practical
and the result of facts alone, assured O'Neal that they
were under the direct protection of Heaven.

"The gude God is favoring the reet. An' though
I'll be sorry when ye're gane, yet, Tom, I feel ye tak
God's blessin'. God is gude," said Janet, feeling she
had been uttering Christian piety.

When the doctor's carriage was out of sight, Janet
again congratulated herself that God was on her side.

"Noo, my bairn, I'll fetch him," she called to Mary
as she ran to her own room, unlocked the door and led
O'Neal to his deliverer.

He paused on the threshold gazing in reverential awe

at the delicate girl who, for pure charity, to save an outcast, had faced the most frightful of deaths.

But to Mary he was not an outcast. With beautiful,
smiling face, with outstretched hands, she was welcoming
a friend. There was no repulsion in that face; like
God's angel's she looked beyond color.

With dry eyes O'Neal had borne the agonies of his life,
but this supreme goodness, this heavenly charity, smote
the rock. On his knees before her he kissed the hem of
her robe, wetting it with his tears, and once more as on
that awful night Mary's hand rested on his head. He
tried to speak, tried to utter the gratitude that overpowered him ; but words would not come. Mary trembled ;
she was turning very pale.

"In Christ you are my brother," she said. "Ah!
how you have suffered. But be patient, endure to the
end, and like Lazarus you shall rest in God's bosom."
More worldly-wise than Mary, Janet groaned at these
words, looking sadly at the Negro from the door where
she stood on guard.

"Puir mon, puir mon, he'll hae mony a hard pillow
before that," she said, shaking her head.

She remembered the story of the negro's wrongs :
she knew what justice he was likely to meet, and could
feel scant comfort in Mary's promised future. But there
was something she did feel—fear ! A sudden sound
blanched her face and took away her breath.

"What's that ?" she gasped. "Hilton !"

A horse came galloping furiously ; some one was at
the gate. Wild with terror she sprang forward, caught
O'Neal by the shoulder and pulled him from Mary's feet.

"Quick ! Hide ! Wad ye peril her life?" she called
to the bewildered man, as not heeding his words or
Mary's startled cry, she pushed the convict into her room
and shaking like one in a palsy, closed her door as Hilton entered the hall.

There was a smile on his face which vanished when

he saw Janet. After several restless days and nights he had successfully argued himself out of his doubts. So great had been the desire to see his daughter that he had left the camp shortly after the day's labor had begun, and here at the very entrance to the house that woman confronted him! Why was she holding the knob of her door with that wild look?

"What's the matter?" His voice was harsh. As it sounded through the little hall it reached Mary, who, startled by Janet's excitement and fearing some danger to the convict, walked to her door. White and trembling she stood there and saw her father.

"Thank God," she cried. "It *is* you, father. I did not know your voice."

Astonished at seeing her on her feet, and frightened at her pallor, her father caught her in his arms, as, turning faint, she reeled and would have fallen. With a look Janet dared not disobey he ordered her to follow, and bade her chafe Mary's hands.

After a few moments, when Mary's face became less deathlike, he put aside the hand that had clasped his fingers, and saying, "In a moment, darling," left her. But Janet was quicker than he. Slipping past him she now stood facing him, barring his entrance to her room.

Was it possible this servant, this woman he had picked up from the dregs of poverty, this creature of his bounty, dared oppose him? He could have killed her. But even in his rage he remembered Mary, and would not again alarm her.

"Move!" he whispered. His face would have frightened one less courageous than Janet. But she stood her ground firmly, bracing herself for what might come.

"Fool! stand aside!" Hilton's voice was husky, his clinched hand was raised involuntarily. Yet he restrained himself even when Janet, reaching back, grasped the knob of her door.

"Are you a thief, that you hide what you dare not

show ?" he said, giving her a rough push. But Janet, all bone and sinew as she was, withstood the blow.

"I am nae thief, ye ken it weel," she said fiercely, and then, more in her natural manner, "Captain Hilton, I swear to ye there's naething o' yours in my room. It is my room while I serve ye, and I wadna hae ye enter. It isna fixed sae early."

"Stand aside, I tell you." But as Janet did not move he caught her arms, tore her hands from their hold, and pushing her away with such force that she fell against the wall opposite, opened her door. Dizzied, she put her hands to her head, but seeing Hilton in her room she ran and stood beside him.

The little room, bare in comparison with the rest of the house, was the picture of neatness. There was no place to conceal anything, for the sunlight streamed on and under bed, table, chairs.

The closet! He tried the door—locked. Janet in the middle of the room, wrung her hands. "Lord, gude Lord," she prayed, "gie us a miracle. Mak' the wood hold."

But in the grasp of Hilton the door yielded, creaked, and with a sharp sound fell open. The woman shut her eyes. She could not see what was coming; she could not look into the negro's face. And Mary! What of Mary! "O God, protect her." Not a sound disturbed the silence. For the first time in her life Janet's nerves gave way. The room spun round; she put out her hand to steady herself. The stillness, the horrible stillness!

"Pah!" Hilton said, and without looking at her, left the room. She staggered to the closet and holding wide the door gazed in. Nothing—no sign of human life—only a goodly pile of household linen and Mary's dainty garments. O'Neal had vanished!

"A miracle!" cried Janet, and fell on her knees.

Passing through the house, looking into all the rooms and finding nothing unusual, Hilton grew more and more puzzled at Janet's agitation. "What was the matter with the fool? Could it have been some woman's freak?" Whatever it was, Mary was ignorant of it. She had nothing to conceal, and his heart grew easy as he remembered her look of glad relief on seeing him. "Innocent child," he said aloud, thinking of his daughter while walking around the house more to satisfy himself than really expecting to find any solution of this mystery.

He stopped at Mary's window. She was lying just as he had left her. With hands clasped and eyes upraised, she was praying. She was all his own, he thought, and felt like the miser who hugs his gold. For a moment he paused exulting in his treasure.

That moment's pause was a wonderful help to Janet, who, rising from her knees called "Tom," waiting, almost expecting an answer. None came, and then she began to look for some explanation for her "miracle."

"Not that I doubt the gude God," she said, excusing her lack of faith, "but if there's left a mark I'll gie nae chance for the de'il to find it."

She looked hastily around, but the convict was not in her room; every trace of his presence had vanished.

"He must hae gane awa', God help him!" As she thought this she ran to the window. Just under it the earth was marked. "He hae jumped frae the window," Janet thought. It would be only a moment's work to rake the walk, but Hilton's step approaching made the simple task dangerous. Presently he stopped, and running from the kitchen door, with quick fingers Janet smoothed the gravel.

"I wadna trust the noise o' the rake," she said, and scrubbing off the dirt, was at her usual work when Hilton stood at the open door.

He watched her awhile and then looked around the silent country. There was not a sound but the hum of insects, the soft twitter of birds and the singing of the kettle on the kitchen fire. What had been the matter

with Janet ? Again he turned to look at her as she went
about her duties. Not seeming to notice that she was
being watched, she was preparing a dainty tray, which
being ready she carried to Mary's room, leaving open the
pantry doors with their shining rows of pots and pans
and pretty crockery. There was nothing there but neatness and comfort. The only suspicious thing in the
kitchen Janet had found undisturbed and hidden more
securely.

"The mon hae gane wi'out a bit," she had said as she
saw the little basket. "Mary wad say the Lord will
send the ravens, but while I'm thankful for all His
mercies, I wish the gude God had sent this basket wi'
Tom." She held it in her hand, and then decided to hide
it, "where Hilton couldna see it to set his evil mind
workin'."

A few moments later when her master appeared and
stood watching her Janet was well pleased with her caution. "A miracle is gude, an' sure it was a miracle how
he went sae quick, but it's better not to be always waitin'
for God's help," she said to herself as she hastened to
Mary's room with her tray.

"He's gane, my bairn," she whispered, "an' prays ye
not to tell." Janet used the moment's liberty, and had
only a moment, for before Mary had answered her by a
look Hilton came in.

The sight of Janet's bruised hand filled Mary with pity.

"Nae, Miss Mary, it's naething. I hurt it on the
door," she said, looking full at Hilton.

He did not notice her, although he felt pleased at her
explanation. It was proof, if one was needed, that
Mary knew of no concealments. Had there been any
concealment ? He scanned Janet with searching eyes.
But the sharp face with long nose and high cheek-bones
told no secrets. She seemed to have no thought, beyond
solicitude that the milk toast was to Mary's liking.

The hour with his daughter was not one of unmixed pleasure to Hilton. Loving her, convinced that her secret was some innocent surprise for him, yet he was not at peace. When she began : "I am better to-day, listen to my secret," he put her off with: "Not now, darling, I must be gone." Then more hurriedly than had been his custom he said good-by, and rode away, turning once to look at the little house, whiter than ever since the autumn weather, soft as it was, had thinned the leaves of the vine that covered it.

CHAPTER XXIV.

RENUNCIATION.

WHEN Janet, closing her door, had faced Hilton O'Neal in her room stood like one in a dream, Absorbed in his own feelings he had heard no sound but Mary's voice, "Endure to the end." To him it was an angel speaking—an angel who rebuked the bitterness he had felt. Kneeling at her feet the negro's soul took a step on that narrow way so difficult to human nature. Then came Janet's sudden cry, her terrified face, her words : "Wad ye peril her life ?" What did she mean ?

As answer to his query, he heard a voice that roused in him every atom of indignant manhood. Hilton ! That slayer of the imprisoned ! Among a thousand other voices he would have recognized that one. Hilton had tracked him to this cottage—was come to gloat over his recapture.

"Not yet, wretch ! Not yet : I'll kill you before the others come."

He tried the door, but some one was holding it. Before he could force it open another voice, another word, sent him staggering backward as if he had been struck,

"Father!" Mary called him "father!"

Was it possible? This, then, was her peril! This forever sheltered Hilton from O'Neal's vengeance. An instant's delay, and she would have an enemy more cruel more remorseless than the blood-hound. He opened the closet door, snatched up his bundle, every article that could tell of his being there, and then with a quick bound jumped lightly from the window to the ground and ran to the clump of trees that with a hedge guarded the back of Mary's garden.

Hiding behind the thick hedge he looked at the cottage. How still it was, how peaceful! What a shelter it had been to him—what friends he had found there! He waited through the day, uncertain from hour to hour what was to happen and on the alert for the faintest sound. The sun moved on to the west and flooded the world with splendor. That light which changed to jewel the poorest stone, but made the outcast more forlorn. He was a thing that dared not show itself, dared not even as a stone, receive the parting blessing of the dying day.

There were now no signs of life about the cottage, and he could not see the road. He did not know whether Hilton had gone, or if he were yet there. And though thus near, he dared not go nearer—dared not, for their sakes, even speak a parting word to those who had done so much for him.

When the darkness fell, O'Neal picked up his bundle and started on his journey. Never more could he have speech with Mary or with Janet. Under the quiet stars he stretched out his arms toward the cottage and with tears called down blessings on its inmates.

The parting over, O'Neal's spirits rose. As he passed

through the quiet country, each step taking him further from that fearful prison and nearer to wife and child, the difficulties he expected did not seem so formidable. The air was fresh, and feeling the strength of returning health, he walked briskly on, until glimmering in the distance he saw the lights of the city. Under some bushes by the roadside he sat down to rest, waiting until the night was further advanced, when fewer persons would be afoot, and thus the chances of discovery be diminished.

The recapturing of convicts was generally left to their owners or lessees, as for each man who escaped a certain fine was paid to the State. Therefore except in rare instances, the general police were not called upon, and if he could get far enough away to avoid recognition of the private force of guards and detectives employed by the camp, O'Neal felt he could be almost secure of liberty. Payment was exacted only for the escaped felon. The dead, the tortured, the murdered—these were of no consequence to the beneficient goddess who presided over the statutes of a free and independent State. Therefore now, and now only, was danger imminent, and even here, thus near the camp, O'Neal began to lose apprehension. Many days had elapsed since that night, when shaking off his chain he had stepped forth a free man. Even now he could feel the thrill of exultation as at that moment ; even now the horrors of that flight rose before him, and he remembered the welcome light which had guided the fugitive. And Mary—" God bless her !" he cried.

Stiller and stiller grew the night. The occasional rustle of a falling leaf or the soft lowing of some distant cow only made the slumbering world seem more peacefully asleep. It was past midnight when with light footfalls and with a heart full of gratitude, O'Neal entered the outskirts of the city of Milton. He had learned

8

from Janet its name as well as all the knowledge she possessed of its locality and surroundings. He had decided to travel at night, buying necessary food in lonely country homes where interest in or knowledge of convicts would probably not exist, and where he, a negro, would be only one among many. His precipitate departure had prevented his using the prepared disguise, which he now could not assume until some chance spring would give him a reflection of his face and enable him to apply a dye Janet had made for him. The town seemed stiller than the country, with its hundreds of houses all closed, its thousands of inhabitants asleep. O'Neal walked in the open street, avoiding the paving stones that spoke too loudly with echoing voice. Even the lamps seemed blinking drowsily and wondering why man was afoot. Suddenly from out of the heart of the town there shot up a red flame, shaming the whitish lights of the lamps and quickening painfully the beatings of O'Neal's heart.

Fire! He stopped, each instant expecting that cry to break the stillness and call to the rescue these sleeping men. But the stillness was unbroken. More and more drowsily blinked the lamps, and the houses with their blank empty windows seemed blinded eyes that looked upon, yet saw not, the deadly peril threatening human lives.

Brighter grew that tongue of flame, leaping up toward the quiet sky and crimsoning the clouds of smoke that attended it. Must he give the alarm? Might he not in calling these doomed sleepers waken an army of enemies? Which one of all that "city full" would befriend, protect, save from recapture the escaped convict? None! He knew it. Angels like Mary were rare in a selfish world. Before him with all its horror rose his convict life. With loving face and alluring voice his wife seemed calling him to her—calling and holding out their child. Must he sacrifice them too? A sob broke from his heart and seemed to tear it asunder. Self-preservation—that was the first law! He ran a few steps and then stopped. Still asleep! All asleep! Higher and higher sprang the flame exultingly licking the air. What was it to him? He *would* go on. He stopped!...

A moment's hesitation, a moment's agony, and then —renunciation!

"Fire! Fire! Fire!" Only a negro shouting along the street—a common fellow with a blanket strapped to his back—but a man with a hero's heart and soul. On he rushed, making for the flames, calling sleepers from their beds, summoning men to the rescue, and where before was silence now trod a hundred feet.

Still calling "Fire!" O'Neal reached the burning building. It was a handsome house, standing in a large inclosure, and despite the flames which were bursting from the side and back, there seemed no one awake. Dashing open the iron gateway, he ran up the avenue to the house and rang the bell, peal upon peal, its noisy voice helping his almost exhausted cry of "Fire!"

A window opened and a man's head appeared. Without hearing his words, if he spoke at all, O'Neal shouted: " Your house is afire. Save yourself!"

A crowd was collecting—a crowd noisy but unable to subdue the flames that leaped in a demon dance over the roof and reached out from window after window.

Presently up the street dashed the fire company. It was willing enough but inefficient in an extremity like this. The puny jets of water seemed only to enrage the fire that roared aloud, and marked its way with crash of fallen timber. As yet the front of the house was untouched, but the smoke and heat were oppressive while O'Neal and a serving man assisted an old gentleman who seemed to be the owner, in removing valuable papers and family plate from a closet in the wall. Dropping a tin box which he had just secured, the old man suddenly looked up to the burning house with a cry of agony.

"God help me!" he cried, "my cousin—Jane Dawson—she came last night—I had forgotten—" and leaving the pile of valuables he ran toward the house.

Jane Dawson! Nettie's protectress! O'Neal's heart gave a great throb. He would save her! "Stop!" he said, holding the old man as he rushed forward. "Tell me which room?"

"There! Save her! and you shall have a thousand dollars."

But O'Neal did not hear. He was looking at a window from which flames were bursting. He saw a woman's face. Even in that moment he recognized it. Pale, calm, beautiful, proud as when she scorned the murderer of Nettie, Jane Dawson was facing her death. Up the stairway, now bending low to avoid a fierce flame, now blinded by the smoke which, in dense clouds rolled through each space, a man was struggling to reach her, periling his live to save hers.

CHAPTER XXV.

A BRAVE DEED.

QUIETLY the heroic woman awaited her fate. She had gone to the door but had been driven back by clouds of smoke and roaring flames that filled the hallway. Now standing at the window she looked down on a sea of upturned, horrified faces. Ladders were placed against the house, but they were too short to reach her. The hot flames, the dense smoke, drove back those who strove to help her. Through the ceiling the fire was eating; she felt the scorching of its breath, smelt the singeing of the blanket that she had wrapped around her. She saw her cousin, Dr. Colton, struggling with some men who were holding him back from the burning house ; he was striving to reach and to save her. She heard his voice, "Jane, Jane, forgive me !"

She knew her hour had come, and knelt to pray.

"Forgive us our trespasses." Hardly had the solemn words passed her lips when a hand grasped her shoulder. Who had dared to pass those flames? She turned and saw against the background of fire a tall negro.

"Be quiet and you will be saved," he said. Tearing a sheet he fastened it around the blanket in which he enveloped her.

"I will let you down from the window. Don't be afraid." He spoke calmly and raised her from the ground. But she resisted.

"No ; save yourself," she said. He did not heed her, but hastily lifted her and thrust her out of the window.

"Your name, tell me your name !" She had pulled the blanket from her face and grasped the window-sill with one hand. "Your name?"

"Tom O'Neal, an escaped convict," he answered with a bitter laugh. Even at that moment in the midst of flame and death he felt the cruel irony of his fate.

The crowd below, horror-struck at the lady's danger, first seeing the negro and then the muffled figure lowered gently, slowly from that burning window, broke into wild cheers.

Had it been whispered that this man was a convict, and his keepers were in pursuit of him, many men would have endangered life and limb in his defense. But for an instant only ! Enthusiasm is not enduring. A moment after, the lady uninjured, had reached the ground, a groan went up from the crowd as the roof fell in, leaving only flames where that black face had been. One

woman fainted and many wept, as each heart thrilled at
the negro's sacrifice, but it is doubtful if besides Dr.
Colton and his cousin, one could be found in all that
multitude, who, knowing what he was, would have sheltered the convict.

———

The morning papers, describing ths destruction of
Dr. Colton's "elegant mansion," alluded to Miss Dawson's miraculous escape.   Very little was said of her rescuer.   But the attention of the police was particularly
called to the report that a very powerful and dangerous
convict had lately escaped from camp Osmerillo, and, so
far as learned, had not been recaptured.   It was possible
that this convict had had some hand in causing the fire
which seemed the work of an incendiary.

With a very pale face Miss Dawson read this article.
The convict had been her rescuer.   It was hardly possible that there could have been two escaped convicts in
Milton.   Appreciating the fearful death this negro had
met in her service, she was deeply hurt at the injustice
done to his memory.

Dr. Colton, walking up and down, anathematized the
newspapers and lauded the act of the dead.

"Convict or no convict, he was the bravest man I
ever saw.   And honest too.   I am surprised he could do
what he did, and be a nigger.   He asked nothing but
rushed in and died to save you.   If there lives any one
belonging to Tom O'Neal I shall consider him a sacred
charge."   The doctor spoke warmly, taking off his glasses
to clear away the mist that had gathered on them.

Nor did he content himself with words, but, ignorant
how else to obtain imformation, put into the journals
throughout the State notices wherein after narrating the
manner of O'Neal's death, he requested the names and
address of his relatives, assuring them that such information would be greatly to their advantage.

Of the negro's death there did not appear the slightest doubt. People discussed it, wondering who the man was, and what led him to brave such a death. For now the daring deed began to belong to the past, human nature sought the motive. Some practical souls chancing to hear of the thousand dollars offered by the doctor, found this motive therein. O'Neal's sacrifice sank into the commonplace, and passing from admiration of his bravery they commented on the power, the greatness, of —money.

At a little distance from the burning house there had been a man who recognized O'Neal as he lowered Miss Dawson to the arms stretched up to receive her. Recognized him—and waited. Unmoved by the negro's bravery he noted his disappearance a little before the roof fell in ; and he believed the convict had escaped.

He watched for a dark object at some door or window of the burning house, intending to arrest and take him back to camp. Then he would gain the reward ! And he who, coldly had witnessed the convict's heroism now felt his pulse quicken as he thought of Hilton's satisfaction and the envious admiration he would gain when he returned to Osmerillo with his prisoner.

This man was Stern, the convict guard, who was most in Hilton's confidence. Patiently he waited for his prey, walking round and round the building.

After a little the crowd of men dropped away, returning to their homes, their own lives. The negro had already begun to belong to the past. They were beginning to forget him, and the deed that had won their admiration. But Stern did not forget. He kept his post, still watching, still waiting for his prey, until the night had gone to join her shadowy sisters and the morning's gray made more dismal the smouldering ruins.

" He is not dead," said Stern to himself, and then believing that some hours must pass before the ruins could be disturbed, he walked rapidly to a little tavern at which he generally stopped. Here he prepared and sent a message to Hilton, asking for a leave of absence, and hinting that he had found some trace of the convict, and if possible would report personally to him by the next morning. Then hastily swallowing a cup of coffee he returned to his post, being of the order of creature that once catching a scent knows not fatigue until the game is run to earth. Men had been stationed in the grounds to prevent trespassing of any kind. Dr. Colton had given orders that no one was to be admitted even inside the inclosure, until after the departure of the men he had employed to search for the negro's body. The search was to be begun at the first practicable moment.

"No matter how he lived, he shall have the burial of a gentleman and a monument that will show to the world that a Sou herner and ex-slaveholder knows how to appreciate a negro's bravery."

"Dat's what de ole gemman said," one of the darkies on guard told Stern after repeating in his own language Dr. Colton's words. "Dat's what he sed, but fer my part, I don't see no good it am gwine ter do a dead nigger. When he's dead he's dead, an' dere am de end. I don't see no good in de blowin' ob Gabrial's horn. An' I tinks de best ting fer Massa Colton is ter gib de money to de colored gemman as is alive an' kickin'."

Stern had been loitering outside the iron railing amusing himself by tossing up and down some small silver coins which the negro had been eyeing rather longingly.

"Are you one of the colored gentlemen who would like a little money?" Stern asked, looking at the darkey with a smile.

"Dat I be. Yah ! yah ! I'se got him," he chuckled, catching one or two of the coins which Stern threw to him. Highly delighted he transferred them to his pocket as Stern nodded to his, " Keeps, massa ?" After a little more playing and the conveyance of a few more coins Stern succeeded in gaining an entrance to the grounds. With a promise " never to let out on a pore ole nig," he was permitted to inspect the ruins before any one else had set foot in them.

" Dese young gemmens has curus ways," the darkey soliloquized, while waiting outside for Stern and watching him as he passed through the stone arch of the doorway and looked up the broad stairs of which a remnant yet remained. It was built of substantial wood. He examined it carefully, going up as far as the steps would bear his weight and looking closely at balustrade and wall for any mark that would strengthen his belief as to the convict's escape.

Then he hurried down again, nodding pleasantly to the darkey who with hands in pockets stood just outside the door as he passed. " Well, massa, am you mos' frough ?" he asked anxiously.

"In a moment. Be quiet and I'll give you a quarter."

" Yah ! yah !" the man laughed, delighted at the thought of the money so easily earned, and Stern entered the large parlors. There the furniture was a mass of charred wood ; the frames of the great mirrors were blackened and cracked, and the glass lay in fragments on the floor.

Stern carefully examined the walls, floors and a closet which was built into the wall. Here upon the floor lay a bit of white paper. He picked it up. It was only a part of a letter, a frail nothing that had escaped the power which destroyed stone and masonry. Again he looked in every direction but found not a sign of what he had hoped to find. Was he mistaken? Was the negro dead ? He walked back to the hall, hurried a little by the whispers of the darkey outside. " I say, massa,

8*

hurry up. Dere's somebody a-comin'." With natural obstinacy and disliking to surrender a fixed idea, Stern, stopped for a moment in the hall and gave another look at the heaps of stone, which lay on the left side of the great old-fashioned double house. Did the convict lie under that pile of rubbish? He stooped, leaned over and picked up one of the smaller stones. It was very hot and burned his fingers. Suppressing an oath as he dropped it he was about to rise, when something caught his eyes. It was only a blackened spot on a fragment of the stair carpet which, somehow, had escaped the fire. It might have been caused by a falling stone, but then the velvet would be singed, whereas this was only soot and looked as if—Stern caught his breath—as if pressed by a foot that had trodden charred wood.

"Hurry, sah! hurry." The waiting negro was growing impatient.

"In a moment." Stern's voice was a trifle harsher. Filled with excitement he fitted his own foot to the mark and then looked around at the blackened and defaced walls to see if there were any further marks he had overlooked.

A little way off, where the soot was not so heavy he saw what, aided by imagination, might be taken for the impress of a man's hand, and at the side a darker shade of what might be blood!

It was blood, for with breath and light touch the soot was removed and that dark mark remained. It was blood!

"He must have been near falling and had thrown out his hand to steady himself," Stern decided, as imitating such a motion, he threw out his own hand. Allowing for difference of size, he felt assured that his conjecture had been correct.

How had he managed to escape? That was the question.

"Damn him, I'll have him yet," said Stern as he threw to the waiting negro the promised quarter and walked away.

There was no one to question except the men who had remained around the house all night. They were sleepy and tired, were about being relieved and "knew nothin' nor hadn't seed nobody," replying rather ill-naturedly to Stern's polite inquiries.

How could he have escaped? This was the question Stern impatiently asked himself, as he traversed street after street, in every direction encircling the Colton place. It was still early ; only an occasional pedestrian shared with him the quiet of the morning—now a woman hurrying to her work, now a laborer ; and now some market wagons lumbered along with their smell of fresh vegetables and their darkey drivers contentedly dozing.

It was while waiting for one of these to pass, that for a few moments Stern stood side by side with an old man, whose hair hung partly over his face, as bent with age, he rested on a stick. Feeling no interest in him yet he looked at him as now he looked at everyone, and he noticed that the hand grasping the cane was copper-colored. The wagon passed, he crossed the street, walked a few paces, and then stopped short. That hand holding the stick looked a strong one, unsuited to the bent figure of the man.

Could it have been the hand of the man he wanted? No—that negro's skin was black as coal.

To assure himself, to leave no chance untried he looked back, expecting to see the old negro slowly coming toward him. But he was not in sight. Stern turned hot and then cold as hurrying to the corner he had left he looked up and down in all four directions. But no old negro was in sight. And then, as if seen in a dream there flashed back on him the figure of the negro when he stood beside him. The breadth of shoulder, the muscles of hand and wrist !

Those were not the possessions of age. And for the shaking, and color, "All that might have been put on. What a fool I was ! I've missed a chance."

Cursing under his breath and hiding his rage with a smile, Stern walked up and down, peering into doorways and looking up every alley. But his hasty search met with no reward

" He is the devil," said the guard, enraged with himself as he thought of the lost chance of the morning. He now firmly believed that the old negro was O'Neal disguised, and nothing but the sight of him would weaken that conviction. With some quiet management he worked up a sympathy in those he chanced to meet, as describing the figure he had seen, he claimed him to be an old and highly prized servant who becoming imbecile had wandered from his home. Several good natured men volunteered to assist in the search, and by promised rewards other helpers were gained—but all without result.

Stimulated by his difficulties Stern took a horse and riding out short distances through the surrounding country, inquired at different houses, describing, imploring, warning or threatening, as circumstances dictated.

But the negroes employed at the different farms were old hands ; strangers were not frequent.

It was only after considerable questioning that one man admitted having shortly before hired a " new nigger." But on hearing Stern's description he said :

" Wal, this one warn't him !" and rode off to a field where some laborers were at work.

Stern followed, scanning the group of blacks, who were obeying the farmer's orders. Ordinary in sze and appearance they bore no resemblance, to O'Neal. Calling to the master, Stern asked :

" Is the strange negro among these ?" To which coolly

replying : " Wal, it 'pears like you is curous, but you ken satisfy yourself," the man went on with the work in hand.

"I will find that devil," Stern swore to himself. But it would take time, and time was not at his disposal unless Hilton would give him a longer leave of absence.

He looked at his watch. It was past noon, and yet so strong had been the instinct of the chase, that he had felt neither hunger nor fatigue.

Riding back to the town, he changed his horse for the one belonging to him, and putting him into a gallop dashed off to the camp.

He arrived at Hilton's quarters as the boy employed to serve him was taking away the dinner. Students of human nature declare that the hour in which man is most easily approached, is that which follows a good dinner. No one serving Captain Hilton would dare do otherwise than well, yet the gruff " come in " that answered Stern's knock did not argue much for the truth of this belief. Hilton's face had a careworn expression unusual to it. Stern noticed this as he bowed respectfully.

" Well, Stern ?" he said rising and shaking his head as if putting from him some disagreeable thoughts. Stern's answer was to give him the morning papers with the detailed account of the fire. " Well," Hilton again asked, as having glanced at them, he threw them aside.

Stern waited a moment as if to emphasize his words.

" I recognized the face of the negro who saved Miss Dawson. It was O'Neal." Hilton started, his frown deepening as he asked.

" And you don't believe he is dead ?"

" No sir ! A man who could work as he did and escape as he did, isn't one to give up life so easily. With less strength, he'd have had time to have left that room before the roof fell in. I kept watch, but there was a crowd and confusion and he could have escaped unnoticed from the building. I believe he's alive and somewhere near Milton. It's reported that a negro first gave the alarm of fire. I believe it was O'Neal, and I believe he started the fire with a view to robbery, but got frightened and tried to cover his crime."

To both of these men, this seemed the natural explanation of O'Neal's bravery. In different ways each felt a personal interest in the recapture of the fugitive.

Hilton desired to retake and punish that convict who was the cause of the hunt passing by Mary's cottage. And Stern longed for the money to be paid as reward.

With compressed lips, and face flushed to a dark red, Hilton looked out over the distant country, and Stern, quietly, stealthily watched him. He was filled with an excitement which he hid under the calm exterior that in the attraction of contrast, first inclined Hilton to like him.

"What is it you want to do?" Hilton asked abruptly, turning to look at Stern.

"I want to capture the nigger," Stern answered in his pleasant manner. And then as if stating some rather agreeable circumstance he added:

"I believe I can do it. He must either beg, work or steal. He can't get far away from Milton. If the country be searched for a circuit of several miles that nigger will be found, dead or alive."

"You think you can find him?" Hilton asked.

"I believe it. I can try." And then Stern added in a heartier voice: "If I once get a trace of him, I'll never let up until he's a prisoner, or one of us is dead."

"Good!" said Hilton.

Opening a secret drawer he took out some notes and handed them to the younger man. "You shall go. I will allow you two weeks' leave. If at the end of that time you are on the devil's track, I'll extend the leave. This money will pay for the beginning. The owners of this property are generous men, and wont object to an arrangement approved by me. Start at once."

"Thank ye, Captain Hilton ; you shan't regret your confidence." Stern's voice and manner were very respectful and Hilton did not notice that his eyes were fixed on the money drawer. Yet hurrying to his quarters Stern's thoughts were on that drawer and its contents.

"The old miser ! With all that money to be so stingy. It wouldn't be a bad idea—" but he did not finish his confidence to the soft warm air, being full of the hurry of preparation.

"If I don't find that devil may I be damned," he muttered a half hour later when with saddle-bags packed he left the camp. Hilton at his office door watched him out of sight.

The evening was a beautiful one. The stars were bursting into brightness out of a sky still flushed by a glorious sunset. The air was fragrant with sweet country smells, the gathered crops stacked in great mounds were ready to the threshing. There were peace, plenty, prosperity everywhere. Yet a deadly struggle was to begin. A man rode away in pursuit, most deadly pursuit, of his fellow-man. A prison more hideous than war could furnish yawned to receive a miserable fugitive. Still standing at his open door Hilton's eyes had wandered to the wood. It hid and yet it brought him nearer to Mary's cottage. Though miles away yet these trees were on the road that led to it and seemed a part of her little domain. How often had he looked at that wood with softening heart, but now he frowned, sighed and then frowned again.

"If I knew she had deceived me I'd strangle her," he muttered, thinking of Janet, of her strange excitement and the terror in her face when he had turned to the closet in which he had found—nothing. Could it be that the woman was a common thief—that she had concealed stolen goods there? He dismissed the thought. Eighteen years of faithful service did not prevent suspicion; it was the fact that there was nothing in the house to tempt her that convinced him. As for money, the woman was exact to the last farthing.

Had there been anything in that closet? He had puzzled over the question, but could recall nothing that would explain the woman's action, and while serving Mary, Janet's manner had seemed to be as usual.

Once—oh, maddening thought!—he fancied that there had passed a significant look between Mary and Janet. He was sure it was but his own imagination, and yet it had haunted his sleep with hideous dreams, and now when peaceful evening covered the earth, tortured him.

CHAPTER XXVI.

LITTLE JIM.

WHEN O'Neal saw Miss Dawson safe in the arms of the crowd below, the linen, untied, remained in his hand; he could easily, by fastening the other end, have swung himself to the ground. But he dared not. Though he had before the eyes of the multitude accomplished what no other dared do, though even at that moment their hearts were athrob with his bravery, he could not trust himself among them. At the window with death in the flames roaring around him, hungering for him, he stood a hero. But down there among them a whispered word, would make him a captive, a felon, a something for children to shrink from, for women to tremble at. For a second he looked at those faces watching him, listened to their cheers, and his heart cried out against his fate. Another second, and down on the floor he groped his way to the door. Battling with flames, shielding his face with scorching hands, he reached the balustrade of the staircase. Of hardest wood, it still resisted the fire, although in great gaps filled in with leaping flames the steps themselves were gone. Closing his eyes and clinging to the balustrade, he slid down, dashing through fire and smoke, until nearly strangled, almost fainting, he gained his feet and staggering put out his hand to keep from falling. He had passed through the doorway of a large room, when with a mighty crash the roof fell in. Parts of it like balls of fire came rolling down the steps, as he reached the closet from which he had helped remove the valuables. Strangled by smoke, with hands torn and bleeding, expecting momentarily a fearful death, his heart cried out at fate's cruel mockery. Hotter and hotter grew the air. Prostrate on the ground he groaned in agony ; better to rush out into captivity than to perish in the flames. He had given up his liberty —for what ? To be strangled like a rat in a hole. " Oh, Julie, my wife !" His heart yearned for her. He felt a mad impulse to curse God and die. Then over the roaring, crackling flames came Mary's voice, and through their scarlet shone the whiteness of her window. Again she was offering her life for his, again she murmured ; " Endure to the end !"

" I will, I will !" he cried, as half-suffocated, he fell senseless.

When he came to himself, the smoke had partially cleared away, the fire was over ; grey dawn was lighting the ruined mansion. But the dawn only brought fresh danger for him, as faint and weak he leaned against the wall. Something resting heavily on his shoulders made him put up his hand, and with thankfulness he found that through all the perils of the night the bundle Janet had rolled up for him was still securely strapped to his

back. Unfastening it he found that the blanket was
much singed and burned in great holes, but the bottle of
dye and the gray wig were in good condition. Inspired
by them with hope and strength, at one of the ruined
mirrors in the great room he covered face and hands
with the wash, and then putting on the wig, no longer
recognized himself. Cautiously peering from the hall
door he saw men who were evidently on guard. Watching his chance, he stole through the hall, down some
steps, out a back entrance, and into a building used as
a kitchen. When steps approached he hid himself, and
then as the watchmen turned and walked away from his
place of concealment, he hastily snatched up some bread
that lay on a tray, and ran unnoticed from the house,
out of the grounds and into the streets. Once away from
the immediate vicinity of the fire, he found the streets
deserted. But just as a feeling of comparative security was enabling him, half-famished as he was, to swallow
some of the bread, quick footsteps echoing in the quiet of
the morning made him spring for concealment behind
the hedge that bordered on the old garden. His heart
stood still, as, cautiously peeping between the leaves,
he recognized the man, who, with watchful eyes fixed
on the smoking ruin, walked quickly on. It was Stern,
one of the cruellest guards in Hilton's camp.

Had Stern seen the fire last night? Had Stern recognized him? These doubts changed almost to certainty
when the convict guard, after some little parley with a
negro passed the iron fence inclosing the scene of last
night's fire, and hastening up to the smouldering ruins
disappeared in the stone entrance. " He is looking for
something. He is looking for *me*," O'Neil said under
his breath, and left the sheltering hedge. There was not
a moment to be lost. Bending over until the massive
shoulders took the rounding of age and the gray wig
concealed his face, he hurried along as fast as he could

with the shambling gait he had assumed. He would reach the country, and there under bushes lie and rest until the day had gone ; night would kindly help him on his way. He turned to where the trees seemed nearest, and walked on. Many feet were now waking into bustle the sleeping town, and among them O'Neal could not so easily detect those steps for which he strained his ears. He had not heard them when, stopping at a corner, a man stood beside him, and he saw Stern. Shoulder to shoulder stood the two men, one satisfying himself with a look, the other on guard, ready to battle for his life. A moment more and Stern passed on, and with a gasp, a hurried glance, the negro ran swiftly down a side street. It was a quiet street, the houses were small, humble, and far apart. Their inmates were at work and did not notice the flying negro. Running in the middle of the road his steps were noiseless, and soon by a fortunate chance he found himself out of the town.

At last he was alone. Breathless he sank upon the ground, resting on the soft grass, gathering strength from nature's breast, calmness from her breath. Overhead were the swaying branches of trees, and around him he heard the soothing hum of insect life. O'Neal had found a peaceful spot where even a fugitive might rest. He took off the hot wig. Here in God's country, out of the city made by man, he gathered hope, and looking ahead, where the paths divided, speculated as to which he should take. If at some quiet farm house he could only obtain employment he would be most effectually in hiding, for in harvest time strangers could not be uncommon. Had Stern regularly started on the search—and this he did not doubt—he would probably look first among the alleys and hiding places of the city. Could a week or so elapse, the heat of the chase would be over, and then not only would he, if so fortunate as to find work, have a little money, but some one to refer to, and possibly by this reference could gain some sort of porter's place at or around the railroad, which would facilitate his return to Julie. At that name tears filled his eyes. Dashing them away he chose the path to the right and walked between sweet hedges over an almost untrodden carpet of grass. There seemed to be a a fatality about this man, for choosing what was apparently the least travelled of the diverging paths, he had hardly gone a hundred yards when he was startled by a child's voice frantically calling, " Whoa ! whoa !" and by the tramping of horses.

"Hold on, Jimmy, hold on !" It was the voice of a woman, and one evidently frightened. " Help ! help !" she screamed.

Parting the bushes and running in the direction of the sounds, O'Neal soon came to an open field across which, wildly plunging, two powerful horses were dragging a heavy wagon. On the driver's seat a little lad of seven or eight was pluckily trying to control the team. But his slight strength had no effect upon the frightened animals, and as the wagon rocked and swung the little fellow swayed from side to side, seeming each instant about to be flung to the ground.

Running toward the child and screaming alternately, " Hold on, Jim !" and " Help ! help !" was a woman, and at some distance following her, came a man with a long whip.

Unseen O'Neal could have passed on, but with no thought beyond the danger of the boy, he sprang forward until meeting the team he grasped the curb, and though lifted and dragged, held on, until by sheer force he mastered them. The child obeying his shout had thrown himself down in the bottom of the wagon, and clinging to the dashboard with a very white face, watched his deliverer.

When the horses, quieted but trembling, glared about with frightened eyes, O'Neal, twisting the reins around his arm, lifted out the child, giving him to his mother, who cried over him and held him to her breast.

She was still hugging and kissing the boy as the man came breathlessly up. He took the child from the woman, lifted him up and looked well at him.

"All right, little Jim, all right?" he asked.

"All right, Dad," and the boy reached out his arms, flinging them around his father's neck. For a moment the man hid his face on the little head, then putting the boy on his feet drew the back of one hand across his eyes, and held out the other to O'Neal.

"You're a nigger, but darn me if you'll ever want a friend while Dick Long lives."

And when O'Neal, saying that the horses were still frightened and needed careful managing, offered to drive them back to the house, Long seemed delighted.

"What! you're used to horses?" he said, and climbing up beside O'Neal watched his handling of the reins. "Ha, ha!" he broke out in a loud laugh, "darn me, but I'm in luck. I was jest alookin' for a chap to drive them horses with some cotton ter the railroad. They're a bit skittish, but they're a nice team. I ain't never seen their like fer kindness. Where did you work? Would you like a job?"

The two questions followed so close one on the other that O'Neal answered the last one first.

"I'd like a job, and I'm used to horses. I can do most any kind of work, but being a stranger have no one to recommend me. Would you take me without a character?"

"Kericter! Darn me ef I ain't seen enough of yourn. I tells yer, ef anything had a happened ter little Jim I'd never held up my head again."

When they reached the house, after securing the horses, O'Neal was invited in "ter git suthin' ter eat." The woman volubly explained how little Jim had "jest climbed up ter wait for Dad, when them vicious brutes started off," while little Jim himself hung around O'Neal, having as his mother declared, "taken sech a shine ter Tom," that when the negro with Long had loaded the wagon the child pleaded to go with him. O'Neal's promise to bring him home safely won the day for Jimmy. Seated on top of a cotton bale and holding to O'Neal's arm, the proud and happy child departed, calling back, "Good-by, Mammy, good-by, Dad," as they drove away.

The team was hardly out of sight when Stern rode up inquiring for the "old negro," only to receive the farmer's rough answer. After inspecting the group of negroes and satisfying himself that O'Neal was not among them, Stern rode back to town, taking a short cut through the woods. Under the shady trees, over the soft green grass he rode, with his mind full of plans for the negro's recapture. He would revisit that farmhouse on the morrow for there was something in the man's hesitation about the "new nigger" hired that had impressed him. And so putting spurs to his horse he galloped off to town and thence to the camp.

At sunset O'Neal and Jimmy returned. The boy was full of delight with his day's ride and O'Neal's kindness. Long and his wife were more than ever pleased with their new hand. O'Neal, tidying up the garden, with the child clinging to him and in his loving ways showing how he had won the little heart, felt almost happy. Good luck was coming to him. This child's affection was a fresh blessing. This little boy was the one to open the way to a happier life. To-day everything had been so fortunate. The railroad at which he had delivered the cotton had a branch road running near Ilanah, and after a little, when by daily deliveries of freight he had become an accustomed figure at the depot, he might gain some chance to work his passage. On the sweet new hay in the stable he slept well, after a kiss from little Jimmy, who stealing away before going to bed, crept beside Tom, and putting his arms around the negro's neck, said :

"Tom, I do love you, and I'm orful glad you've come. Good-night," and then he ran back to the house.

The little fellow's tenderness filled O'Neal with gratitude. Waking with the sun he was busied about the stable, attending to the horses and proving himself worthy of his place and the confidence of his master. When Dick Long came down, the stable work was all done.

" Come to brekfas', Tom," he said. " The ole woman sez as you shall eat your vittals with us. I ain't so sure Jimmy ain't a been coaxing her. Bnt at any rate I wos ter tell yer. An' I'll tell yer another thing. I'm pleased with yer, and as long as yer does yer duty I'll keep yer ter work. Is that a bargain ?"

A thankful heart and bright outlook for the future sweetened the coarse food. After the meal Tom returned to the stable to harness the team, while, much against his will, Jimmy, was not allowed to accompany him.

With hands in pockets and very wistful eyes the little fellow was about to go on some errand for his mother, when a stranger rode up to the house. It was Stern. He had decided to make an early visit to the farmer ; and by arousing his fears gain permission to examine each negro employed by him. Full of childish curiosity Jimmy began examining the stirrups and saddle, while Stern, dismounting talked to his mother and father. Finding something about the saddle to which he was unaccustomed, Jimmy turned for an explanation just as Stern was saying :

"This convict, Tom O'Neal, is a most dangerous man, of great strength, and rather superior in appearance. He knows, once found, there is no escape from the penalty, which he has increased by breaking out of prison. I warn you for your own good. He is a thief, convicted of stealing.   Not only your property, but your lives are not safe if you harbor him."

Stern's pleasant appearance had ingratiated him with the woman, who offering him a chair, asked, " Won't the gentleman set down ?"

Graciously declining the invitation Stern watched the man.   Dick Long's face was puckered with doubt and hesitation, as looking down he struck his boot with the long whip he had taken in his hand when waiting for O'Neal to drive up with the wagon.   After a moment, he said :

" Wal, stranger, I knows this nigger I hired ain't no thief, fer last night he could a took all I had, an' this mornin' everything's safe."

" Well, sir, I don't say your man is Tom O'Neal.   I only ask to see him," and then Stern went on to mention the penalties prepared for those who harbored convicted felons, until Mrs. Long, growing nervous, said, " Why, Dick, there's no harm in callin' Tom.   Here, you, Jimmy !"   But Jimmy was nowhere to be seen.   With beating heart and frightened face the little fellow had been listening to their conversation.

Tom ! why that was his friend.   Tom saved his life ! They shall not take him to prison.   They shall not call him a thief.   His lips quivered, his eyes filled with tears, he was about to beg his father to drive that horrid man away, when his breath stopped, his little heart almost broke.   His mother, his own mother, said, " Call Tom up !"

" No, they shan't neither, they shan't catch my Tom," thought the child, and unnoticed he slipped away behind the house, then running to the stable as fast as he could, he threw himself sobbing violently into O'Neal's arms.

" What is it, my boy, what is it ?" Tom stopped har-nessing the horses to soothe the excited child.

" Tom, Tom, there's a man up there looking for a

thief, and moth–mother says he can see you. O Tom, Tom, he will take you to pri–prison. And then I wo–won't see you any more, my dear, dear Tom."

O'Neal put the child on the ground. But the little heart was too full, the little arms held fast.

"Don't, don't let him take you, Tom. Do–don't !"

"I won't Jimmy, but you must be my friend. Stop crying and look at Tom."

The child lifted his tear-stained face, gazing up to the black one looking earnestly at him.

"I am the Tom O'Neal that man's looking for, and if he finds me I'll be taken back to a horrible prison. But, Jimmy, dear little Jimmy, you'll believe Tom when he tells you he never stole anything in his life. I was sent to prison but I am not a thief. Good-by, my dear little boy, good-by. You won't forget Tom. God bless you. Good-by."

He took the child in his arms, kissed him, and then gently unclasping the arms the little fellow had thrown around his neck, laid him on the sweet hay and—fled.

CHAPTER XXVII.

MAN'S INGRATITUDE.

AFTER much parley, Stern, aided by Mrs. Long, convinced Dick that it was safer to let the new hand be seen. Acting on Stern's suggestion, they decided to walk to the stable where the man was at work instead of summoning him to the house. Stern believed this to be the way to surprise the negro, and Long unwillingly yielding, felt less shame in thus conducting the inspection. Only yesterday the negro had saved the life of his child, and now he was turning him over to prison.

"It ain't true, I know it ain't true," he said aloud, trying more to reassure and excuse himself than to convince Stern.

But Stern answered: "I hope, Mr. Long, you are correct." And then in silence they proceeded to the stable.

Outside, tied to a post, stood the team partially harnessed. The stable door wide open showed nothing but neatness and careful tending.

Glancing in and remembering its previous condition, Long felt more than ever ashamed of injuring so efficient a workman. "I ain't goin' in," he said doggedly, turning away his face as with a look of triumph Stern entered and examined the building.

Into each stall, through the yard, around each stack of grain he went and found nobody. Nobody but a little boy lying face downward on a pile of new-mown hay.

"Why, that's our Jim. Jimmy!" and Mrs. Long who, through curiosity had followed Stern, now in motherly concern leaned over her child. Sobbing and crying, the boy could not answer her questions or Stern's, who tried coaxings, bribes and even threats. The little fellow's words were so indistinct, so vague, that feeling he was only losing time Stern walked impatiently away. The mother, left alone, had no better success. Either the child knew nothing of Tom, or he would not tell; little Jim was true and loyal to his friend.

The negro's disappearance, joined to Stern's belief that he had harbored the convict, aroused the fears of Dick Long. Remembrance of the service rendered was lost in the fear that he had been dealing with a felon. Expecting to find himself robbed in some hidden manner, he summoned the laborers from the field, ordering them all to unite in the search for Tom. It made a holiday for the men, who with jests and laughter drove pitchforks into stacks of grain and piles of hay, and searched every nook and cranny around the farm. But the only result was the certainty that however much convicted of stealing, Tom had taken nothing from his new master.

"It was only because he had not time," Stern assured Long, who shook his head, looked grave and said nothing. He may have been listening to little Jimmy. The child, exhausted with crying, now leaned his hot face against his father's and whispered in his ear :

"How could yer, Dad, how could yer, when he saved my life ? He ain't no thief, he ain't stole nothin', an' yer said yer'd be his friend."

While the men beat bush and meadow, hunting for the convict, O'Neal, within sight and sound of his pursuers looked down as they passed and repassed under the tree where, covered by luxuriant foliage, he was concealed. As for an instant after parting from the weeping child he stood hesitating at the stable door, there seemed to him no shelter so near as this great live oak, that, forming the corner mainstay of the stable, stretched its huge branches protectingly over the child of its adoption. Voices and steps approaching gave the negro little time for consideration. He climbed up the rugged bark, high above the stable roof, where, finding a branch upon which the dark leaves grew thickest, he extended himself full length upon it. The dark color of his clothes made no contrast to the wood, and he hid his face among the leaves. Here he felt comparatively secure ; and lying thus for hours nearly motionless, he had full opportunity to moralize on man's ingratitude. From his observatory he saw men on horseback dispatched in different direction and surmised that they were messengers sent in warning to the neighborhood farmhouses. He heard the mid-day bell for dinner, and after the half hour's rest he saw the laborers return to the field.

"They have given up the hunt for the day," he thought.

But Stern did not give up the search, He walked round and round, once even climed half way up the tree. It was not until night was advanced that O'Neal had a chance to leave his hiding-place.

Stiff and sore he slipped to the ground. He was so exhausted that he resolved on the rather daring plan of taking one of the horses, which after he had put some miles between himself and the place that but yesterday was offered for his lifelong shelter, he could then turn loose to find its way homeward. He looked up at the low frame dwelling-house with a light shining in one window.

" They are on the lookout for a thief," he said bitterly, and then little Jimmy's sobs and tears, little Jimmy's warm affection were remembered, softening the hard uprising of human nature.

He tried the stable door. It was locked, but with his great strength it was no difficult matter to force the worn-out iron. The hasp fell off, the door opened, the sweet odor of hay floated out, and he heard a neigh from one of the team he had that morning tended with care and pride. A lover of horses, and an adept in managing them, he had no difficulty by soothing sounds and motions in quieting the dark bay that seemed to recognize him. Leading out the horse, and putting a log against the door to keep it steady, he smiled bitterly at the thought that in the morning should the horse be missing Long would believe the worst that could be said of the negro he had harbored. Letting down bars and striding across fields, he found himself at some distance from the house, when striking the road, he mounted and galloped at full speed for life and liberty. The horse bounding beneath him, the cool air rushing by, brought a sense of exhilaration. After all, he was well, was free, and even if he were being pursued he had met friends, and good ones ! This animal that every now and then proudly arched its neck beneath its rider's hand was glad to serve him. So the eyes that looked up to the dark blue sky with its myriad of stars, were full of gratitude.

It was like giving up a friend, when, leaping to the ground, he tightened the girth more securely and then turning the horse's head whence they had come, gave him a little cut and called " Home." But the parting grew harder ; for the animal, springing forward under the sting of the willow, went only a few paces, then turned, came back to O'Neal standing in the road, and rubbing his head on his shoulder seemed to ask him to be his master.

" I can't, old fellow, I can't," said the negro, and then, ashamed thus to requite this affection, he gave him a sharp blow of the whip. The horse reared, plunged ; another lash, and like an arrow off he flew, back to the farm house.

Little Jimmy, first to awake, wandered out with pale face and swollen eyes, and found the tall bay at the stable door in the early morning. The blanket wet with sweat and the muddy legs showed that he had made a long and hurried journey. The boy, although a little afraid of the great beast, unstrapped the girth, hid the blanket, rubbed off the mud, and led the horse back to his stall before his father was astir or there was any other witness to big Jim's return.

" You won't tell, Jim, you won't tell," little Jim whispered, standing on tiptoe and peeping over the neighboring stall at the tall bay, who contentedly grinding his corn seemed to have forgotten the whole affair. And then as he thought of " dear Tom " the little fellow's grief broke out afresh. In the stable his father found him still crying.

"I say, Jimmy, git up and don't be sech a baby," Long said in a rough voice, but the hand on the boy's shoulder was gently drawn away, and when the child had run to the house in answer to his mother's sharp call Dick Long, whose fears had been awakened by the broken lock, but who had found everything in order, looked after the little fellow, saying : " I'm darned ef I don't feel near as bad as Jim. I wonder ef Tom *was* a thief?" Time passed, and Long went about his daily tasks, thinking sometimes of the negro who never came back. Little Jim watched for him often at sunrise and at evening, sometimes called out his name in lonely places, listening, almost fancying as children will that a rustling leaf, a falling nut, was token of the friend who had so quickly won his heart. But Jim grew older and the memory of Tom became fainter and fainter, and perhaps would have died out altogether put for the wonderful gossips his mother would have with any chance visitor, about the convict they had housed " unknownst " to them. She "jest kep' her eyes open," she would declare, "and the nigger didn't hev no chance." Then Jimmy's indignant heart would give a bound and he would cry : "Mother, you know Tom warn't no thief, and he saved my life."

But gradually the memory of the negro faded out of their quiet lives, with that of the " nice young man," Mr. Stern, who rode away the morning after big Jim's return.

Stern, convinced that the " Tom " hired by Long and the convict were one and the same, had gained something. The man lived ; and his reported dangerous character would bar the possibility of work or food being given to a stranger by any one in the neighborhood. In fact, every strange negro was and would be for some time under suspicion and liable to arrest.

There was not a person except little Jim who was not in sympathy with Stern, and as he rode from house to house repeating his cautions and renewing his promises of reward many an honest fellow grasped his hand cordially and wished him safely back again with his recaptured prisoner. Thus leaving a guard behind him, Stern, rode on through the country, following the clews that were sometimes so many as to bewilder rather than assist. Yet with the bloodhound tenacity he kept on. His leave of absence had been extended by Hilton into a month, two weeks of which had passed without finding the negro. The harvest time was in O'Neal's favor; laborers being in demand, many negroes were afoot seeking employment, and it was hard to decide which was the convict. Night after night Stern cursed the black skins and himself when, after a hard day's ride in following up an exact description of the negro, he would come upon a stranger contentedly eating his pork and cornbread outside of a farmhouse door.

It was after one of these fruitless errands that Stern's luck changed. Turning into a lane that led to a lonely house he asked for dinner and food for his horse.

Growing restless while waiting for the leisurely movements of the housewife he walked a little distance away to a spot where a spring bubbling out of some rocks trickled over a pebbly bed into the meadow below. Without plan or thought he followed it until in a clump of trees it formed a pool over which a man, a negro, was stooping to drink.

At his step the negro raised his eyes, sprang to his fet, and Stern faced O'Neal. For an instant the negro stood bewildered. With hand pressed to his head and hollow eyes he looked at the man, who, in triumph, grasped his arm.

"I have you, you devil!" cried Stern, and though much smaller and slighter, he seemed more than a match for the emaciated creature before him.

Sleeping under hedges, eating when and where he could, now staying hunger with bits of mouldy bread, now with raw corn, and only rarely obtaining a meal, O'Neal was not far from starvation.

He recognized Stern, and his brain filling with phantoms, created around him the convict camp, its guards, its dogs, and the hundreds of miserable faces.

Was he once more among them? Then this flight had been a dream, and the dream from which, exhausted, he had just awakened, was reality.

It was not until Stern, still grasping his arm, began to fasten on his wrist the handcuffs which since he had started on his search had never left his pocket, that the truth came back to O'Neal.

With a sound half groan, half laugh, he dashed them aside and flinging his arms around the white man would have crushed him, but that athletic and watchful Stern met him in this fierce embrace.

Locked together they fell to the ground in desperate struggle. Freeing one hand Stern felt for his revolver, but that instant had nearly been his last.

Throwing him back, O'Neal tightened his grip and with a gasp the white man lay motionless. "Now,' shrieked O'Neal as he snatched the revolver, " Now is my chance, you murderer of prisoners."

His shaking finger had touched the trigger, his gleaming eyes were like a madman's. Suddenly he staggered to his feet, and looked around. The revolver hung loosely in his hand, his eyes were fixed in a sightless stare. His wife's cry—her words " he is not guilty "—rung in his ears. Mary's charity arose to warn him back from crime.

Miserable he was, miserable he might be, but a murderer, never ! He flung away the tempter, and running, hiding, was once more a fugitive.

CHAPTER XXVIII.

COULD THERE COME REQUITAL ?

WHILE O'Neal, surrounded by difficulties, was slowly making his way to her, Julie, his wife, in failing health and fading hope, had fallen into a melancholy that left very little of that intelligence, which, considering her opportunities and ancestry, had been remarkable. Had her husband died in the ordinary course of events, she would have doubtless felt a life-long grief. But to see him unjustly branded as a thief, to know that the future for which both had striven was lost to them and that their child was heir to something worse than slavery, preyed upon her mind until reason became unsettled. " Save your husband "—it was the one thought of her life. She would see faces smiling at her, hands pointing the way to his deliverance.

After that early morning when Mr. Day, striding past, had called out his parting words of cheer, she would stand at the gate at dawn, at sunset, would even run out at midnight, fancying that she heard that firm, light tread and Tom's heavier one beside it.

" I'm coming, Tom ; welcome home !" she would waken Mammy with the quick, nervous cry, and the good old woman calling from her own bed : " Hush, Julie, chile, you'll wake de baby," would fall asleep again, unconscious of the ghostly figure at the gate watching, watching, for what came not.

Daily Julie went to the post-office for letters. But the one sent by O'Neal had been mislaid by the coachman intrusted with the commission, and the one written by Dennis informing her of her husband's escape had been carelessly overlooked, and was now on its way to

9*

the dead-letter office, while the "Mrs. Julie O'Neal" to whom they were addressed grew "queerer an' queerer," people said, seeing her gradually sinking into melancholia.

Perhaps this would have come as the natural result of the blow her husband's conviction had been to her. But it is a lesson to the careless, a sermon to the negligent, that so slight a thing as a mislaid letter may help break a human heart. With her baby in her arms Julie would go up to the court house and singing the minor strains abounding in negro melodies, would walk up and down under the trees. She was so gentle, so unobtrusive, and her voice was so sweet, that she was seldom molested. Sometimes she vaguely heard the whispered comments of children who would gather in a curious little group and say to each other, "Dat's de crazy ooman."

Once, Brown, coming to attend to some matters, found her within the inclosure. He did not recognize the trim-looking girl whose skin was already changing to that death-like hue which sometimes in the negro accompanies mental affliction.

"Yer'll hev ter go outside, my woman," he said. But with nervous hand she caught his arm and whispered eagerly: "Oh, let me stay. I'm waiting for his trial. It's Tom O'Neal, my husband. He's not guilty, he's not guilty." Brown gulped down a great sob and moved back a step or two trying to hide the tears that started to his eyes.

"I'd a most forgot the pore gal. So that's what she's come to. That's what the law has done. Pore niggers, it do seem a shame the State don't pertect 'em. It gives 'em law, but monstrous little justice!" He leaned against a tree shaking his head as he looked at her. She was watching him. The sad vacuity of her eyes had changed to eagerness, such piteous eagerness, it would have touched a harder heart than the bailiff's. She looked cautiously round, and seeing no one went quickly up to Brown, holding the baby toward him as she spoke :

"He's innocent. On my child's life I swear it. Do you believe me? You do believe?" And when Brown, sobbing now in good earnest, answered : "I—I do, my pore gal—I do," she took his hand in her hot thin one.

"Then tell the Judge," she whispered, "tell him to set Tom free."

It was only by promising her he would do this, that Brown persuaded her to go back to Mammy's house. He looked down the street until the slight-figure in dark calico passed through the little gate of Mammy's neat garden.

" Pore gal, pore gal !"

Brown walked home thinking all the way of the negro and his unfortunate wife. When, with a wild outcry the young Browns rushed to meet him, he held as many little hands as he could, and then, surrounded by the others, told of the meeting with "pore Julie."

"Pore Julie," the children cried in chorus, shaking their heads in unconscious imitation of Dad.

Little Meg did not speak. She hung behind a step or so and quietly wiped away her tears in a noiseless fashion peculiar to the staid little girl who was so great a contrast to her sisters and brothers. These wild ones, their pity soon forgotten in fun, did not notice that Meg's eyes were redder than usual. But kind old " Dad " did. He took his little girl in his arms, holding her on his breast, when the noisy band in obedience to their mother's order had gone to bed.

" Don't ger grieve, Meg," and he patted her cheek. " I knows yer can't help it—tender little heart—but don't yer grieve. I'll take yer to town ter see pore Julie. My ! but ain't she got the cunningest little nigger I ever sot eyes on."

But Meg did not see Julie for many days and weeks.

When at last she went to Mammy's house the old woman was alone with the baby.

"Julie's gorned," Mammy told the sympathetic little girl who took her own handkerchief to dry the tears that trickled down the kindly black face.

After meeting Brown, Julie grew more and more restless. She wandered about the town and one morning, much to Mammy's surprise, put on her bonnet before she had eaten breakfast, and softly touching the old woman's arm as she stoopod over the fire, said more naturally than she had for some time spoken, "Mammy, I'm going to walk out to the cabin."

Mammy lifted her head and looked perplexed." Why, Julie, chile, dere ain't no use a-goin' dar, only to griebe yourself."

"Mammy, Mammy," and she burst into tears, "I think I will grow stronger if I can look at the house where I was so happy with Tom."

"Well, chile, go an' de Lord bress de journey"—for Mammy felt that Julie's tears were a healing flood. "An' now, afore you goes, jest take a little mouthful, that's a good chile."

Always gentle and yielding, Julie tried to eat. But the effort and delay only excited her, and Mammy preparing a lunch for her, told her "she had better start afore de day grows too late."

She took her baby in her arms and the lunch in her hand. Mammy followed her to the gate, and then returning for her basket of clean clothes went along the same street. A little way from the door she found on the pavement the paper of lunch.

"Dere!" and stooping she picked it up. "De pore chile's los' de lunch! Well, well, de Lord knows whar she gits de bread as is her staff, for she don't eat nuffin' an' is jest fallin' off ter skin an' bones. Pore gal, she's failin' fas'. I'se afeard sometimes she'll fergit an' drop

de baby. He *am* a nice young un," and Mammy's face
was full of smiles as she thought of the little child that
had crept into her heart.

Hurrying the mid-day meal Mammy rested a little
from her ironing, expecting that Julie would return.
The hours came and went but Julie did not come. The
old woman stopped her work a dozen times to look out
of the door and up the road. But Julie was not in sight.
Over and over the old woman counted on her fingers.
" Well, Julie had jes' two hours ter go, dat makes two,
and two hours ter come, dat makes four, an' den two ter
stay, an' dat makes six." This calculation was perfectly
correct and ample time for the trip, yet ten hours had
gone and no Julie came.

" Lord, Lord, I hopes nothin' ain't happened ter her,"
and a great fear began to fill the honest old heart as
Mammy thought of the baby.

It was not until after sunset that she could stop her
work. " Well, it ain't no use," she said, " I jest can't keep
on ironin' when I feels my heart a-bustin." And for the
twentieth time she went to the door. At the gate stood
Julie.

" Lor, Julie, chile, whar you bin ?" Mammy ran to
the gate to meet her. But something in Julie's face
dampened her pleasure. She looked a moment at the
poor girl.

" What's de matter, chile, what's de matter ?" she said
as she took the baby from its mother. Julie not noticing
that she no longer held the child still kept her arms in
the same position and made no answer. " What's de
matter, Julie, chile ?" Mammy asked again.

But still Julie did not speak. Her face was like that
of a corpse, except that the eyes were full of terror—a
terror that made her shake all over and gaze back across
her shoulder intently, as if she were looking for something. Mammy took her hand and leading her into the

kitchen mude her sit down by the fire and gave her a cup
of tea.   It was only then that she seemed to realize where
she was, and lost a little of her strange manner.

"It's gone, Mammy, it's gone," she said in a sepul-
chral whisper.

Busily feeding the infant with bread and milk, Mammy was not looking at Julie, and intending her words
more to soothe than question her, said : " What's gone,
Julie ?"

"The house, our cabin.   I could not find it."

At this answer, Mammy started suddenly, nearly
dropping the cup of food.   She felt sure that Julie was
crazy.   The hope she often discussed over her ironing,
"dat de pore gal 'ud git well if Tom only comes back,"
left her as she looked at the pale face of the mulatto,
the thin figure bent forward with folded hands extended
on her lap, and sad eyes gazing into the fire.

"Clean gorn," the old woman said under her breath
to the solemn baby, who, satisfied with bread and milk,
seemed to have no other desire than to watch Mammy's
face.   "Clean gorn, pore gal," and Mammy shook her
head and said as a nurse might to a sick child : "Julie,
Julie, Mammy 'll go wid yer to-morrow.   We'll fin' de
little cabin where you an' Tom use ter be happy, an'
where de Lord'll send you eider happiness agin, or de
joys ob de Hebenly Jerusalem."

With hopeless eyes Julie looked at her, and sighing,
murmured :

" Mammy, God has forgotten us."

Mammy striving to administer a lecture against
"sech sinfulness," mingled with sure promises "of de
glory dat's comin'," broke down completely under a
second look from those sad eyes, and still holding the
baby went into the yard to have her "cry out."   But
Julie did not stir, did not notice her absence.   The next
morning, however, when Mammy, dressing the baby

"spic an' span," as she said, held him up for his mother
to see, Julie brightened, she even smiled. Yet her mind
was not clear, for when the moment came for starting
she took the shawl Mammy had put near the sleeping
child, and holding it tenderly in her arms, smiled and
spoke to it in the soft tones mothers believe best suited
to baby ears. Mammy, seeing this, felt easier, even while
it wrung her heart. "You jest come 'long wid Mammy,"
she whispered to the copper-faced philosopher, who in
his quiet content seemed to approve the arrangement.
"You jest come 'long. Ole Mammy'll take care ob you
till your mudder comes back to herself. I'se feared dat
will nebber be," she said under her breath, not wishing
to take the infant too deeply into her confidence.

The fresh morning air and Mammy's kind words
revived Julie. Presently she looked at the shawl, then
at Mammy, and recognized the fact that the old woman
had the baby. She stopped, put her hand to her head
and looked once more at the shawl.

"How did it happen?" she spoke to herself. "I
thought I had the child." Then turning to Mammy she
offered to take him. But Mammy was afraid to give him
up.

"No, no, chile, you jest pick Mammy some ob dem
pretty flowers," the old woman said, and a moment after,
singing a sad little melody, Julie began to gather the
feathery grass weaving it into graceful wreaths. As they
neared the place whereon the cabin had stood, she ran
forward, losing her breath and stopping bewildered,
pushing back her sun-bonnet, gazed around. It was
thus Mammy saw her as she hurried along.

"Wal, I reckin I'se clean gone too," Mammy said,
looking at the ploughed up ground where the little cabin
had stood. All that remained of the negro's home was
a pile of logs.

It was simply the removal of a useless cabin, a few

old logs that stood on ground for which there was possibly still due some payments. At all events, it was the property of a convicted felon and an eyesore to the rich and powerful. Therefore, what more natural than that it should have been pulled down and thrown aside? It is an example of nature old as the days of the man who coveted the one field. But reasonable as such actions seem to their perpetrators, no excusing reasons suggested themselves to the two women standing side by side on the spot where once had burned the hearth fire of an humble home.

Julie, poor shadowy creature, whispered incoherently, her pallid face grown more pallid, her sad eyes more hopeless ; and Mammy's short comfortable person seemed to gain dignity as her honest heart swelled with indignation.

"De rich hab robbed de po', but de Lord's vengeance is a-nigh." She shook her closed hand at the distant house of the Eaton family. Could there ever come requital? Would a day fulfill the old woman's words until they should stand as prophecy? Now their only effect was to bring forth a laugh from a gay young gentleman, who, riding across country had jumped his horse over the fence near the two negresses. His face flushed with dissipation, young as it was, demonstrated one of the saddest phases of life—self-indulgence.

"Go it, old woman. We'll stand as much of that vengeance as *you* can bring," he called out insolently.

This salutation, considering that he belonged to the wealth and power of the state, and the old woman to the miserable black element, should have overpowered her with its condescension. But although she knew him to be that " Mars Eaton " who had caused all the misery of her friends, although she knew not what he might do to her, she looked up at the young heir to great estate with unflinching eyes.

"Oh, you're spunky, are you?" and perhaps to

frighten her he touched the spur, making his horse spring forward.

But Mammy stirred not. She trembled a little, thinking her hour had come, and tried to pray. The noise made Julie turn. She looked at the horseman with vacant eyes, which changed to recognition as she said: "Mr. Eaton." She did not utter another word ; did not bid him look upon his work, nor did she raise her voice calling upon justice to abolish those statutes that have in reality disfranchised the negro.

These laws, enduring for years, have almost destroyed the power to criticise, or desire to amend. And this in a State where their continuance is so much to the interest of the ruling element. Interest is a powerful lever with law-makers ; and where the oppressed have no voice, no representation, their rights are readily forgotten. These two, the mulatto and the young *roué*, represented each a class, existing, it is true, throughout the world, wherever is found helplessness and the unrestrained evil in man.

Even though the "nigger" was to him a domestic drudge, fitted for and created to slavery, Mr. Eaton felt a little uncomfortable under Julie's steady gaze. The sadness of the thin figure and of that pallid face made him wince, as he looked upon them here on the desecrated hearthstone of the home where she had seemed fair enough to strike his fancy. She was evidently ill ; involuntarily he pitied her. He tried to laugh it off, being prone to joke on serious subjects. But there was little to assist a joke in the figure before him.

"What's the matter?" he said, feeling sure that if any of his friends could see him they "would make no end of a time" over it. "What's the matter, Julie? Are you sick?" As she did not answer he grew impatient. "I say, leave off staring. And if you want your money for the part of the land you owned, the governor'll give you

a fair price. I'll see he does the generous thing by you."
Still she did not answer.

"Are you dumb? Lost your tongue? Well, Julie,
here's a dollar for the little nig," and tossing a coin to
her he turned his horse's head, riding swiftly away and
cursing to himself at "her damned impudence." For
O'Neal he had no thought, no pity. He could not forget
the fact that that "nigger" had dared to strike him. It
was to revenge himself that he took the suggestion of
an associate, and with the assistance of his body-servant,
who had a private grudge against O'Neal, turned the
negro over to the law to be punished as a felon.

The elder Eaton had been ignorant of the plotting
against the negro. While he would surely have killed
an ex-slave for striking a white gentleman, he would not
have lent himself to any underhanded scheme. His prosecution of the negro had been a fair one, so far as he was
concerned. He had been robbed, and determined to
make an example of some one. The little field owned
by O'Neal close to his residence was a constant annoyance to him. He had several times offered to buy it, but
the negro having received it partly as a legacy from his
dead master, had not wished to sell. After his conviction, Mr. Eaton, in looking up the title, found some legal
flaws, and so the rich man quietly possessed himself of
the land, acting in accordance with the law in seeking
for all claimants of property, and holding himself ready
to pay its price. He felt not only justified but absolutely
generous. It was easy for him to pour balm upon his
conscience. The question of the negroes' affection for
their home did not occur to the rich man. He did not
give the negro credit for any of the finer feelings, and
would have been angry indeed could he have seen
Mammy, as with the face of an outraged woman she
stooped and picking up the coin flung it violently after
his eldest son.

"Take your dollar," cried the old woman, trembling now with indignation. "Take it, you man who 'sults de miserble you has made, an' larfs at de hearts you has broke. Dere is justice in de Hebens even for de black folks, an' dere's hell fire even for de whites."

Julie had fallen on her knees. She hid her face and seemed praying. Presently she bent over, took a handful of earth and kissed it passionately. Then she rose.

"Come! Come! Mammy, I'm going to the Governor to ask Tom's pardon."

She spoke so quietly that the old woman, whose short lived anger had given place to tears, answered: "Dat's right, Julie, dat's right. You'll get it sho'. An' now, honey, let's go home." For Mammy belonged to the natural order of nurses who never irritate the sick by needless opposition.

That night Mammy kept the baby in her own bed, as Julie without noticing the child, had fallen asleep soon after their return. She looked so peaceful when Mammy glanced at her before putting out the light that the good old soul felt relieved. Tired herself, she slept until daybreak, when she wakened with a start and put out her hand to find the baby lying warm and snug on its pillow.

"Well, I'se glad o' dat," she whispered, "fer sho' I tought dere was a sperrit roun'." Frightened at she knew not what, she went over to Julie's corner to look at her. It was still dark in the little room and she passed her hands cautiously over the pillow. It was unoccupied. More and more alarmed, she ran to the window and raised the calico curtain.

Julie was gone! The black silk dress Tom had given her for her wedding present and which a few days after the baby's birth Mammy had brought in to town with the rest of her clothes, was no longer on the peg where it had been hanging; and a neat little bonnet Julie used to wear at church was also taken, as well as Mammy's blanket shawl.

With trembling fingers the old woman slipped on her clothes and ran out of the house. Up and down the streets she ran looking for Julie and inquiring at the cabins of their friends. She was not to be found. Unable to spare another day from work, Mammy begged a negro she knew to go out to the spot where the O'Neal cabin had been.

"She's dere, I'se sho' she's dere," Mammy said, trying to quiet her anxiety.

But she was not there. And though the kind old woman kept up the search for days, nothing was heard of the poor girl.

"Well, chile!" Mammy with many a groan and head shake stated the case to the grave baby. "Well, chile, you is got no fader an' no mudder now. Only Mammy, pore ole Mammy. But I promises, ef yer'll only jes' keep good, Mammy'll be de same as fader, mudder an' brudder."

Whereat, to her mingled wonder and delight the copper-colored philosopher raised up his voice in a strange unearthly crow. It was the first baby sound he had ever emitted except an occasional faint wail, when some pressing need was neglected beyond infantile patience.

"Well, well, he's de knowingest chile," ole Mammy appealed to the kettle, " he jes' 'cepts de sitiwation."

A knock startled Mammy from contemplation of the baby's wisdom. Putting him on the bed she ran to the door and opened it to Dennis.

"Bress de Lord, bress de Lord !" and then to enforce her obligations on Deity, in louder tone. " Bress de Lord, I say. I'se dat glad ter see yer. I tought yer wos a sperrit. Sit down, please, massa, sit down," and she dusted and redusted the newest of the two old chairs.

It was pleasant to be welcomed back, for Dennis had but just returned from Milton, having been busied in collecting material for the work which had been the original motive for the trip through the mineral district of Georgia.

"Where is Julie?" he asked, after a little.

"She's gorned!" and then as to Meg Brown Mammy told of Julie's disappearance.

"Poor girl!" said Dennis, after listening to the little story which lost nothing of its sadness in Mammy's simple words. "Poor girl!" It was all Dennis could say. He thought of O'Neal, the dangers he had braved, the risks he had run. And after all should he reach his home he would find his wife gone! Even should she be recovered in the body, who would bring back her mind, her memory? The tender little scene between these two, when Julie had kissed her husband's hand as in the dock he waited for his trial, came before him. And then the negro's agony when bursting the inclosing rail he had clasped to his heart his fainting wife! Dennis sighed heavily as he asked :

"Did Julie receive the letters I wrote?"

"No, massa."

"Not even the few lines I wrote telling her of O'Neal's escape!"

"'Scaped! Has he 'scaped?" The old woman held her breath for fear the walls might hear. "How did he get to do it?"

"God alone knows how he managed what seems almost impossible. But he has escaped, and up to the time I left Milton he had not been recaptured. I have hired a man to send me word as soon as he is retaken. This has to be managed privately. You see, Mammy, these convicts are not in charge of the State, but of guards hired and paid for by the parties who work the convicts. The State does not seem to know much about

them ; and cares less," he added in a bitter undertone.
And then, as the old woman's eyes were fixed on him
with the wonder and inquiry of a patient child, he explained that only for the escaped are penalties exacted.

"How O'Neal not only managed to escape but to
remain undiscovered is a marvel, all the more as I have
reason to know that extraordinary efforts were made to
recapture him.   And after all he has endured, Julie has
disappeared !   It is most unfortunate."

"Dat's so, massa." Mammy heaved a great sigh.
And then with motherly pride she said : "But jes' look
at de baby."

"Yes, he is a nice child," said Dennis, desiring to
please Mammy, who watched his face as she held up the
young philosopher. "A nice baby," and then he wondered if all infants had the habit of looking so much
wiser than their elders.   He sat thinking, trying to form
some plan by which with the limited means at his disposal he could bring Julie back to her friends.

"Mammy," he said suddenly, "I'll see Brown. He
might suggest some way of tracing Julie.   I believe she
has gone seeking the governor.   Poor girl !   Even with
her wits about her, it would be a hopeless task.   As it is,
she will probably be lodged in some charitable institution.   Poor girl, poor girl !   As for the cabin, I'll have
it rebuilt.   Mr. Eaton will probably pay for the ground
he has taken.   It was a gross injustice, but that will not
change facts, nor is it sufficient reason to make the rich
give back their rights to the poor.   Probably the best
plan will be to get as good a price as we can for the
ground.   I'll call on Mr. Eaton or his man of business.
If Julie should be wandering about she might find her
way to the cabin even if she forgets this place.   It has
sometimes happened that those in her condition retain
old memories."

While Dennis spoke more to himself than her, the old

woman listened as if Solomon and all others accounted
wise could not approach the knowledge of this one-armed
carpet-bagger.   She trusted him, she knew he was her
friend, in fact the friend to every helpless creature that
came in his way.   And women, high or low, educated or
ignorant, are more or less governed by affection.   Whom
they love seems always wise to them, so the old negress
in her humble way was but a further illustration of the
sex, that, disclaim as they may, are in one manner or
another, according to his nature, the blessing or the
bane of man.

CHAPTER XXIX.

IN THE DUSKY SHADOWS.

AFTER burning the midnight oil writing, writing,
writing, until with head aching and side throbbing he fell into sleep and dreamed of Mary,
Dennis wakened early in the morning.   He had no time
for lounging, for long reveries, for watching the curling
smoke of his pipe.   He made to himself no more bitter
commentaries on the folly of noble impulses.

"Not a moment to waste," he said as he thought of
Mary, and of Janet's dark figure barring the way to her.
"O white dove!   When next your wings would bring
you to me there shall be a nest awaiting you."   And then
laughing, he roused himself from a reverie so bright it
had nearly robbed him of half the hour so valuable to
him.

After his modest breakfast he walked out to the
Browns.   The little cottage without a child in sight
seemed still asleep as Dennis, fearing that illness might
have visited the happy family, hastened his steps.   But

the sight of Mrs. Brown dissipated such thoughts. Fair and comely she looked with her sleeves rolled up and her round arms whitened by the flour of the bread she was vigorously kneading. "Good strong muscles, too," Dennis thought, remembering Meg's pleasure at Tim's having escaped the switching.

"Lor sakes, is it you, Mister Day," and she bobbed him a courtsey while she filled her pan with the snowy balls of dough. "Law sakes, it is really you? I'm real pleased; I can't a'most help it, though pleasure *is* a sin. But that shawl; however did you know I wanted one? I has worn it five times ter meetin', an' feels mighty good in it. As fer them chillerns they was *the* most delighted when the box comed. An' now I hopes you'll stay ter dinner. I'll get up suthin' nice. Lor sakes, I've been so shamed o' the supper you took with us! Nuthin' but bread an' butter. I'd got mad with Brown about it, but what's the use o' gettin' mad with him? It don't do no good. Now yer'll stay, won't yer?"

"Thank you, Mrs. Brown, but I can't stay. I've just walked out to see Mr. Brown in reference to that unfortunate woman who since her husband's conviction has lost her reason."

"Pore critter! Brown told me. I ain't no hand fer niggers, but I ain't one fer treatin' 'em like dogs. Well, ef yer won't stay yer'll fin' Brown in the pertater patch. Good mornin', sir, good mornin'." She stood watching Dennis after he had taken leave, admiring his vigorous stride as he made his way to the field of potatoes.

"Well, well, he do walk nice. An' what a handsome face, with them clear blue eyes! I declare he's a fine-lookin' feller, an' as fer that arm he's so easy like, one never misses it, till one feels a little queer a-shakin' a lef' hand."

Dennis came up to the field at a moment of wildest fun. Taking advantage of "Dad's" position, as on his

knees he dug away at the potatoes, four of his youngsters, headed by the madcap Nell, were posing upon his
back. In vain he exposulated, threatened, begged; on
his back they remained, nearly throttling him with their
arms around his neck.

"Wal, thar's nuthin' fer it but to do like the donkey
with the hay," and suiting the action to the word Brown
rolled himself on the ground. Over and over, shouting
with laughter, went the happy fellow until with a
triumphant "thar!" he arose amid deafening applause.
Even Meg turned away to hide a smile, for, perched on
his shoulder, covered with mud and with a long strip of
calico flying from her torn dress, Nell still clung.

"Wal, wal, Nell, you beats 'em all," said her proud
and delighted parent, as he turned to Dennis, who had
leaped the fence and joined him.

"Your sarvant, sir, Mr. Day. I'm proud to welcome
you back." Brown looked first at one hand and then the
other with his jolly laugh. "I wish I could give yer a
hand-shake, but bless me, atween these chillern an' the
taters my hands is nothin' but mud."

"Mud and all, I'll take it," said Dennis, clasping the
hand in a friendly grip, while the children standing
about looked "candy" as hard as children could. Miss
Nell, seeing that none was forthcoming, suggested it
under her breath, much to Meg's horror.

"Why, Nell, how could yer," said the little girl,
blushing with shame. But Nell, nothing discomfited,
possessed herself of a parcel Dennis produced, saying,
"For all of you." And then he took Meg's little hand
and slipped into it a tiny purse.

"O please, sir, you're too good!" Meg flushed with
pleasure. "I'm sure you've already given me too much.
I never seen anythin' so nice as the work-box you sent
me."

"Careful Meg!" said her father, patting her head.

10

"Now them others has lost everythin' o' theirs. Jest look at 'em !" And he proudly pointed to the spot where in a heap the family of Browns were diving into the paper bag and munching the candy. Brown contemplated them for a moment with his hands clasped behind him, and then sitting beside Dennis on the wooden fence, gave his whole attention to the subject of the unfortunate Julie.

" I tell yer what we kin do, sir. I've a friend down at the capital ; I'll jest write him ter be on the lookout fer the pore gal. Sometimes these pore, weak-minded critters do happen ter meet with lots o' kind folks, an I do think Julie had a way as would tech most hearts. It do seem onlikely that she sickly as she was lookin' when I seed her, could make sech a long journey and on foot. Did she have any money ?"

" I think so—a little. Mammy says there was a purse in Julie's pocket. There may have been a few dollars in it."

" Wal, Mr. Day, I'll jest look out and write ter all I knows on. P'raps we'll fin the pore critter nigher home."

And then with howls of regret from the children, who began to consider Dennis a blessed mine of candy, he bade Brown good-by.

Dennis shortly called at the office of Mr. Eaton, who, represented by his business man, paid a moderate sum for the O'Neal property. Then Dennis bought a strip of ground outside the Eaton inclosure, upon which he ordered rebuilt the cabin for Julie.

It stood a little way off from the road under a tree that resembled somewhat the one that had sheltered it during the happy life of the O'Neals. Following Dennis' directions Mammy stocked the closet with groceries, and locking the door, hid the key where it had been the custom of Julie to keep it. The money paid by Mr.

Eaton was given to Mammy as a fund for the baby, for a windfall had come to Dennis in the shape of a check from his publisher, who was delighted with the first part of the work forwarded to him. It was more money than Dennis had been possessor of for a long time. He walked the streets looking into shop after shop, seeking a gift for Mary. Until he found something that would speak to her of him, the money fairly burned in his pocket. Janet should have a new dress of fine wool. But Mary, what could he give her? Finally, one day to his delight he found among a store of old paintings a small one that delighted him. It represented a white dove flying low, near the shore of a lake. Blue shone the water with here and there a glint of sunshine upon its peaceful waves, while against the dark green background of trees the bird stood out in beautiful relief. It was a small picture, a gem, and the purchase made a great hole in his little fortune. But he who has not felt the delight of being impoverished for her he loves has lost one of life's truest pleasures. There was hardly as happy a man in all Georgia as that carpet-bagger when writing Mary's name on the wrapping of this picture he enfolded it in Janet's dress and directing the parcel to "Mrs. Janet Wilson, to be kept until called for," expressed it to Milton. Then he wrote a little note to the same Mrs. Wilson concerning the parcel at the express office, and praying at the end for some tidings of Miss Mary, whom he would consider it his highest privilege to serve. He trusted that even if the letter should not be forwarded to the little cottage fifteen miles out from Milton, that perhaps in the town there might be some one who, knowing the Scotchwoman, would, when the letter should be advertised, tell her of it. And then with renewed energy he returned to his work. These articles were making for him a reputation in a small way, and feeling himself slowly mounting to success he was debating the pro-

priety of a short visit to Milton. There might be some
interesting things in its neighborhood that would prove
valuable to him in the study to which he was devoting
himself. And then he laughed outright, acknowledging
in his heart that this was not what was drawing him to
Milton,—but Mary, Mary; whose face seemed smiling
on him from her rose bower.

There had come no answer from Janet, no acknowl-
edgment of the parcel. And since that little picture
went to his beloved, he had grown so envious of it, so
full of longing, that he resolved he would follow it.
Perhaps she might care to see him. Had she not said,
" Come back."

He had just arrived at this conclusion as he opened
the morning papers and read the card of Dr. Colton concerning the death of a convict named O'Neal.

" Dead !" Dennis's hand dropped and his heart gave
a throb of sympathy and then of admiration. After all,
there was compensation in life. For this man, unjustly
judged, unjustly punished, by his own nobility must live
in every noble heart. No fear now for the future of his
child, or for the support of his unfortunate wife. The
name of Colton was well-known throughout Georgia, as
representing both its wealth and aristocracy. Here was
another reason why he should go to Milton and go at
once.

Yes, he would start this very evening. He was fully
decided now, and he picked up his letters which with the
paper, he had just brought in. The postmark and
writing on one of them made Dennis start. It came from
Newton, Vermont, his old home. In the address, weak
and wavering though it was, he recognized the writing
of his uncle Seth. Years had passed since he had seen
it ; years, since the morning when the army mail being
delivered, there came a few lines from the old man, telling of the death of the wife of his youth. He remembered

each word and the tears which had rushed to his eyes making him hurry to his tent that his comrades might not see. " Dennis Day, your Aunt Selina is dead. She blessed you with her last breath. But for me—how can I forgive a lad that leaves his home and breaks the heart of a woman who loved him as a son? What right has a boy like you to be a soldier ?"

How often he had read it, how often in the stillness of night when on guard, or lying wakeful by the camp fire, had he stifled the sobs that would come as he remembered that never again could he see Aunt Selina's kind face. The letter from Uncle Seth had given him many a miserable hour. And from that day to this he had never received a line. He had written several times, for he knew that under a rough exterior Uncle Seth had a gentle heart. But no answers came, and fearing to be considered as trying to conciliate one who had grown rich, he ceased to write. Now a flood of old memories rushed over him, his hand trembled and a mist rose to his eyes, nearly hiding the written words :

" DENNIS DAY : I swore I would never write you another line. I swore I would always remember your ingratitude in marching to the war and breaking your aunt's heart. Doctors may say she died of consumption, but I know she never held up her head after the day when you marched off with the rest of the fools.

"A nice mess you have made of your life, losing your arm, getting all crippled up with wounds, and breaking as kind a heart as ever beat in a women's breast. What good have you done? Can you see it ?

"As far as papers go, there's not a day I don't read something that makes me ask, ' Did the Yankees win? Or were they whipped ?' And as for the niggers, it's all very well to call them free, but if there's any truth in published statements their freedom don't seem to have given them any rights. Their votes are worth about as much as blank paper, and if I didn't sometimes read of some of them being killed at an election, I would think they had voluntarily resigned their franchise. But for you—the pride of Selina's heart, to say nothing about what you might have been to me—for *you* to stay South and be called a carpet-bagger! I'm so ashamed I've almost had a fight with that brother of mine about it. Not one of them but all turns his nose up at a connection of the Hunts being a carpet-bagger! It is not a bad name, Carpet-bagger, but I think fool suits you better."

Here there was a break in the letter. And then in weak, tremulous characters was added:

"Come home, Dennis. The doctors say I can't live long. And boy, I want to see you once more. I hate all the others toadying around. You may not have money, so I inclose two hundred dollars.

"Your uncle,   SETH HUNT."

"Poor old man!" Dennis sighed. Had his uncle been poor he would not have waited all these years. For his aunt's sake he would have seen him. But to carry back a maimed and useless body, to be taunted hourly with his poverty! No, that had not been possible. He folded the crisp bills, putting them into his pocket, and resolving not to touch them. He had enough money to take him to Vermont, and perhaps when there, would have time to finish the second part of his book, when he could obtain money from his publishers. He wrote a few lines to Dr. Colton telling him what he knew of the wife and child of O'Neal. Then he hastily threw some necessary articles into a valise, of which articles the MS. was far the most important and bulky. Closing the door he left the key with Mammy, and receiving a hearty "God bress you, massa," from the old woman, started for the North.

On the road he telegraphed to his uncle, and arrived

one evening about dusk at the city, which when a boy he
left a little town. A carriage was waiting for him. He
had recognized the driver Nat Green, a type of the tall,
thin, long featured Yankee. The old man walked up and
down peering into strange faces, passing and repassing
Dennis until, catching sight of the empty sleeve, he
stopped :

" I s'pose yew aire Dennis Day," he said with the
nasal Yankee twang that had for so long been unfamiliar to Dennis. " I don't calculate thar's more'n one
man here who's lost his right arm."

So that was all that made him known to an old
friend ! Without giving him a chance to speak Nat
went on : " You're uncle's goin' fast but wants orful tew
see yew. My, my ! but there's little left o' the han'some
lad I taught tew ride. I'd never ha' know'd yew."
Holding his whip before him the old man surveyed
Dennis as if seeking some familiar features.

" Nat !" Dennis grasped his hand, " my memory is
better than yours, or you are less changed, for I knew
you at once, and right glad I am to see you."

" Wal, wal, it *is* kinder nice tew hev yew back," and
Nat's face lightened and brightened at Dennis's hearty
greeting. " An' now that yew smile an' talks yew
dew look more nat'ral. But we'd best hurry. The old
man ain't none too patient."

Nat held open the carriage door. But when Dennis,
tossing in his bag, took the seat beside the driver, Nat
was delighted. " Jest like himself fer all the world," he
said, as climbing into his own seat he gave Dennis's
hand another shake. " I'd know yew now, yew young
rascal, allus ready tew talk with Nat. Dew yew recol-
lect the times yew hid in the barn tew listen tew Nat's
stories when the school-bell had rung and Seth Hunt
was fumin' and frettin', sayin' yew'd never win the prize.
But yew did, Dennis, yew did." And again his hard old
hand gripped that of Dennis.

"Arter all an arm don't make a man, an' yew're the same Dennis with your warm-hearted ways. How we hev missed yew. An' the old man's bin gettin' queerer an' queerer ever since your aunt died, till sometimes ef I hadn't allus bin used tew him an' knowed he was all right clean down tew bottom I'd ha' left. Aunt Selina, she was a good woman, none better; an' now she's dead the old man sets a store by her, though she hed tew work orful hard while she lived, a milking cows an' what not. But Seth Hunt's got orful rich sence the town growd up all over the old farm, an' my! sech a lot o' lovin' nieces an' kinfolks as hev sprung up! They're' waitin' now fer his money. But nobuddy ken tell how the money's goin'. I hopes yew don't look fer none?" And Nat gave a quick side glance out of the old eyes that despite age and wrinkles had lost none of their shrewdness.

"I don't look for it and I don't want it." Dennis spoke a little sharply. He knew that old Nat liked him, that his words were intended as a warning against building up false hopes. At the same time he felt the natural pain of a proud, sensitive nature that finds itself at the very outset met with doubts of its sincerity. And then he smiled. After all it was only the Yankee reverence for the almighty dollar, and Nat had meant kindly. "No thought of money brought me here, Nat. I came just for love of the old man. And though, believing me poor, he sent me two hundred dollars, I haven't touched a cent of it, and mean to give it back to him."

"Two hundred dollars! phew!" and Nat gave a whistle. "I didn't calculate the old man set quite so much store by ye. That's oncommon generous o' him. Now don't be a fool an' give it back. Two hundred dollars o' good money ain't tew be throwed away, an' I calculate it's the most yew'll see o' his money. Keep it, Dennis, lad!"

But when Dennis shook his head Nat chuckled;

"The same," he said, "the very same. Carin' no more fer a dollar than fer a penny. A good lad an' warm-hearted, but foolish, foolish."

Still it was a folly that made Nat's heart warm to him as occasionally chuckling, he glanced out of the corner of his eye at Dennis, who was looking about him with surprise at the handsome streets.

"How changed everything is," Dennis said, when passing row after row of handsome residences, they came to a large inclosed property that in the midst of the populous town seemed a park.

"I calculate yew'll find not much change here," said Nat, as the handsome iron gates were opened and the carriage rolled in under great trees. "Seth's been offered a cool one hundred thousand fer this, but I reckon he'll hold on tew this bit o' land as long as he lives, an' longer ef I knows anythin' about it."

While Nat was still talking the old farm-house came in sight. It was unchanged, with its long low porch and the two cherry trees before it into which so many times Dennis had climbed to feast on the luscious fruit. All leafless now they stretched out their bare branches in welcome to him, who when last under their shade had been young and full of hope.

For them, youth would return with spring blossoms, but for him—

The carriage stopped, the door opened, a neat maid held it aside for him to pass. A stranger! There was no one to welcome him. The kind old aunt who had grieved at his going was gone too. "Tick, tick," in the same heavy tone that had warned him of study hours, the clock in the hall spoke of the olden times. How small it appeared in comparison to those childish days when as a giant it had looked down on him. "Tick, tick," it was welcoming him, wondering how he had grown so tall, and pointing out other old friends. With a mist before his eyes and a swelling heart Dennis saw the same old chairs, the wooden settle and all the unchanged furniture of his childhood's home. How much more durable than immortal man, were these bits of wood fashioned by his hand !

But he had not much time for thought, for the maid, coming out of an adjacent room, was just about to deliver a message when a sharp thin voice hushed hers. " Dennis Day, come here !" Walking past the curtseying maid, Dennis entered the sick room and falling on his knees by the bed kissed the thin hand held out to him.

" My boy," said the old voice whose sharpness was lost in trembling, " my boy," and the other hand was laid on Dennis's bowed head.

There was a silence in the room, while the loud tick of the old clock seemed telling of the life that was passing away. Dennis had caught a glimpse of that shadowy face on the pillows and struggled hard to keep back his rising tears. He could only remember this uncle as a stout and ruddy man, loud of voice and quick of temper, but in spite of sharp words, with a kind, true heart. He remembered that when his pale mother, widowed in her youth, had no home, Uncle Seth had opened his door, Uncle Seth's wagon had been sent to meet her and had brought her here to die. He remembered that when Aunt Selina had taken in her arms the dear younger sister who was so pale and sick, and had sobbed over her, Uncle Seth had said : " Don't be a fool, Selina," and then lifting him from the floor had pressed him to his breast. And he had seen tears in the " grown man's " eyes, and had wondered at them, boyishly. How he had tried to keep from crying himself, and when he couldn't, Uncle Seth had held him a moment in his arms, and then in a rough voice saying, " be a man," had put him at his mother's feet, patted his head and strode out of the room. He could remember an endless number of kind deeds, and the sharp words that had never hidden from him his uncle's true nature.

And now all that remained of that strong man was this ghostly figure on the bed. Louder and louder ticked the clock, ticking away his life. Presently, with something that sounded as a faint echo of his old impatience, Seth Hunt spoke.

"You're wasting time, you're wasting time," and then with the tremble coming back to his voice, "Look up, Dennis, you great fool of a boy, look up. I want to see your face." And when Dennis raised his head the old man stroked the hand which held his own and something like the shadow of a smile lighted the ghostly face.

"You've been a great fool, Dennis, a great fool. How you've changed! What a handsome lad you used to be! Great fool, great fool," the old lips kept on murmuring. But there was nothing but tenderness in his face.

"To think you never came till I was dying, and wouldn't have come now if I hadn't sent the money. Did you get it?" the old man asked quickly.

Dennis's answer was to take the two bills out of his pocket and put them within the clasp of the thin fingers, that, released from his hand, were plucking nervously at the counterpane.

A smile, like the shadow of some amusing thought, passed over Seth Hunt's face. "And so you were too proud to touch the old man's money. Yet I calculate you're as poor as poverty. Well, so much the more for charity," and again that smile. "Put away the money in my box on that chest of drawers. Perhaps it'll be your last chance to refuse honest dollars."

Dennis's face had flushed hotly, but having followed the old man's directions he came back to him and drew a chair to the bedside. "Uncle," he said, "I'm not rich, but I've managed to get on and owe no man a cent. Now I intend to do better and make some money."

"How'll you make it?" A sneer came over the old face, shadowy like the smile.

"Writing," Dennis answered.

"Bosh," said Seth Hunt. A pause and then he heard again the old voice, grown sharp and querulous now. "If you'd come and asked me I'd have put you in a good business. But that hard head and obstinate pride I suppose, they kept you back. And now it's too late. You've made your bed and you must lie in it."

"That's all right, uncle; I'm not complaining of my lot. I know I brought it on myself. And yet—" he hesitated.

"Spit it out," said the old man, and Dennis was surprised to see that the faded eyes could look so sharp and angry. "Spit it out," Seth Hunt repeated, as Dennis still hesitated.

"And yet, uncle, though I call myself fool oftener than you can, if the war were to be fought over, I'd have to go. It seemed right to me then, it seems right now. I no longer feel the hopes that made my boy's heart glad. I no longer dream of gaining a great name and making you proud of me, for I know a soldier can do faithful duty and gain little reputation. And I live where I see constant examples of its uselessness, in the war's results. I live where life and property are not safe, should one enter into politics and strive to make a party other than the one upheld by the wealth and power of the State. I live where there are laws as ruinous to the negro as was ever slavery; yet, uncle, if the war were to be fought over I would have to go. It would be my duty."

Dennis had spoken very gently, not wishing to anger the sick man. But something like a flush darkened the old face and his uncle's eyes were turned away. The old hand had fluttered as if it, too, wanted to be freed from the touch of this obstinate young man. But Dennis would not let it go; he held it warm and close.

"Don't be angry, uncle." No answer from the old lips which he could see were trembling.

"Don't be angry. I've come all this way just to see you. God knows I've wanted many a time to come. But my unanswered letters made me think I would not be welcome. I knew you were rich, and I was poor. Had you been poor I would have come back, and have been a true son to you. Working for you would have given a motive to my life which until lately has seemed so useless. I would have been happy working for you, for I can never forget how kind you were to a wretched little orphan."

The old face began to work nervously, and one thin hand was held up as if to bid Dennis say no more. But Dennis did not see it. His head was bent over the hand he held, and on it fell a tear that could not shame manhood.

Silence again, broken only by the ticking of the clock. And thus these two remained until the maid coming in with nourishment for the sick man lit the lamps that drove away the dusky shadows.

CHAPTER XXX.

THE WILL.

THE coming of Dennis seemed to revive the dying man. "He slept better than he has for a month," Nat whispered to Dennis as he lay back in an easy chair at his uncle's bedside. Yet every time he had stirred during the night he had seen his uncle's eyes fixed upon him. "Don't go, since you've been so long coming," Seth Hunt had ordered, when Nat, who was to sit up that night had said :

"P'raps, Dennis, yew'd better go to bed ; yew're tew hev your old room."

But at his uncle's wish Dennis had remained by the bedside and slept well enough in the great arm chair Seth Hunt had ordered to be rolled in for his nephew's use. Despite Dennis's entreaties, the old man had tired himself in directing arrangements for his nephew's comfort. Therefore the faithful old servant was jubilant when the morning found his master much better.

There was an influx of Hunts during the day, from Archibald Hunt and his two daughters to a very plain old-maid cousin who all her life had spoken the truth to and quarrelled with Cousin Seth. There was not much vigor left in the old man, and Miss Susan Hunt had only gentle words for him now, as she first bowed to and then shook hands with Dennis in a cold limp fashion. For Dennis kept his seat at his uncle's bedside, held there by an impatient, "Stay, I tell you," when he moved to make room for the others. "Let them come in here. They bothered me enough before you came," Seth Hunt said peevishly when the maid announced, "Visitors for Mr. Day." So in they came. Strong, wiry Archibald Hunt making a strange contrast to the pale ghost on the bed.

"Glad to see you so well, dear Seth," said Archibald, looking down on his brother, whose only answer to this affectionate greeting was a gruff "Humph!" as he turned his head away, not condescending to notice the two young ladies whom Dennis found difficulty in recognizing as little Sophie and Miranda Hunt. Sophie was very pretty and spoiled by the fact. She laughed a little at the awkwardness of shaking Dennis's left hand. Seth Hunt turned on his pillow.

"One arm's better than two useless ones," he said

sharply, looking at the two pretty members with the neatly gloved hands that were crossed on the young lady's velvet pelisse.

But the old gentleman was so nearly gone that beyond a slight smile and blush his words awakened no feeling in any but Dennis, whose heart they touched, proving as they did his uncle's affection.

A few days passed and Seth Hunt recovered so far as to surprise Dennis by being on the sofa when he came in from his own room, where he had gone to write an important letter. The old man wore a gay dressing-gown that harmonized ill with the pale, wrinkled face.

"Not dead yet," he said with a chuckle. "Are you sorry I'm keeping above the ground, so you won't have a chance to fight over my money."

Dennis flushed as he answered:

"I've nothing to do with your money, uncle. It doesn't concern me, and I don't care for it. But I do care for you."

"I believe you, my boy," and the old voice trembled. "It's a comfort to know there's one who won't lie to get the dollars I've been so long saving."

Seth Hunt lived a month after his nephew's arrival— a month during which he could not bear to have the "boy" out of his sight. And although his heart was with Mary, although every moment lost from his work delayed the time for winning her, although letters came from his publisher first asking then demanding the second part of his MS.; Dennis put everything aside to soothe the declining days of the man who had sheltered his youth.

"You'll not be disappointed, my boy, that I have willed my money to charity?" his uncle said to him one day.

"Uncle Seth, don't let us talk any more about money. I am glad you have settled the matter. Now put it out

of your mind. Don't think of it. To me you are not the
rich man but the kind uncle who befriended my dying
mother and educated her son."

And Seth Hunt's only answer had been to put his
hand on Dennis's hair as he leaned over the sofa.

"Handsome, curly hair, Dennis. Your aunt was so
proud of it. And now it's all that is left of your good
looks."

After this the money was never again mentioned between them. One night when sitting by the fire in the
same gay robe which made the pale old face more
ghastly, there came a change over Seth Hunt.

The room was perfectly still, Dennis having closed
the door so that the loud-voiced clock would not disturb
his rest. As daylight faded and shadows came out of the
dusky corners the invalid whispered, "Dennis," and
grasped feebly his nephew's hand. Suddenly with a
nervous grip he rose up on the sofa. Dennis sprang
nearer and knelt beside him. "I'm going, Dennis!" he
said in a louder voice than usual, and Dennis, seeing the
thin figure quiver a little, put his arm around him as the
old head fell forward on his breast.

———

The funeral was over. Dennis with crape on his hat
had shaken hands with Nat, and now, bag in hand, entered the old-fashioned parlor where the Hunts were assembled in deepest mourning and very quietly discussing
the probabilities of the will. Dennis bowed and spoke
in a low tone to Lawyer Jones, who with a package in
hand—doubtless the mysterious will—had just cleared
his throat to make a short address.

"Mr. Jones, you asked me to say 'good-by.' I am
in haste to catch the afternoon train for New York."

The lawyer, a small spare man dressed in black, looked
over his heavy gold-rimmed glasses in surprise. "Why,
Dennis, my boy, you are in great haste."

"Yes," Dennis answered as his face grew red. "But you see I've no claim on any of them now Uncle Seth's gone. They are anxious to have me go, and I'm equally anxious to be gone," he said, with the smile that made his face attractive.

"Dennis, I think it is your duty to remain." The lawyer spoke aloud in his deepest voice. He was heard all over the room by every Hunt ear, that, unable to catch Dennis's words, was far from soothed by Mr. Jones's very audible reply. Every Hunt nose took a slightly disdainful curve, as each Hunt wondered why on earth there should be any reason for detaining the one connection that the family was ashamed of—not only because of his lack of "property," but because he was, what they blushed even to think of, a carpet-bagger. Without at all considering the feelings of the family, Lawyer Jones went on :

"Really, Mr. Day," said the lawyer, " I think that the respect due to your uncle's memory should make you remain and learn his last wishes."

"I will remain since you think it right, for I want to show my uncle's memory every respect." Dennis, too, spoke aloud, as taking a chair near the door he turned to smile at old Nat, who entered at the moment and placed himself behind the young man's chair. The old fellow was much broken since his master's death, but in all his grief he managed to hate "them stuck-up Hunts," and to think that Dennis, one-armed, carpet-bagger and all, was "heaps higher than them." He could not get over a certain mortification, that the lad he had been so proud of should be only a "carpet-bagger." Before Dennis's coming and after the reading of many newspapers he had concluded that a carpet-bagger must be a "darned mean thing," and often wondered how the boy who had been the soul of truth and honor could have fallen so low. But after he had seen Dennis the man, after he had

looked into his honest eyes and had·felt the old true ring
in every word, Nat swore privately that "whatever them
papers might say, he knew one carpet-bagger who was a
gentleman." Just now, hating the whole Hunt family
for their cool treatment of him "who should ha' been
heir if Seth Hunt hadn't been so queer," he stood up like
an old soldier behind his chair.

It is probable Nat's opinion was not of the slightest
consequence to the Hunts. The only one of them who
noticed him was pretty Sophie, who with smile of
amusement whispered to her sister Miranda : "I wonder
who next will come to hear the will ?"

Lawyer Jones untied the red tape that bound the
package, selected a small envelope and broke the seal.
Expectancy was at its height : Nat and the carpet-bagger
were forgotten in the eagerness to know what was to be
done with Seth Hunt's millions.

"Ladies and gentlemen—" the lawyer paused, and
unable to contain themselves in quiet, there rose the
sounds of a soft fluttering of dresses, an uneasy moving
of chairs, as each auditor fairly held his breath that not
a word might be lost.

"Ladies and gentlemen—"

"I shall die if he says that again," Sophie whispered
to her sister. But she did not die, although Mr. Jones
once more prefaced his remarks with :

"Ladies and gentlemen, the will I am about to read
to you was drawn up fifteen years ago by Mr. Seth Hunt
and read to Dr. Lumber and myself, who, in the presence
of each other signed as witnesses thereto. One week before his death Mr. Hunt having sent for Mr. Lumber
and myself, with his own hand wrote this document
which I will read to you before breaking the seal of the
original will, which has for fifteen years been lying in
my safe. When this shorter document was being written and witnessed Mr. Dennis Day, by request of his

uncle Mr. Hunt, went from the room and out of the house, Mr. Hunt choosing this moment for the absence of his nephew, as it was a characteristic of deceased to keep each member of his family in ignorance of the manner in which he intended to dispose of his property."

There was a slight murmur of approbation from the Hunts. Nat advanced a step nearer Dennis's chair and wished for the thousandth time " old Seth hadn't been so queer."

Clearing his throat as if to gain greater power for the heavy voice, the lawyer read on :

"NEWTON, Vermont, December 2, 18—.

" I, Seth Hunt, being of sound mind, do hereby confirm in each particular the will made by me fifteen years two months and seven days since, which will is and has been in the keeping of E. F. Jones, after having been by me sealed in the presence of J. Lumber, M.D., and E. F. Jones, attorney-at-law."

There was a little more rustling of dresses, a little more moving of chairs, and then perfect silence as a moment after, the seals were broken and the will taken out of the large envelope :

"NEWTON, October, 18—.

" I, Seth Hunt, being of sound mind do declare this to be my last will and testament. To my brother Archibald Hunt, a man of whom any brother should perhaps be proud,"—here Mr. Archibald Hunt with an audible murmur of " dear Seth," for an instant's space buried his face in his snowy handkerchief. But he raised his head as apparently regardless of this exhibition of brotherly love, the lawyer read on—" A brother who now that the old farm is increasing in value takes such kindly interest in my investments, and is so

generous with advice ; to Archibald as a testimonial of
my appreciation of favors that I have never accepted, I
hereby bequeath the sum of—" here something must
have maliciously choked Mr. Jones, for while M. Archibald Hunt, still holding his superfine handkerchief
listened eagerly for the amount bequeathed him by the
dear deceased brother, a full minute was lost as the lawyer coughed.   Finally the throat was cleared and with a
little appologetic bow Mr. Jones went on—" the sum of
$200, this being exactly the amount I once asked of him
as a loan and he with great feeling, owing to utter
inability, refused me (although at the time he was considered a man of wealth).   It is to prevent his ever
having a like trial of his tender nature and being obliged
again to refuse such a loan to some unhappy poor rela-
ive that I now bequeath this amount to him."

There was perfect stillness except for the crackling of
paper as Mr. Jones turned the page.   Mr. Archibald
Hunt stood erect and stiff as the stiff gray hair brushed
carefully up to conceal the shining baldness on the top
of his narrow head.   An angry flush darkened the palish
yellow of his skin, and a grim smile replaced the expression of grief that his countenance had worn.

" Look at pa," Sophie whispered to Miranda as she
dutifully hid her smile behind her small black glove.

Dennis could almost have smiled too.   The words,
so like Uncle Seth, seemed as if spoken by him. "Bravo,
old boy," he said under his breath.

Archibald Hunt was a successful merchant, and his
wife a leader of fashion in the town where Dennis's boyhood had been passed.   They had tried to patronize
Uncle Seth and Aunt Selina, an attempt that always
enraged the quick-tempered farmer, who rarely went to
see his rich brother.   He made one visit the year the
crops failed.   Dennis could remember that Uncle Seth
after some impatient words had decided he would borrow

the $200 from one who could so easily lend. He had
come back red and angry. There had been a good deal
of timber cut, and when it was sold Seth Hunt had gone
about whistling—an unusual thing for him ; so unusual
that Dennis with a child's curiosity had asked his aunt
why it was, and she with a smile had answered : " Seth
finds he did not need his brother." In listening to his
uncle's cynical words these circumstances came back.
He forgot the present in old recollections until the
lawyer's voice uttering the names " Sophie and Miranda
Hunt," brought it back to him. The bright flush on
Sophie's pretty face made him hope that Uncle Seth had
not disappointed her. Apparently with no other interest
than to read distinctly Mr. Jones went on : " To my two
nieces, who even now are being taught to look out for
the main chance, I bequeath $400 each, hoping it will be
enough to buy each a dress when they are educated into
the extravagance and wastefulness their parents think
necessary to a rich man's children. To Susan Hunt, my
cousin, who was too honest to marry a man she didn't
love and too ugly to get the one she did, I leave $10,000.
To Nat Skinner, my faithful friend, I leave $10,000. To
J. Lumber, M. D., and E. F. Jones $5,000 each." Then
followed bequests of $50 each to every known relative,
mentioning each by name. Dennis's name was not included. With all these bequests less than $45,000 had
been disposed of, and Dennis wondered what particular
charity was to receive the large fortune that remained.
He looked around the room full of disappointed faces,
lighted up by the beaming one of the ugly cousin. He did
not turn to Nat, for he knew by certain sounds behind
his chair that the old man was crying. Still holding the
open will in his hand the lawyer began to speak :

" As you are doubtless aware, the sum total of the bequests in this will of the late Seth Hunt does not exceed
$45,000, and as you perhaps know the estate, owing to

the great advance of property in Newton and fortunate
investments, amounts at lowest calculations to $1,500,000,
the bulk of the property yet remains to be disposed of.
It was owing to this great increase of value that Mr.
Hunt drew up the short document that was read in your
presence previous to this will."

And then after a little pause as if to make his words
more impressive and to increase the family regrets, the
lawyer continued to read the will :

'Now that my family is disposed of, and doubtless
are blessing my memory, I will carry out my long-
expressed determination of leaving the bulk of my
money to charity.   To my mind charity means love, and
though I have shown mighty little of it, there is still
one left above the earth that my heart warms to, a young
fellow who gave up home and all prospects, to be a
soldier ; who is, I have heard from old comrades, bat-
tered and maimed in body. I forgive him the disappointment he caused me, for I believe the young fool meant
to do his duty.   And if he outlives me I would like to
think that there would be left as my heir one of the few
I have ever known who was too honest to lie. To this
boy or man, Dennis Day, I bequeath, only excepting the
legacies stated in this will, every cent I possess, or ever
shall possess, all my real estate, mill property, all and
every kind of property in which I have, or ever shall
have, any interest, share, right or title. Of Dennis Day
I ask that he shall retain the house known as the Hunt
farmhouse, with all its belongings, just as he receives
them at the time of my death. I ask that if he desires a
larger dwelling house he will add to this without changing its original shape and that he shall settle a portion of
the estate to be annually devoted to the repairing of the
old house.   This I also desire shall be made incumbent
upon any heir or heirs to whom he shall will, or who

shall inherit from him, this estate.   If Dennis Day dies
before I die, I leave all my property, with the above re-
strictions, to his heirs or heir.   If Dennis Day dies without issue, I then leave the whole property to found and
maintain a home for old men and their wives, where they
can live together.   I desire the Home to be built where
my dwelling house now stands, the old house to be retained intact and added to as the estate warrants, in substantial stone.   And I desire each old man and woman
shall have made to them a suitable allowance.   If Dennis
Day shall survive me, and finds the estate warrants it, I
desire that he should give a sum toward such a home, a
sum not large enough to impoverish him, but sufficient
to start such an enterprise, and inspire some other old
cross-grained fellow like me with an idea what to do
with his money.   And here declaring this to be my last
will and testament, I affix my name and seal.

SETH HUNT."

Dennis sat speechless.   There was a blur before his
eyes and in his ears a rushing sound.   All that money
was his!   He who for eighteen years had just managed
to live, had become a millionaire!   After the first bewilderment was over his heart gave a great throb.

Mary!   No need to wait now.

He sat with eyes on the floor until roused by some
one fumbling for his hand.   He looked up and saw
Nat.

"Dennis—I—" Nat could not speak another word.
He covered his face with his hand to hide the tears of
honest joy at the lad's good luck.

Dennis threw his arm around Nat's shoulder for a
moment ; then with a sob the old man broke from him
and out of the room.   The lawyer and doctor shook
hands with him and whispered their congratulations.
The Hunts, finding Dennis Day the millionaire quite

different from the same man when poor, advanced to extend to him the family hand.

"Look at him, Miranda," said Sophie. "I believe he knew it all the time. That was why he looked so proud." And then her father having cordially invited Dennis to stay with them while he arranged matters, included his daughter's wishes with his own. "Sophie and Miranda may be able to persuade you. They have always retained their cousinly affection for you."

Sophie smiled and blushed, letting her plump little hand rest in Dennis's and emphasizing with the barest possible squeeze her "Do come." With thanks Dennis declined the invitation. But youth and prettiness exact a certain homage, so he escorted the sisters to their carriage, standing bare-headed as they rode away. Mr. Archibald Hunt walked to his office, his legacy being too small a cause for longer indulgence in grief.

In the old parlor Dennis held a long conversation with the two friends of his uncle.

"But, Day," said Dr. Lumber, with whom Dennis had always been a favorite, "if you devote one-third of the estate to this home for old people you surely will be robbing yourself."

"No," Dennis answered firmly, "I will then be far richer than I ever hoped to be. Besides, if I didn't do at least this much, I should always feel as if I had robbed my uncle of as noble a monument as man can have. Take this in hand for me; draw up the papers; I'd like to sign them and see the thing started, for—" and he hesitated, then flushed—"I must go South by to-morrow noon at furthest."

"What is your pressing business, Dennis?" Lawyer Jones asked with a twinkle in his eye. "A lady?" And when Dennis flushing still more, looked both handsome and happy, the lawyer laughed outright.

"Well, well," he said good-naturedly, "we all feel

the same when we are young. Maybe it is the best part of life after all."

A little more argument and the matter of the "Home" was decided upon. Then were repeated some last words from Seth Hunt, which not wishing to make obligatory he had left as messages. He wished Dennis, unless it proved disastrous to his interests, to keep up the mills. They had taken many of his later years to establish, and he would like to think they were running after he was dead and gone. And also, if Dennis were willing, he wished him to take the name of Hunt. "I would like," he had said to the lawyer, "to think the old name would linger in the old house, and that there'd be Hunts of a better stock than Archibald's brood."

Leaving the lawyer in charge of the property Dennis started the next afternoon for Georgia and—Mary.

Nat drove the wagon that carried him to the train. "Bring your wife back with you, lad," Nat said, and Dennis, looking proud and happy, nodded to his old friend as the train rushed out of the station.

What a wonderful change this money made! It was the magic wand that would lay at Mary's feet the wonders and beauties of the world. Mary's father should have the half of his fortune. He must leave his present occupation. A driver of slaves! and Dennis shuddered as he thought of the horrors of the convict system. What could he do to brighten the lives of those miserable blacks? It was a depressing thought, that however strong his desire to help, before such a wrong he stood powerless. A sin against a people the people only could remedy, a crime in legislation, legislation must change. No one man could modify law, however unrighteous. But perhaps one man might speak to many, and by bringing facts before their eyes waken them to the desperate needs of a class they should protect. And Dennis Day in the first delight of his new fortunes, vowed himself to this crusade against injustice, this war in behalf of the oppressed.

------♦------

CHAPTER XXXI.

HE IS MY FATHER.

MARY amid flowers, in perfect innocence, with peace shining in the depths of her beautiful eyes, had grown to womanhood, knowing no sin, nor the shadow of evil, loving only her father and Janet. She had in quiet content reached that age when in the busy world girls are wives and mothers. Suddenly, out of the far-away dreamland there had come a man with frank face and winning smile, a man with manly thoughts and noble impulses—and straightway Mary's heart was won. Quick throbbing, changeful blushes, smiles, sighs and even unbidden tears that were sweet as bitter, replaced her calm. The coming of Dennis had been the first, the great event of Mary's life. And the others, how quickly had they followed ! The convict with his miseries written on his face, Dr. Colton, his courtly bows and varied compliments.

All passed in thought before Mary, as leaning on the gate she looked down the road and waited for her father. Now and again she cast a wistful glance at the dusty way which had brought her a new friend. " He will come; Dennis will return," she said to herself with low voice and blushing cheek. And then sadness came over her as she thought of her father's changed manner. Why did he oftener sigh than smile ? Why would he not listen to her secret about Dennis ; why did he put her from him with "not now," each time she began to speak of what had made her so happy? She wanted him to see Dennis with her eyes, to feel for him what she felt. And the convict! She wanted to tell him of the convict. There would be no danger now the poor man had gone. Why did Janet still bid her to be silent? And why was Janet always pitying her? "My puir bairn, God gie ye strength!" was now oftenest on her nurse's lips. Somehow the sun seemed hidden by mist—there were tears in her own eyes.

"Father is in trouble, I fear," she said, and softly sighed. Then turned her face to the other road and dreamed of Dennis.

Janet from an open window watched the graceful figure at the gate and trembled for Mary's future.

Two weeks had passed since the burning of Dr. Colton's house. He announced it to Mary with covert allusions to the new mansion he intended to rear, hoping to win a beautiful girl to accept it as her home. And when Mary had said she hoped so, if he desired it, the doctor had had much ado to keep himself from then and there asking her to be his. But that mysterious father! Dr. Colton must consider a little longer. He was not quite ready for another shock of the nerves; Janet had given him one when she had opened the door for him, and he had in his new graciousness spoken to her of the fire and the death of the convict. They were uppermost in his thoughts with wonder at the man's successful effort to save Miss Dawson's life. To his astonishment Janet grasped his arm.

"Dinna ye tell her. Dinna ye tell Mary o' the convict," she whispered. Though in offended dignity he had tried to shake her off, she had held fast, until he was absolutely obliged to promise.

And now Janet as she stood watching Mary was thinking of the negro she had periled so much to save.

"Puir Tom, puir Tom! A naiger but the soul o' a

mon. An' to think he should hae died the night he left
this house ! To what purpose has God made sae noble a
mon, an' gied him a black skin ? There must be a place
where the wranged get their rights.   And though Mary
says we maun forgive, I fin' my ain heart hard as a stane
to them wha wranged that naiger.   Weel, weel, I maun
do something or I'll rub off my ain nose wi' weepin',"
said the Scotchwoman as she looked around Mary's
room trying to find a speck of dust, or the slighest thing
out of order.   But white and fair as the girl herself was
this snowy chamber with its fluttering curtains and the
soft couch with its dainty pillows whereon for all these
years Mary's golden head had rested in innocent
slumbers.   Giving an extra dusting and putting into
fresh order what was itself perfect order, Janet with
another glance at Mary went into the garden behind the
house to repair the damages of the morning's storm.
Although October had nearly gone the air was warm as
summer and thunder storms were frequent and violent.
They filled Janet with superstitious awe. "There's something wrang coming," she would whisper to herself as
the darkening clouds would foretell a storm.   The first
muttering of thunder, the first flash of lightning would
send her to her knees in the middle of the room, while
Mary, coming at her entreaty, would stand at her side
gazing in wondering admiration at the raging elements.
There was no fear in her heart, only awe at God's power,
who held all nature in the hollow of His hand.

There was, however, some cause, some reason for
Janet's nervousness.   Hilton's change towards his child
was only too apparent. He now came at hours the most
unexpected.   Sometimes he would come daily ; sometimes days would pass without a visit.   To Mary he
spoke little, receiving her caresses sometimes in moody
silence, and again with a love that hurt her as he clasped
her fiercely in his arms.   Janet he never noticed except

to scowl at her. A less brave woman would have been frightened, would have kept out of his way. But Janet knowing he suspected something, and not being able to tell what, rather courted his notice, hoping that he would be angered and would turn on her.

"He can but kill me. An' he'd find it nae easy job," she said to herself as she gathered together the ruined plants of her kitchen garden and throwing them into a basket carried them outside of the fence. "Wad he kill her?" She stopped to think, trembling and turning pale as she saw that unconsciously she stood beside a tree the lightning had shattered and felled. "Wad the lightning kill the tree? It has mair heart than he." And with a shudder, a vow to watch well her bairn, she went into the kitchen and began scrubbing with all her energy, hoping to drive away her fears. It was thus life stood with Mary, as, still at the gate with head leaning on her clasped hands, she dreamed of Dennis. A smile was upon her lips, a light in her eyes that made her most beautiful. She was so absorbed in dreams that she did not hear an approaching carriage until its occupants, a lady and gentleman, had seen and commented on her.

Dr. Colton had leaned out and saying, "Look, Jane, there she is at the gate," had moved aside to give the lady place. Miss Dawson seeing that fair face was surprised and pleased:

"She is lovely, Charles, I commend your taste."

An instant later the startled girl had looked at them, blushing a little as with graceful bow she opened the gate.

"A lady," Miss Dawson had whispered to the delighted doctor, who jumping to the ground took Mary's hand and presented her to "My cousin, Miss Dawson."

Even at the moment, while charmed with Mary's grace and beauty, Miss Dawson could hardly forbear smiling at the thought that her cousin was actually in

love and contemplating marriage with a young girl who
to him had no other name than Mary.   When his cousin
had proposed this visit she had embarrassed him by asking, "Do you intend marrying this young person?"
And he, despite his sixty years, blushing as might a boy
at his first escapade, answered, "I—I—think of doing so."
When to her natural questions concerning the girl's
family and connections he had been unable to make
satisfactory answers, she had raised her hands and brows
in horror, as she said : "My dear cousin, I hope you
don't intend to make a misalliance."   She had feared that
some designing woman was about to make a fool of her
cousin and had determined in her pride, to deliver the old
gentleman from any such meshes.   But the sweet girlish
face of Mary with its delicate features and snowy skin,
the tall, slender figure, and above all her perfect grace
and simplicty, charmed Miss Dawson and convinced her
that the girl was, as she whispered her cousin, "a lady."

"Nothing plebeian here," she thought, as following
Mary into the pretty parlor, Miss Dawson sacrificed
breeding to curiosity and glanced through the door of
Mary's room.

"Lovely, lovely," she said to herself.   "There can be
nothing here to hide.   Whatever the father, he must
come of good stock.   Possibly he has lost his fortune,
or is a little dissipated."   These were faults that might
be excused.   The Coltons were rich enough not to seek
wealth, and dissipation was generally considered a gen-
tlemanly vice.   But for the Colton family to receive a
plebeian !   Never !   So thought Miss Dawson as she
talked with Mary.   Presently she ceased criticising.
Listening to the girl's thoughts and fancies, finding her
ignorance but innocence exalted, this young creature
was attracting the elder lady as no one had ever before
done.   With softening face and tender eyes she looked
on this stranger maiden who had set throbbing the ma-
ternal heart inborn in all true women.

Jane Dawson had never married, because, as she had candidly answered when sometimes pressed for a reason, she had never found a man who combined those qualities she required in a husband. Charitable and generous as she was, her gifts were generally bestowed through some medium—she had never liked the contact of misery. Once a little negress had crept into that proud heart. Pleased with the intelligence of Nettie and the affection which had sprung from some capricious attentions to the child of her servant, Miss Dawson became personally interested in her and had planned her future with tenderness. When the girl's misfortune came Miss Dawson had shocked some of her circle by her stanch support of the "criminal," and after Nettie's conviction had never rested until she obtained her pardon. The scene at the convict camp, and the horror of Nettie's death had greatly affected her. But she belonged to the type of Southern women by whom nothing is more avoided than a feminine leadership of any progressive movement. Thus while she stood ready to use a great portion of her wealth in the cause of humanity, especially in benefiting those convicts whose too apparent miseries awakened her pity, she did nothing to call public attention to this particular feature of the law. She dreaded to draw upon herself public notice, and she feared that such action by making public the methods of private institutions and bringing into prominence many injustices of established law, would cast odium upon that party which from time immemorial had been supported by the Coltons and Dawsons.

Nettie's death followed so closely by the heroic conduct of the convict had filled her with doubts. And though she believed that the majority of convicts were justly condemned, the cruelty of their treatment, the inequality of punishment accorded to negro and to white, disturbed the calm content of her life, and thus heart

was battling against pride. This interior conflict made
the lady have greater need of tenderness—a need that as
she clasped the hand of Mary made itself felt with redoubled yearning.

Dr. Colton blandly surveyed the two. Since Miss
Dawson approved his choice, there was no need for
further hesitation. He would at once speak to the young
lady and—With an impatient exclamation that passed
unnoticed, Dr. Colton came back to the fact that he did
not only not know where to find the mysterious father,
but that he did not even know his name. And there
stood Jane Dawson, after professing herself so shocked
at his neglect for not insisting upon this information,
there she stood chattering away just like any ordinary
woman ! Why didn't she ask it now ? How long would
those two stand gazing at each other ? It might amuse
them but it certainly was tiresome to a spectator. He
never knew that women found each other so interesting
—and the old gentleman looked disconsolately at the
gathering clouds that now were obscuring the sunlight.

Miss Dawson really had forgotten all about Mary's
parentage, and even Dr. Colton's proposed marriage,
which now that the girl had touched her own heart
seemed desecration. Mary feeling a strong attraction to
this lady, of whose like she had dreamed when picturing
to herself the majesty of queens, was quite content to
look without speaking. At last Dr. Colton, unable to
retain his vexation, turned to Mary, and with a bluntness
most unusual said :

"Miss Mary, you have never told us your father's
name."

Mary started, smiled and blushed. "My father's
name—do you not know it ? Henry Hilton."

"Bless my soul !" Dr. Colton took off his glasses,
wiping them nervously and putting them on again,
simply because he did not know what else to do. The

only Hilton he knew was a man employed by some friends of his to superintend a coal mine in the vicinity of Milton—a man of whose cruelty to the convicts, he had heard, and to whom, utterly ignoring the fact of any responsibility belonging to his aristocratic employers, Dr. Colton gave the full blame for such cruelty. He who had many times shaken the hand of the owners of the mine, now trembled with nervous horror at having so nearly offered his own to the daughter of the superintendent. He looked helplessly at Miss Dawson. Her face was very pale. Could that Henry Hilton be indeed the captain of the convict guard? Again she saw those miserable wretches. Again she held Nettie's dead body. Again that negro's face seemed to look at her from among the flames. With a shudder her eyes came back to the girl, who with hands pressed to her heart gazed in bewilderment at Miss Dawson's changed expression. So perfectly innocent, so perfectly ignorant she looked, it could not be she knew her father's occupation.

"Do you know your father's business?" she asked.

"Oh yes," said Mary, " he superintends a mine where the men are happy in their work, and don't fear the darkness of coal pits, knowing how greatly their labor benefits the world."

" Mary." Miss Dawson took her hand and held it between her own. There was no question of her duty in the lady's mind. Clearly it was right to show Mary the horrors of her father's occupation. Clearly it was her duty to take this lovely creature from such vile association, or at least to give her the opportunity of leaving it. She could know nothing of the world, this young girl who had said that for many years she had not walked beyond a circuit of a few miles around the cottage, and who had always been attended by a servant whose interest it was to keep the child ignorant. Certainly if she knew her father's occupation she did not know its dis-

11*

gusting, cruel features. Yes, she would break these facts
very gently to this girl who so attracted her. If Miss
Dawson thought of the longed-for companion she would
gain in Mary she did not admit it to herself, was not
even aware of it.

"Mary, have you heard of those miserable beings
called convicts?"

"Yes." Mary's face changed and tears sprang to her
eyes, tears of pity as she thought of Lazarus.

"Child," Miss Dawson's voice was trembling "you
may have heard but you have not seen, and until you
have looked on them you cannot realize the crimes
against common humanity, the guilt of all concerned in
such barbarous cruelty."

"I have seen," Mary answered, no vestige of color
now in face or lips, for before her in all its misery came
the negro's figure on that fearful night.

"You have seen, and still remain here, still take as
support the money earned by such brutality!" There
was amazement in the lady's face and voice, as letting
fall the hand she held, Miss Dawson drew away from
Mary's side.

"What do you mean?" With brow drawn in trembling frown and eyes black with a horror dawning upon
her, Mary looked at the lady,

"Mean! That your father, Henry Hilton, is at the
head of a convict camp; that Osmerillo Mine is a horror so great, its cruelties are so vile, it almost makes us
question the watchful power of God; that you, if this
man supports you, are living upon money gained in a
manner as brutally cruel as could be shown by any
hired torturer of human beings!" Carried away by
feelings Miss Dawson's voice rang out clear and strong
each word falling like a blow on the gentle heart before
her. Mary's slight figure swayed as if falling. Dr. Colton put out his arm to support her, but she steadied her-

self against the wooden pillars of the verandah. The old doctor had been very uncomfortable during Miss Dawson's excited speech. He had been impatiently wishing that woman would do something else than fuss or kiss, and rather congratulated himself that after all no woman had right or title to him. But Mary's pallor and faintness touched the man's heart, and made him desire to protect her.

"Jane, she is ill. You have probably judged her harshly," he said, as with astonished face Janet appeared at the door and looked from one to the other.

"Gude God! What's wrang!" she cried. Mary had turned away, but something in the drooping head aroused Janet to fury. She sprang down the steps, nearly knocking over Dr. Colton as she passed.

"My bairn, what is it?" she asked, tenderly putting her arms around the girl.

"Janet! O my father!" It had come, the blow Janet had dreaded. These "grand folks" had come to this little cottage to break a girl's heart.

"What richt had ye to tell her?" She turned her face from the head resting on her breast and over her shoulder glared angrily at the visitors. "Why should ye come out in a' your bravery to break the heart o' an innocent lamb? She didna mak' her feyther. She knew not aught that could spot *her* godliness. Shame on ye, mon! ye come wha' ye werena' sought. Shame on ye, woman, wi' heart o' stone!"

Filled with regret at her misjudgment Miss Dawson did not heed the loud voice and angry looks of this servant, and a thousandfold more did her heart yearn toward the maiden who without one word of reproach had received from her a cruel blow. Releasing herself from Janet's embrace, but holding for support to her faithful arm, Mary turned to enter the house. Until Janet spoke there had lingered a hope that all this might be a cruel dream. Some mistake had been made, her father must be a good man! But Janet's anger had left no remnant of anything but grief. Suddenly deprived of that perfect trust that had made life beautiful, the girl needed solitude wherein she could hide her wounded heart and gather thought and purpose. For the first time she must think for herself, for the first time seek out and do her duty. Obedience, the ruling virtue in her character, was now become a sin, but the voice of that Christ she had grown to worship would show her the right path.

"Mary," said Miss Dawson, "forgive me. I have lived in a world where innocence like yours is unknown. An hour ago I wished for such a child as you, and now I ask you to become my daughter, to bear my name and be heir to my fortune. I am a lonely woman, but I possess not only wealth enough to give you every desire, but influence to obtain a position for your father. Both shall be yours if you will but accept them. Will you come to my home, will you gladden my life?"

Janet's wrath had changed to delight. At last her bairn might have rank befitting her. Already in her imagination she was decking out Mary in silks and velvets equal to those of the "gran' leddy." "Speak out, my bairn, speak quick. Tell the leddy ye'll tak' the offer," she whispered coaxingly in Mary's ear. But her hopes had a great fall when she saw Mary's face. "She willna' tak' it," Janet muttered, longing for some power to compel her to accept.

"I thank you," Mary said, "I thank you for your kindness, but my place is with my father. The greater his sin, the more need he has of his daughter. He will leave this—this business. I know he would not break my heart." Her voice faltered. "Perhaps for him I may ask your help. Besides," and as she made this plea tears fell from her downcast eyes over the white cheeks, "as he did everything for me, perhaps this sin was for my sake." Miss Dawson put her arm around the girl and kissed her brow.

" I will come again," she said. " And if you need me, this is my address." She put a card into Janet's hand. Following Miss Dawson, Dr. Colton with a bow, to Mary, entered the carriage that drove rapidly away, carrying with it Janet's dreams of grandeur. Then heavily massing clouds, the sighing winds and a few drops of rain brought Janet back to the dread reality of another storm.

"Come into the house, Mary," and she kissed the girl's cheek. " I couldna' lang be angry wi' ye. But ye were foolish not to tak' the leddy's offer."

A flash across the darkening sky, a muttering of thunder, and a frightened, " Come quick, Mary," from Janet, stirred the girl from her stupor. Slowly she went up the steps and entered her own room. Janet would have followed her but she turned at the door. " Not now, kind Janet, I want to be alone," and gently pressing the hand Janet had raised in expostulation she fell on her knees at her bedside.

For a few moments Janet stood in doubt. Then came a brighter flash, a louder roll of thunder. Running hastily to the window she closed and fastened it. " Ye maunna' stay i' the draught," she said, and then paused ag in. Unwilling to leave Mary, and yet unable to deny her right of solitude, Janet was in a quandary. " Surely God wadna' hurt sae sinless a lamb." There was another flash of lightning. " There isna' harm could tech her. Nae fear o' Hilton in sech a storm. I'll gang to my ain room." She started, then turned, came back and stepping softly had nearly touched Mary's shoulder to rouse her to listen. She would beg her to let her old Janet stay, and watch over her. She dreaded something. What was it? Was evil coming to Mary? Again Janet advanced, but the sight of that still figure with hidden face stopped her. Another flash, another roar of thunder, and Janet, leaving her door wide open that she could hear Mary's call, crouched down in the middle of her own room with eyes tight shut to keep out the fearful lightning.

CHAPTER XXXII.

SHE HAS BETRAYED YOU.

RIDING through the gathering gloom, unmindful of the wind that bowed the trees from side to side, unmindful of the heavy raindrops that fell on and around him, unmindful even of the lightning's glare that made the frightened horse stop and tremble, or of the thunder that roared wildly around, Hilton was coming to his child. The storm though great in violence did not compare with that inner tempest that tore his soul. From the moment when looking into Mary's eyes he had seen a thought, a feeling for another than himself, contentment had died for him. Her willingness to confide in him did not soften the fact that something outside of himself had given her happiness. Try as he might he had been unable to satisfy himself that this secret meant some childish freak. The girl's face had altered. The clear eyes softened by dreaming fancies were not raised as often in frank love to his. He dreaded her confidence, he dreaded to be assured of anything that would stand as a barrier between them. Therefore he had deferred the day for learning Mary's secret. But now he could not longer remain ignorant. Now there had arisen a doubt whose bare possibility made a madman of him. Either this doubt must be banished forever, crushed by Mary's truth, or— No ! He could not think of the other possibility of that question. Its bare suggestion called up every devil out of hell.

Plunging his spurs into his horse's side, he dashed on. Foam falling from the creature's mouth flecking its breast as with frightened eyes it gazed on the storm. That morning a letter had come from Stern to Hilton. He was still in pursuit of O'Neal. "The more I think over the matter of that nigger's escape, the more sure I feel that O'Neal must have been hidden in some house outside of Milton. Before leaving Milton after my return from the farm where I am convinced he had escaped by the connivance of a child, I searched pretty thoroughly the nigger quarter and the nigger records. Could find no trace of O'Neal, nor could I hear of any one who had seen such a nigger. The fellow is too remarkable in size and strength to have remained unnoticed even in a city like Milton. I believe when he first got into the town he started the Colton fire with a view to plunder. This, as you will remember, was discussed between us. Since you have extended my leave I shall work harder yet for the nigger's recapture. If I do not soon succeed on this side I shall take the train and go to the man's home." This and much more Stern had written. It was all about the work in hand, O'Neal's recapture. But one phrase would not leave Hilton's memory. "O'Neal must have been hidden in some house outside of Milton." Over and over again, gathering suspicion with every utterance, he repeated these words. Janet's terror, the glance between herself and Mary, were barely thought of at the time, but now were remembered with an oath. Riding through the storm he heard nothing, saw nothing, until the horse stopped at Mary's gate ! Hilton did not look up. With his scowling face bent forward and eyes fixed on the ground he led the horse to a little shed at the side of the cottage. Fastening there the trembling, frightened creature, he entered the house, and shutting the door behind him he stood for a moment in the silent hall. The stillness, the perfume of flowers, the atmosphere of purity of Mary's home surrounded him with their softening influence. Insensibly his face lost its fierce gloom, his breath came more quietly. He stepp'd to Mary's door and looked at his daughter as she knelt in prayer. The lightning flashed upon her lovely face, her upturned eyes and clasped hands. She seemed a voluntary victim offered in sacrifice. For what was she offered, of whom was she the victim?

" Mary."

She sprang to her feet, to his arms, and weeping fell upon his breast. He did not ask what made her weep, although in all her life he had never before seen her thus agitated. But to his heart he strained her in such fierce tenderness that he almost stopped her breath. Abhorrent as were his crimes, still she loved her father. The Christ she adored had prayed from the Cross, " Forgive them, for they know not what they do." And she weeping on her father's breast, was praying, " Lord, Lord, forgive him, and let the punishment fall on me." Thus had she prayed as unnoted roared the storm, and Hilton looking on, wondered at her devotion. Still with his arm about her he led her into the sitting-room. He placed her in a chair where the lightning would reveal the minutest changes of her face, and himself in shadow with his arms folded on his breast gazed on her. There was upon him a premonition, almost a certainty, of what was coming.

She did not raise her eyes. With drooping head and clasped hands lying in her lap, she was still weeping.

"What is your secret, Mary?" He had tried to speak gently, but his voice was harsh, and in the darkness his face was working nervously. Her secret! Absorbed in this great sorrow, her father's sin, she had almost forgotten the pure joys of her life. Ah! she could not tell him now of Dennis. Her tearful vision could not hold his face. That most miserable creature, who had fallen at her feet imploring mercy—his figure blotted out every other. Was that misery her father's doing? Was his terror the outcome of her father's sin?

"Oh, father, leave the convict camp! Oh, father, repent of that sin!"

She had fallen on the ground before him. She strove to clasp his knees with her arms. He pushed her off. Curses were in his mouth, but as yet he would not curse her. He had only to lift his hand, and he could kill her, who, kneeling at his feet, looked up imploringly at him. But he would not kill her. Not yet; though the lightning flashing on her face had lost its gleaming white, tinged, in his maddened fancy, with her blood.

"What do you know of convict camps?" he asked.

Hoarse with suppressed passion his voice took on the tone of the thunder that roared outside. The lightning flashed continuously, and the heavy rain beat on the windows. She could not hear his words, she could not see his face. But loving him with all her heart, she plead against his sin. "You will leave this life, dear father. You will not take money made in such a horrible way. We will work together and together expiate our sins."

Very sweet and clear was Mary's voice; so clear, so unlike the din of the storm, that each word reached her father. Again she moved toward him, striving to clasp her arms about him, striving to show by her tender caress how she loved him. But again he pushed her off. Then leaning over her that she might hear him, though wilder and louder roared the tempest, he asked: "When did you see a convict?" Within his soul there roared a storm so wild he could no longer dally with the truth; know it he must and at once. He glared furiously at the white figure at his feet and still—oh, strange humanity!—hoped where he knew hope was vain. There was no fear in Mary's face, no tremble in her voice, as she uttered the truth which destroyed man's semblance in the man before her, making him brute.

"Father, I saw a convict the night the dog sprang on me. I hid him in my room. I knew you would have protected him had you been there."

Gasping with rage, while on throat, face, head stood out the veins swollen in fury, Hilton caught her up, and then dashed her on the ground. The wind shrieked, "Kill her, kill her, she has betrayed you!" The thunder roared it, the lightning wrote it in lurid flame. He sprang forward, murder in his heart. His hands touched her, his fingers grasped her throat, as bruised, suffering and yet most loving, she was slowly rising to her feet.

It may have been a flash so fearfully bright that it tore the black sky in jagged edges of blinding light, or the thunder that seemed to rock the house ; it may have been those pure eyes that still looked at him in tender love ;—whatever the power that stayed him he loosed his murderous hold on Mary's throat. "Quick! leave me, leave me forever, or I'll add the thought of your murder to the hell I endure!" and grasping her shoulder, he pushed her from the room, from the house.

Out into the storm Mary wandered, now in blinding darkness, now dizzied by the vivid lightning. She was not conscious of movement, did not know that, stumbling in the muddy ruts, beaten by the pelting rain, she was running as she had never run before. She had seen murder in her father's face, and in that awful moment had prayed for a soul in peril ; and now filled with gratitude that he was spared the crime, she yet trembled with excitement. "He did not mean to hurt me. O Lord, no, no! It was the evil spirit, like that Thou did'st cast out of the boy. Save him, protect him, have mercy on my father!" Exhausted, panting for breath, she stopped for a moment, putting out her hand in the darkness and touching a tree. There was a vivid flash, and she saw

before her a wide road almost submerged iu torrents of
rain. Where was she? Where was Janet? Another
flash, and then a torch of fire came from the surcharged
clouds striking the great tree. With a crash it fell
across the road, and beside it, white and motionless,
lay the body of a girl.

CHAPTER XXXIII.

"THE SPERRITS O' HILTON'S SINS."

THE same flash of lightning streaming through the
windows of that little cottage revealed a madman
at work, a madman desecrating, destroying.
Dashed to atoms on the floor lay each fair token of
Mary's presence. Janet with terrified face stood in the
doorway.

Between each burst of thunder, each flash of light
she had listened in vain for Mary's voice. "She is in
prayer," she thought. Another crash, another flash, and
Janet's eyes would be shut tight while her "God save
us!" had less of petition than of horror in it. After that
roar of thunder so loud, so fearful, Janet started up. "I'll
e'en gang to Mary. She is safe, I weel believe. But
there's something I dread, and I dinna ken what."

Just then a flash and then another, in quick succession delayed her. Recovering herself and shutting her
eyes she hurried to Mary's door, where, aghast at what
she saw, she lost all horror of the storm in this greater
horror before her—Hilton with fierce hands destroying
the home of Mary. Hilton in fury! Where then was
Mary? Janet's breath seemed to stop, her heart to cease
its beating, as with eyes upon the floor she sought for—

Mary's body! But it was not there. There came an
instant's relief to the tension of her nerves, and then
with a return of that same horror she rushed from room
to room, then out into the garden, seeking, seeking,
what would madden her if found.

"Mary, Mary, Mary!" she shrieked, and listened for
the faintest moan. The storm was subsiding. In the sky
there were now a few clouds amidst which, serene and
beautiful, hung the clear cresent of the fair new moon.

Janet ran a little way down the road, then back
again, starting with horror as at the side of the house
she stumbled over the body of the dead horse. It was
hidden by some bushes. Perhaps, perhaps, Mary too
might—No, she dared not think it, dared not even conjecture such a possibility. Running into the house she
came out with a lantern and searched beneath each bush.
Into the celler, the spring-house, everywhere—but no
Mary. Then she rushed back again to Hilton, grasping
his arm fiercely.

"Where have you hid her? Where is she? Where
is Mary?" She shook him roughly. But he made her no
answer; he only looked at her like a drunken man, who
hears but does not comprehend.

"Where is she?" Janet shrieked the words, in her
fury catching at his throat. He struck her away, and
without a sound ran from the house and down the road
toward the convict camp.

"My bairn, my bairn!" sobbed Janet. The desolated
house was strewn with broken bits of glass and wood,
with torn shreds of cloth; these ruins were all that remained of Mary's fair nest. "I maun find her. Aye,
though I walk off shoes and feet, I'll never rest till I hold
ye in these arms, my bairnie, my bairnie."

As she spoke Janet hurried to her room and lifting
a plank under which she concealed her money, took out
the roll she had saved ready for her yearly deposit in the

Milton bank. She looked around, intending to make up a small parcel of necessaries, but everything was destroyed. The closet door was wrenched from its hinges and lay on the ground, trampled and broken. The dainty ruffled laces of her darling were a mass of rags.

"De'il! de'il! you de'il o' a mon! The raging lion is mair after God's likeness. I wad curse ye wi' the fire o' hell, but if she were i' Heaven 'twad grieve her gentle heart. Mary, oh my Mary!"

Without hat or shawl Janet left the place where for so long she had loved and served its fair mistress. At the gate she stood irresolutely looking up and down the road towards the convict camp. "No, she wadna' gang there if she went afoot." And turning away from the road to the wood, she faced the one that led toward Milton, the road which Mary had watched as Dennis disappeared. Janet walked on, calling often and stopping to listen. At last with a heavy heart she gave up hope, resolving to go to the city, report Hilton and have him arrested, charged with the murder of his child. The tears were still pouring down her face, and though the wind blew chill, she did not feel cold, being too full of grief at Mary's loss and rage at her cruel father. The narrow road had nearly reached the wider public one when she turned to look at the little cottage. How lonely it was! how desolate!

"Wi'out my Mary it is nae mair hame. Wi'out her for me the warld is bare. Good-by, wee house, ye war bonny, but now ye are a grave."

She hurried on, absorbed in grief, until she splashed into a mud puddle that lay where the roads joined. It was to reach something firmer than the boggy ground that she scrambled on the trunk of the great tree that lay across the road. "Anither death, anither friend gone," said Janet, crying bitterly even while she wrung the muddy water from her skirts. Under this tree she had been used to wait for a chance ride on a passing wagon when she made her annual expeditions to the city. And to it, with all her parcels, would she return, Hilton's orders being that no wagon or carriage should go down the little road leading to the cottage, which road thus remaining in evident disuse did not tempt exploration. And now all was gone. Mary, home, even this good old tree had been thrown down on the very day when Janet had lost everything else.

"I knew these storms wad bring sorrow an' sin," she said as wiping away the tears she held up her gown, trying to see by the waning light of the moon if she had rubbed off the mud. Perched on the tree she had nearly lost her balance. She threw out her hand to save herself, catching at a bunch of twigs and leaves that had sprung out from the side of the great trunk. But young and tender as they were, they gave way beneath her, and her hand falling through them touched something else, A slipper! She held it to her eyes and then on her knees pulled aside the boughs and tore away the leaves. It was Mary's slipper. Even in that dim fading light she recognized it. How had it come there? Was there any other token?

Suddenly she stopped her search, noticing what in the first moment's agitation had escaped her. The slipper was warm. Was it from the heat of her hand? She put it to her face. Her hand was cold. Then that warmth must have been from Mary's foot. She was not dead! "Thank God, thank God," cried Janet. Up and down the road in the growing darkness she ran calling on Mary. There was no answer but the wind's cry. Oh! for a light to see the ground! Oh, for one trace of her foot! How could she have come so far? She who in her whole life had walked but short distances and never alone had gone outside of her own garden. Janet strained her eyes to find a footprint. It was useless. There was nothing for it but to return to the cottage for the lantern. Breathless she entered the desolate house, shuddering at the eerie sounds made by the rushing of the wind through broken doors and windows. Snatching the lantern that lay just where she had felt it, she ran out again.

"The place is haunted," she muttered. "If it be with no real ghosts, it is wi' the sperrits o' Hilton's sins. If I find the trace o' her foot, he hasna killed her, but I'll gie my life he drove her forth. Sae tender a lamb i' sech a storm!"

As she spoke Janet with head bent toward the ground, was hurrying along searching the road whence she came.

"I hae found it!" she screamed, kneeling in the mud and fitting the slipper to footprints, that amid the muddy puddles kept their shape.

Wild with joy, through mud and water Janet ran, finding here and there the marks of that little slipper. But those were all—there was no Mary, no further sign of her. The morning found Janet still searching, but beyond the fact that Mary must have walked to the tree, and therefore her father was cleared of her murder, Janet knew nothing.

CHAPTER XXXIV.

TWO LETTERS.

IT was raining fast when Dennis reached Illanah and taking a carriage at the depot drove first to the post-office and then to Mammy's cabin. So misty with rain were the windows and so musty was the old carriage that he let down the glass, enjoying the sensation of the dampness on his face. Those wet drops beat against a breast filled with joy. He could not imagine the moment when he had not loved Mary, so truely a part of himself had she become. Thinking of her he forgot to open the parcel of mail matter which had been handed him by the young clerk. He still held it, when the carriage stopped at Mammy's door. The old woman looked out and then ran to get her cotton umbrella so that " massa would not wet hisself." But " massa " was inside the doorway, altogether indifferent to the rain on hat and shoulders, before Mammy could coax her ancient treasure to open.

"Dere, sit in de corner, you obstinate ole ting." She gave the umbrella a shake, and then with delight in every line of her good old face wiped her hand carefully on her spotless gingham apron before touching the one Dennis held out to her.

" Massa, you'se grow'd hansome sence you bin gone. You allus was a fine gemmen, but now I could a'most light a candle wid de sparkles in yo' eyes."

" Thank you, Mammy," said Dennis with a laugh " And now I want your eyes to sparkle too. I stopped to see you to get my key and to tell you you are not to work any more. Just play lady and tend that solemn little chap on the bed."

" Wha', Wha', massa, what you means?" Mammy asked in amazement.

" I'm rich, Mammy, I'm rich. I look on you as one of my best and oldest friends, so you must share my good fortune and be independent."

" Lord, Lord ! De jubilee am come ! Hear him ! Honey, does yer hear him ? De massa say we is ter be dependent, we's ter be dependent."

And she tried to induce the baby to give one of his rare " crows " as a congratulatory huzzah. But the philosopher was not to be shaken out of his gravity ; he kept his eyes most unflinchingly fixed on Dennis, doubtless debating in his own mind some deep problem.

"He's jest thinkin' it ober," said Mammy, trying to excuse him, and then putting him on the pillows she threw on her shawl and saying "I'se gwine to light yo' fire," hurried out of the door.

She was on her knees blowing up the bright flame when Dennis, having stopped to pay the coachman, entered the house. He threw his mail on the bed, which was white and neat as possible, and praised Mammy's kind care as he looked around the little room.

"Here, old lady," he called her from the kitchen where she was getting the coffee pot ready ; and putting a roll of money in her hands he said : "That's all yours and the baby's. You shall have as much every month."

"Why, massa, massa !" and then trying to laugh, trying to thank him, Mammy burst out crying. It was only a minute, however, before she wiped her grateful tears on the corner of her apron and beamed on "massa" with happiness in her face. "Why, why, massa, I'se feared I'll grow too proud wid de riches ob dis world."

"I'm not afraid of that, old lady." And then almost hesitating to cloud her enjoyment he asked : "Any news of Julie ?"

"Lor', Lor', I mos' forgot to gib you—" busily searching in the great bandanna folded across her breast, she drew forth something wrapped up in a handkerchief. "Here am de letter Massa Brown brought fer you, massa. Julie's foun', but loss agin !" And good old Mammy shook her head and sighed heavily, while Dennis, who had already begun to untie his own mail, not expecting anything but newspapers, and perhaps a scolding letter from his publisher, tossed it aside and sat looking at Mammy, who unfolded the handkerchief until finally the letter was produced. The envelope, post-marked at the capital of the State, had on it a few lines from Brown saying that he kept this letter for Mr. Day and regretted the news was not better. Dennis opened the letter and read it to Mammy's accompaniment of groans and tears.

"DEAR BROWN:—I know I saw the mulatto woman. So sure was I that I took her home to my wife, who really acted like a brick. But the unfortunate creature got away. I have kept a sharp lookout but so far have not seen or heard anything of her. I found her in this wise: It was the day of the Governor's reception, and pushing through the crowd, hurrying up the steps came a pale, thin, mulatto woman. She had a pitiful look about her, and really, though her dress was old and worn, was more ladylike than many a better-dressed and whiter woman in that very crowd. I jest kept my eyes on her, for I said to myself, p'raps that's the nigger Brown's been writing about. And then I fell to wondering how she could find her way down to Augusta. It's a long distance for a woman and a poor one too. While I was a thinking, the woman reached the door, and the nigger waiter dressed up in a fine new suit said : Git back. No niggars 'lowed.' The woman begged to go in. She spoke low but distinct. P'raps I was trying hard to hear, but at any rate I caught almost every word. How she did pray to be let in. 'It's not money I'm asking for. It's a life I want, a life I'm begging for.' There was a wild look in her eyes, yet she seemed to know what she was saying. I was waiting to hear her give her name, waiting to have some proof that she was the one you wanted. But, Brown, it did set my blood boiling to see the airs that black nigger waiter put on with his own color ! He just pushed her aside, threatening to call the perlice. The woman looked frightened, looked to see if a perliceman was coming and caught something closer in her arms. I thought it was a baby,

but I'm blamed if I didn't start when I saw the poor critter had just a shawl holding to her breast. I knew then
it was Julie, and started forward under pretense of getting her away and preventing disturbance. I intended
taking her home to my wife. But as she turned she met
a party of young bloods coming up to see the Governor.
They were laughing and as jolly as gentlemen generally
are when they have just about as much as they can carry.
The last thing I expected was to see the pale mulatto
girl catch hold of the gayest of the lot, Mr. James Eaton.
He comes from your parts; his daddy's mighty rich,
they say, and this young man's the greatest beau of the
season. But he didn't like the belle he'd caught this
time. If ever I saw a nigger fluster a white it was that
same mulatto woman. I could have laughed at him if
her face warn't so pitiful. But there warn't nothing
mealy-mouthed about her words. She spoke out as plain
as could be, and said: 'You've caused all our misery, set
my husband free! You know he's innocent—set him
free as you hope to be saved!' He tried to shake off her
hand, but I'm blamed if he could. She stuck fast, and
the gay young fellows around began to chaff and laugh.
But the poor nigger did not seem to hear; her eyes were
fixed on Mr. Eaton, who turned red and white. To make
matters worse one of the old grandees came up, jest in
time to hear the nigger's words. 'Oho, young man,
thought I, 'your cake's dough for that old man's daughter.' But I'm blessed ef the old gentleman didn't side with
the young one, calling out 'perlice! perlice!' I was handy
so I took off the poor critter, who was whispering
to that roll of shawl. I declare I never saw anything
more pitiful than that nigger. As the old gentleman didn't
make a regular complaint I jest took her home to my
wife. After all it's the poor as helps the poor. For my
wife, who, what with my rheumatiz and our Sallie's sickness, had used up every cent, just gave to the nigger

woman as if she had a fortune. First she made her eat. I never saw any one so hungry, but all on a sudden she stopped and seemed to forget. I couldn't stay long, so as soon as I saw my wife getting out one of her own calickers to give the nigger, I jest walked away thinking I might be richer, but I'm darned if I could ever have such another brick as my old girl. In the evening I was off duty, and little Sallie begged I'd take her round to the Governor's to hear the music, for there was to be a grand ball. It was a real cold night, but I tell you the music was fine, and to my eyes my little Sallie a-jumping up and down with her face just shining with pleasure was prettier than all the fine ladies rolling up in their carriages and trooping up the stairs with their long trails a-sweeping behind. I couldn't help thinking how many shivering folks could have been kept warm by them yards and yards of stuff that was just sweeping up the pavement. Well, after Sallie got a little tired she wanted to take a peep in the windows and then we'd go home, she said. So I put her on my shoulder while her little heels kept time to the music. I was busy keeping off the crowd when suddenly Sallie began to cry ; 'Oh, daddy, daddy, there's the poor colored woman.'

" There sure enough on the steps was that unfortunate critter looking mighty neat in that clean calicker of my wife's. But when I once saw her face with the bright light from the open door shininig on its misery, I declare, Brown, I felt like crying with little Sallie. There on the stones the poor nigger knelt. I couldn't hear her words, but her looks were enough as she tried to catch hold of the ladies as they passed. But they none of them seemed to listen. 'Let's take her home, papa,' sobbed my little Sallie. I tried to reach the poor critter, but before I could, two of the force had grabbed her up and carried her off. Sallie and I tried to catch up with them, but the crowd was great and before we managed to get away the woman and the officers were out of sight. I went as fast as I could, for I feared she'd be put in the stockade over night, and if ever there's a beastly, cruel wrong it's the stockade business. It is a crying shame to throw poor devils in that hole and let them be at the mercy of a set of wild beasts, for some of the prisoners ain't a bit better, and are they to blame when they know no matter what happens no one's to be punished ? I declare the cruelties I've seen them do to new prisoners fairly makes a man's blood boil. But I was too late, Brown, the poor nigger was sent to the stockade. I tried to get her out, but the man in charge ain't a friend of mine, so there was nothing for it but to wait until the morning. I went around very early, but she was gone—where, I couldn't find out, nor what cruel trick they had played on her. But there was a deal too much wicked laughing among the ruffians in that den for me not to know they had ill-used the unfortunate critter. I'm almost as sorry as you are about the poor nigger, and I do think the State ought to break up this stockade business. I only hear of the convict camps, but this stockade I see every day, and it's a crying sin. Good-by, old fellow. I hope Mrs. Brown and the little Browns are well, and that you are having easier times than we are down here.

"Yours with respect,   R. M. WHEELER."

'Poor Julie !" Dennis looked at the little window with the rain pouring on it. The drops seemed tears at the unmerited misery of that negro family. These laws were terribly unjust ! Again he vowed he would devote both time and fortune to the righting of the wronged.

Mammy stood patiently waiting and watching. The unconscious pathos of her face touched him deeply.

" Well, old lady," he roused himself from the unpleasant reverie, "you and I will make the youngster happier than his mother and father."

"'Deed we will, massa, deed we will." And with another "God bress you," she went back to the baby. In spite of his own happiness Dennis was depressed by the sad news concerning the mulatto. It was a hard world for the negro, the innocent cause of war and now the victim of that war's odium ; where was his chance for a better future ? Slowly, to dissipate thought, Dennis untied his bundle of mail matter. But the first letter was the only one read. His face had flushed and brightened at the postmark, and the cramped, uneducated writing made him exclaim: "From Janet." He tore open the envelope, turning white at the first words :

"Mr. Dennis Day :—Mary has gone ! Where, God only knows. But if ye wish her half as well as ye say, ye will come and help in the search. I am stopping at the hotel with Miss Dawson.   Janet Wilson."

He looked at the date. The letter was a month old. Where was Mary ? Had she been found ? Did she believe him faithless ? Was she dead ? No ! this could not be. And yet at thought of the possibility there settled upon him the numbness of despair. He looked at the clock, and caught up the paper to glance at the time table. With a swift team he might reach the station in time for the southern bound train. The station was at some distance from Illanah, but money could hire horses.

"Thank God for the money !" he said, and snatching up the bag that lay just where he had thrown it on entering, he hurried out of the house. He thrust his head into Mammy's doorway and tossed some money on the table. "Good-by," he called, "I may be away some time. Have Brown keep a lookout for Julie." He had disappeared before Mammy could answer. She stood at her door, watching him as he dashed down the street into the livery stable, whence in a short time a carriage rolled out and rapidly disappeared.

"Lor, Lor, wha's de matter now," Mammy whispered to herself. "My! how white his face was. I hopes it ain't no trouble, for Massa Dennis am a gemman, 'a real gemman.'"

CHAPTER XXXV.

THE SEARCH.

THE sun was shining brightly, the streets were gay with people, as Dennis, pale and haggard, looked out of the window of the hotel in Milton, where, having sent up his card, he was now impatiently waiting for Janet. After a few minutes which seemed an age Janet came. Stiff and prim and looking years older than when he had last seen her, the Scotchwoman bowed her head, nor seemed to notice Mr. Day's outstretched hand.

"I have been away from Illanah ; I returned only two days ago, and started for Milton as soon as I had read your letter." He spoke hurriedly, and then waited, hoping, fearing, to hear of Mary. But Janet did not mention the name nearest to both their hearts. With her eyes on the ground she said slowly, as if to herself "Then he wasna' fause."

"False ! Janet ! I love Mary. A fortune has just been left me, and all the pleasure I felt in it was for Mary's sake. It was poverty alone that drove me from her." His face had flushed with his impetuous words, and his eyes shone with a light that touched Janet even more than his words.

"For Mary !" she said and then began to cry in a

quiet way as if it had become a habit with her. "My bairn is nae mair, nae mair."

"Dead !" Dennis grew ashy pale and dizzy. Then while a determined look replaced the horror of his face, "Are you sure she is dead ?" he asked.

"Sure !" Janet's eyes fixed on space were dulled by tears that seemed to have washed out all color. "We hae heard naething, found nae trace, and now a month has gane."

"Janet, never say she is dead until we find her body. I believe she lives, and I will find her."

Janet, who had been sitting in a hopeless fashion, at his words gazed earnestly up into his face. He looked strong, brave, determined ; he seemed a lover who would keep his word. She caught his hope and sprang to her feet, while something of their old sharpness came into her eyes. "An' if ye do it ye are an angel sent frae God. Ye are worthy o' my bairn."

"I will find her, Janet, if it takes my whole life. If she is above the earth I will find her, if buried I will find her. But she is not dead. I am sure of it, I feel it, I know it."

"God grant it, God grant it." Grasping his hand Janet looked eagerly at him. In silence they stood a moment as if binding themselves to this service, this obligation. Then placing a chair for her Dennis inquired into each particular, the finding of the slipper and of the traces of Mary's feet. Janet had on reaching Milton been aided in her search by Dr. Colton and Miss Dawson. Each public institution and private home had been examined, advertisements had been inserted in the papers, and the police put into requisition ; and for all result— nothing.

"Is that all ? Did you lose hope after so little had been done ? Oh, Janet, if you had been a man, a man who sought the woman he loved, you would know the search had only begun. Good-by; I shall take it up just where you left off."

"Mon, mon, ye a'most mak' me laugh wi' joy." Dennis had taken his hat and was already at the door. Janet followed him, half-laughing, half-crying. "See," she said, "I hae grieved sae lang, an' now ye are sae fu' o' hope I am a'most afeard. But come, afore ye gang, an' see Miss Dawson an' the doctor. They are baith Mary's friends. I will tell ye a' about them anither time. Can ye not wait noo to see the leddy?"

"Not now, Janet. I must begin the search. Each moment's delay is so much wasted time. I will stay at this hotel and see your friends at my first leisure. Keep up hope. Mary will be found."

And down the stairs he went so quickly Janet held her breath for fear he would fall. "He has gi'en me new life," she said, as with something of her old manner she went up the stairs and rapped at Miss Dawson's door.

"What is it, Janet," the lady asked, startled by Janet's excited face.

"Miss Dawson, I hae hopes."

"Hopes!" The sadness of the lady's face was changed to an excitement almost equal to Janet's, for these hopes could have but one reference—Mary. Since that morning when distracted by grief, not knowing upon whom else to call for help, Janet had burst in upon Miss Dawson with the news of Mary's loss, the lady had been a kind friend to the Scotchwoman. She had made her stay at the hotel, giving her some light duties that she might not feel dependent, and had aided her both with money and personal effort in the search for the missing girl. Proud to a fault, Jane Dawson was too true to excuse an error, even to herself. And she now felt she had been greatly in error in precipitating sorrow upon that innocent girl. It was small comfort to know that she

12*

had acted from a sense of duty. It had been a cruel duty, and harshly fulfilled. While each was ignorant of the facts of Mary's departure from her home, all felt it had been caused by her knowledge of her father's sin. No proceedings against Hilton had been begun. Janet's finding the slipper yet warm at such a distance from the cottage at the very time when Hilton was destroying the traces of Mary's presence there, precluded any thought of his having killed his child. After some consultation Dr. Colton had ridden out to the convict camp, and had been politely received by Hilton. At the first mention of his daughter's name his face had clouded ominously and saying, "Sir, I know nothing of that person since she left my care," he dismissed the subject. When Dr. Colton persisted, and losing patience at the strange father's silence, threatened, Captain Hilton said :

"Every man is allowed to manage his private matters. You are taking great liberties with a stranger. If you have any case you can call the law to your aid. But for me, I order you to go!" and trembling with passion almost equal to Hilton's, the doctor had to summon all his pride and good sense to his aid to prevent him from striking the man. He had regained his coolness by the time he reached Milton. On discussing the subject with Miss Dawson, they agreed that in a legal process against Hilton much would be lost and nothing gained. So they decided to make a thorough search for the girl. But as the days rolled by they lost hope, and Janet sank into the despondency from which Dennis had just roused her.

"I hae hopes," she said again, walking up and down the room in her agitation. "Dennis, the one-armed mon—ye mind him, Miss Dawson ; 'twas he my Mary's heart went out to—he has come. He says he will find my bairn. An' oh, he looked sae strong, sae brave, I canna but believe him. I hae thought him fause, I hae slandered him afore ye, but I could a'most ha' kissed the groun' at his feet, when I saw his love for Mary shining in his ee."

These were not very logical reasons for Janet's hopes —certainly not sufficient ones to brighten Miss Dawson's despondency ; yet when, just before dinner, Dennis's card was sent up and at the lady's invitation he came to her sitting-room. she too caught some of his strength and felt cheered by his hope. He was handsome, strong, brave and loving ; these are wonderful arguments with a woman. Even the fact that Mary's lover was a " carpet-bagger," a fact which he very frankly stated early in their acquaintance, did not entirely deprive him of the lady's favor. It certainly was trying to the doctor on his return from the hospital, where he had gone for an important consultation, to find a young man taking the lead in the matter of finding Mary. And it was more than trying to hear Jane Dawson, who knew his feelings and intentions toward Mary, calmly speak of the stranger as " Mary's lover." But after a few days, when the vigorous measures instituted in the search for the lost girl gave them all a certain excitement, if not hope, the doctor too began to rely on this " audacious carpet-bagger," as he had angrily called him the first time he had talked him over with his cousin. He too began to listen eagerly for the quick, light tread of Mr. Day and to fidget a great deal more than the " fussy women," if the dinner hour passed without Dennis's handsome face enlivening their table. After awhile they all began to depend on him, and, their interest in Mary being the first bond, grew to like, admire and even feel affection for this " audacious carpet-bagger." As for the man himself, he passed many a weary, anxious hour. Keeping a brave face and brave hopes to cheer the women and the old doctor, he felt sometimes very near despair. But he would not give up the search.

He employed a force of ten men, and after some drill-
ing had an army of quiet, efficient workers, the first law
of whom was perfect secrecy.   The advertisements were
kept up, but Dennis had little faith in them although he
trebled the offered rewards.   It was his theory that Mary
must have fainted or was perhaps injured by the falling
tree, and had been picked up by some passing country
wagon.   Her own perfect ignorance of the world, even
of the name of Milton, the city nearest to her home,
would be one great difficulty in her way should she have
striven to find her friends.   As for the names "Colton,"
"Dawson," "Hilton," "Janet," what would they be but
sounds to country people who had never heard them?

It was possible that whoever had taken her had a
motive in keeping her concealed.   It could not be gain,
or some steps would be taken to let it be known a lady
had been found.   It might be that she was ill, and he
leaned against the wall pressing his hand to his throbbing side, which had not lost its old fashion of aching in
sympathy with anxious thought.   It might be that she
was dead.   A blank came before him, life itself seemed
over as this possibility arose.

"No! it it is not that! She is not dead!"

He would not admit such a thought to his mind.
He hurried from the house, and taking a horse dashed
out of town at a breakneck gallop.

Acting on his theory that Mary was concealed in some
place in the vicinity of Milton, Dennis having given
each man his district, had ordered that each house and
building should be thoroughly inspected.   The manner
was left to their own discretion, secrecy alone being en-
joined.   As the men were paid liberally, and as abundant
money was furnished for expenses, and, moreover, as a
reward almost fabulous was promised to the fortunate
finder of the missing lady, the little band was indefati-
gable.   Added to these facts the certainty that they were

as a body and individually under the personal inspection of Mr. Day, who seemed ubiquitous, filled the men with the spirit of emulation than which nothing is more inspiring. A month had been spent in incessant and unremitting labor, and, except the certainty that within an area of fifteen miles Mary was not to be found, nothing had been discovered. Mr. Day's orders for the continuance of the search were quietly given and quietly received; the men, among themselves voting him " darned plucky," went about their business. Miss Dawson and Janet, when Dennis reported results, were inclined to take the despondent side, but gained fresh courage from Dennis's determination to keep on, and his firm belief that Mary would be found.

The necessity for his being away from Milton, as the scene of his labors grew more distant, depressed Miss Dawson extremely. She had grown to like this young man, so lately a stranger to her, to depend on and trust him as she had never before done to man. He seemed to unite those qualities she most admired, and feeling a tenderness for the missing girl, she had rejoiced in his love for Mary. There had been sincere regret in the lady's eyes as well as in her words when he left her.

" Mr. Day, I can hardly tell you how much I shall miss you."

" Thank you !" Dennis smiled with pleasure at her kind words as he held his hand out to Janet.

" Good-by, Janet. Remember you are not to lose heart, ' he said, and hastening from the room he took all cheerfulness away with his brave face. There was little brightness in his expression now as he rode along the highway absorbed in thought, and yet keeping a sharp lookout on every passing wagon — hoping, always hoping, to see something that would tell of Mary. As he came to the little side road down which he had once walked to her cottage he turned into it. He would visit

once more that which had been her bower. He saw it
afar off, gleaming white in the sun. But when he came
nearer, the broken windows, the destroyed garden, the
ruin everywhere filled him with bitterness and grief.
Where was she, that angel who, looking from her roses,
won his heart? Where was she? "Oh, fool, dolt not to
have taken her, when like a white dove of innocence she
would have flown to my breast," he said, as over the
broken gate he entered the garden, and walked through
the empty rooms once hallowed by her presence. Of
that fair girl not a relic remained ; there was ruin, deso-
lation everywhere. Crushing back the grief that was
almost dispair, he mounted his horse. " I will find her,"
he said, looking away from the ruined cottage, "I will
find her. She is not dead."

CHAPTER XXXVI.

DINAH.

RAIN, rain, rain. Old Mammy looking from her
window thought the rain would never cease.
"I reckon it's de'struction ob de world," she
said to the wise baby, whose wide-opened eyes followed
her every movement. Mammy had become an object of
interest to all her friends and neighbors. Hearing of her
good fortune, the colored gentry had called to congratulate her, and many a bright quarter found its way to the
pockets of her needy brethren. As for the warm cups of
coffee and pipes of tobacco that were enjoyed besides
Mammy's fire, they would have impoverished any one
but a " millinere," Mammy said as with delight she
showed the baby their riches. There came a knock at

the door, and hiding the old tea-pot that was her saving
bank, Mammy called out, "Jes' come in." The door
opened and a thin mulatto woman entered. "Lor,
Dinah, chile, am dat you?" said Mammy. "Jes' sit
down dare an' I'll get up the nicest hot coffee you'se
ebber seed." Dinah took one of the new chairs bought
with Mammy's "fortune," and sitting on its edge, began
to rock herself back and forth. She did not speak until
Mammy, having put the kettle on, lit her pipe and sat
down opposite her. Then, still rocking and keeping her
eyes on the fire she said :

"Nebber hab to work eny mo'! I'se heard de news,
an' joys wid yer. De Lord hab remembered yer in your
old age." Dinah's voice, full and resonant, made her
slowly uttered words seem like a hymn she was giving
out.

"Yes, yes, chile," sighed old Mammy. "I'se berry
grateful, but I'd rudder work til Gabel blows de silber
horn, dan to see dem I lubs like my chillern suffer as dey
hab done,"—at which words the baby, whom Dinah's
voice had waked from sleep, raised up his voice and
crowed. "De wisdom ob dat chile!" Mammy said,
shaking her head. But Dinah did not notice the "chile,"
nor Mammy's last words.

"Mammy, Mammy," she said solemnly, "you looks
de gibt hors in de face. It am right to lub yo' chilern.
Dey is good nuf in dere way, dough some times it's a bad
way. But yo'd better tank de Lord fer de blessin ob de
money. I calls yo' degrateful. I tell you, Mammy, you's
in need ob 'legion. Yo'd better jine de church now
yo'se got de time ter pray an' de money ter pay de dues.
Fer I tells yer ter lib on de fat ob de lan', an' nebber no
mo' hab ter slabe am mighty near the salbation time."

Mammy tried to speak to assure Dinah she was
grateful, but Dinah would not give her a chance.

"Hol' on, honey," she said, "I'se de flo', an' I'se a

messenger sent from de Lord. I wants yo' ter jine de meetin'. Ef de rain'll ebber stop we's ter hab de grandes' meetin' out under de grobe ob live oaks, whar' de holy men'll wrestle wid de debbil, fer yer souls. I'se gwine ter de meetin' ef I habs ter starbe a mont. I'll be dere ter jine my shoutin' wid de holy ban' 'til it reaches up ter Hebben an' bangs agin de wall. De time is fixed fer de week dat ends dis mont an' is de beginnin' ob de nex' an' den wid clean hearts we'll be ready, we'll be ready fer de holy Christmas time."

More singing than speaking, Dinah had risen to her feet. She still kept up her swaying motion, and her eyes glowed with excitement. She had pushed her damp sunbonnet back on her shoulders and even with the gay handkerchief around her head looked like some weird prophetess gazing into the misty future. Mammy still seated had taken her pipe from her mouth and was earnestly watching Dinah.

"Ho, Mammy, dis camp meetin'll be a glorious day fer Dinah. I'se spectin' Cæsar 'Gustus, my sister's chile. He's struck wid de Lord an' has jined de preachers. You 'members de little boy I sent Nort to school? I'se wukked faithful all dese years to eddicate dat chile, an' now I can take de Lord's pride in dis precious fruit. He writes me dis," and seating herself she drew from her bosom a letter written in a small clear hand. "See, he is edicated, writes like a book. I starved, but he ken read an' write. Glory hallelujah!" Her voice had risen almost to a shout, exciting old Mammy who putting her pipe on the stove began to catch the spirit of the moment and with folded hands kept time to Dinah's voice with the rocking of her body.

"Listen," said Dinah, speaking lower and more quietly. "I knows it ebbery word. I has heard it read, and dough I can't read, nebber having de merciful chance, I 'preciates de blessin'. Pride's a sin afore de Lord, but sho' de Hebbenly satisfaction in de larnin' ob dis boy is like de whisperin' ob angels, when I knows de work ob dese black hans hab done it all." Dinah gave her sunbonnet another push, and holding the letter carefully upright repeated it from first to last to her admiring audience of Mammy and the baby.

"Dere, Mammy," and once more on her feet, Dinah triumphantly waved the letter aloft. "Dat's what I has libed fer. Ter see dis boy, my sister's chile, growed up ter be a preacher ob de Lord, a reader ob de Gospel. I feels like standing on de house-tops an' sendin' out de shouts ob victory. Oh, ef his mudder could ha' libbed ter se de day!"

Swaying backward and forward, her voice ringing through the room and her eyes widened as her excitement increased, to Mammy's simple vision she seemed inspired. Catching Mammy's hands in her nervous ones, she looked at her with those wild eyes and in a low monotone chanted: "Sister, will yer jine?" and then louder and higher: "Will yer jine de Lord? Repent, oh sinner, repent!" Mammy fell on her knees, weeping for sins which in her true life had never been committed and sobbed, "I will, I will!"

"A bran' snatched from de burnin'. A sinner gained to de Lord!" Dinah chanted the words as standing by the hearth she towered above Mammy kneeling at her feet. In the half madness of religious fervor, with her long arms sawing the air, she seemed taking part in an incantation. Suddenly she began to sing, filling the little room with her vibrating voice:

> "Jine me, den, on de Ribber Jordan,
> Jine me wha' de waters meet.
> See de Hebbens open gently,
> Showin' us de golden street."

Mammy overpowered by the woman's wild enthu-

siasm began to groan and cry, while the solemn baby on
the bed stared harder than ever.

"Fare de well," Dinah chanted, as taking Mammy's
hand she lifted her to her feet and swayed her back and
forth with her own motion. "Fare de well, sister; de
Lord hab teched your heart. Hol' Him fas', hol' Him
fas'. I'll meet you in de promised lan'. You'll be dar !
You'll be dar !" For a moment she fixed on Mammy her
fiery eyes and as the old woman sobbed, "Yes, yes, I'll
be dar," Dinah turned and with the unopened umbrella
grasped tightly in her hand walked rapidly down the
street, muttering as she went. Unmindful of the pouring rain, looking straight before her with an intense
fiery stare, her calico dress, blown by the wind and
wetted by the rain, flapping about her, she was a fierce
wild figure, a thrilling type of negro enthusiasm.

Poor old Mammy was overpowered by the sense of
wickedness. "I'se a sinner, dere's no doubt ob dat," she
said, shaking her head and mourning her own lukewarm-
ness. She was called from her doleful contemplation of
her "sinful state" by the philosopher, who, whatever
Mammy's opinion might be, thought her the most amiable
person in the world, as he very plainly showed. He
ceased crying the moment she took him in her arms, and
smiled up into her face in the "knowin'est way," the old
woman said, when forgetting all about sins and sinners,
she followed God's law in her motherly love for the
orphan.

———

There was a week of great excitement among the
negroes. Not only in Illanah but for miles around the
negroes were preparing for "de great meetin'." For
though the season had advanced into the winter months
there was no sign of winter in the soft air and sky of
perfect blue.

"De Lord Hisself is workin' fer de strayin' souls,"

Dinah said, as throwing aside all other duties she gave her whole time to "de great work." Her tall thin figure and vehement gestures, her chants, hymns, and more than all those fiery eyes, stirred the enthusiasm of the negroes. She never tired, but passed continually from cabin to cabin, coming often to Mammy, whom she conjured not to be a "backslider." The old woman had had some misgivings about leaving Illanah, feeling herself left in charge by "Mars Dennis," and always expecting the return of Julie. It was only when "Mars Brown" promised to look after the O'Neal cabin himself, and Meg volunteered to keep the keys of Mammy's house, and "Mr. Day's too" that her conscience was set at ease. And now in her cabin, all ready to start, she was waiting for the wagon that was to take her to "de harvest ob de Lord," as Dinah called the camp meeting. A huge basket packed with a week's provision stood near the door in friendly companionship with a large carpet sack, a relic of "de ole miss," Mammy's former owner. On the bed the baby sat and stared. He too was going to the meeting, "gwine ter jine de ban'," and if appearance is index to feeling, was fully impressed with the gravity of the occasion. "Mars Brown," and little Meg had come to see Mammy off and take possession of the keys. Brown had at once taken into his kind heart the old negress and the orphaned baby.

" You see, a-fillin' o' Mars Dennis's orders, I has lef Julie's cabin all fixed up wid pervisions and just the nicest chickens a pickin' roun' ter make de place look like home. Ef ye would jest see dey don't starve, and dat de dus' don' lay too heavy on Mars Dennis's rooms, 'case he comes un'spected like!" Brown promised he would walk out every two days to the cabin, and Meg said she would "see to the dust." Mammy was still thanking them when a large country wagon drove up to the door. It seemed filled to overflowing with black faces looking out through every possible aperture of the white canvas covering.

"Why, there's no room," said Brown.

"Room! dere's lots inside," shouted some one from the interior of the wagon.

"Mammy, Mammy," cried several voices. And then Dinah's voice was heard rising clear above the noise: "Come, Mammy, come, I'se waitin' ter lead yer to de promis' lan'." Mammy no longer hesitated, but helped up by Brown was comfortably seated near Dinah while in the wagon's marvellous capacity was found room for the basket and carpet sack. Putting the baby on her lap Brown shook Mammy's hand. "Good-by, old woman," he said kindly. "Have a good time and keep easy. We'll look after everything." And little Meg on the door step waved her hand and smiled.

"Good-by, I tanks you bofe. God bress you," Mammy called out, as Dinah led the hymn in which the negroes joined. To the accompaniment of their melodious voices, mingled with an occasional groaning, the wagon rolled out of town.

CHAPTER XXXVII.

"I HAB DONE WID LIFE."

THE place selected for the camp meeting was a grove of magnificent live oaks about seven miles out from Ilanah. Hundreds of negroes were assembled. The grove seemed a miniature city with its myriads of tents and the numbers of people in constant motion.

The night before the formal opening of the meeting Dinah passed between the rows of tents saluting alike friend and stranger.

"You is all one to me," she said. Her eyes burned with inward fire and her face was blanched by intense excitement. "You is all one to me. Am we not de chillen ob de Lord? Am he not gwine to sabe us? Yes, dough it be by de fiery brimstone, dough we walk frough de ocean ob bitterness, ef you repents you'll be sabed. See! See! from de Hebens shines de eternal light." See! See!" And raising her long thin arm she pointed afar, while with fixed eyes she seemed to see what was hidden from her eager listeners. From tent to tent, from group to group, she went firing the imagination of these simple hearted creatures, until when raising her clear, melodious voice she sang a hymn familiar to all, hundreds of voices followed hers. Some frightened souls shouted aloud their sins, some fell face downward to the ground, and some jumped high in the air and screamed in wildest excitement. Quiet old Mammy with the wondering baby in her arms, felt herself on the strong tide of a rushing river. "I feels de presence ob de Lord," she called out as loudly as she could, and her call wakened echoing cries from numberless sympathetic hearts. While the cries were at their loudest, Dinah sprang to her feet and extending her arms shouted, "Hush!" Those near her were immediately stilled, so powerful was her magnetism. The wave of silence went on until all in that excited crowd had caught the whispered "Hush, hush!" of Dinah's wonderful voice. Then in the stillness, in a whisper that thrilled her hearers the woman sang:

> "Sleep, sleep! dat de flesh be ready,
> Sleep, sleep, dat the sperrit may be strong
> Sleep, sleep! for de clarion ob Gabrel
> Is gwine to call you, in the golden morn.
> Sleep! Sleep! Sleep!"

Hushing her voice to the softest sound, with arms

outspread and face lifted to the moonlight, she slowly retreated from the sight of the awestruck crowd and disappeared in her tent.

As the rising sun brighted with its glory the beautiful grove, Dinah's voice, clear as " Gabriel's horn,' wakened the sleeping multitude. She stood on a fallen tree, with long arms extended before her and tightly clasped hands that moved in regular rhythm to the music. The sunlight falling on her upraised face and wide opened eyes, added to their intensity. Not far away on a rude platform, with head bent down and hands crossed on his breast knelt a man in prayer. Swiftly, gently, fearing to disturb his devotions and unconsciously in their movements keeping time to Dinah's song, the negroes came from their tents and row after row formed around the platform. Each heart felt the influence of that silent prayer, that attitude of absorbed devotion, as each negro took his place besides his kneeling fellow. Dinah's voice seemed miles away ; fainter and fainter came the sounds, yet so wonderfully sustained, so artistic had been the effect, that after she had ceased and was prostrate on the ground in a half trance of religious fervor, the air seemed still vibrating with her words.

" Glory, glory, glory hallelujah ! De Lord hab remembered de sinner ere He dies ! "

The very beating of their listening hearts were saying the words, when rising from his knees, his face exalted by prayer, the man walked to the edge of the platform and holding out his hands asked a silent blessing on the praying multitude. He was a young man of medium size, with the dark brownish skin that is most common among his race. His features were of the ordinary type, but his forehead was high, and somewhat redeemed the plainness of the face, that had, moreover, an additional gift in the extreme sensitiveness that now made his lips tremble. But the mouth, full as it was, did not show coarseness of nature, and his eyes, soft and black, were full of tears. Unuttered were the words of prayer that moved his lips, and perfectly quiet were the kneeling figures before him. Then in a voice full and deep, and with something of the vibratory power that made Dinah's so effective he cried :

"Arise, for the Lord speaks unto you !"

As if they had heard God's voice, the negroes started, some with eyes rolled up until only the whites shone in their dark faces, some with hands clasped and gaze fixed on the preacher, some striking their breasts and groaning. Their faces were filled with religious emotion, so true, so real, that the sentiment exalted, obliterated, mere accident of feature and skin. There was a moment of silence then the preacher gazing at them broke into an impassioned address.

Eloquence, mighty eloquence wakens admiration, but feeling, thrills. One sways the mind, the other moves the heart. This negro uttered only simple words—words a child's intelligence could easily grasp, yet so intense was his own feeling, so thorough his own truth, that had statesmen been his auditors they might have felt their hearts quickened. They too, perforce, would have glanced inward as conscience stirred from its lethargy would have called, "Can you bear this test ? Can you stand this judgment ? Do you believe ? Or are you a Pharisee, a hypocrite ?" Tears were rolling down the preacher's face, but he did not notice them.

He fell upon his knees, and then after some moments of silent prayer gave out the hymn. Above the weaker voices Dinah's thrilled, and as the music rose the negroes became more and more excited until the moment came for entrance to "the sinners' pen," when so many rushed up that there was not room to accommodate them. Jostling against each other, groaning, weeping, striking their breasts, their religion was more demonstrative than the fastidious would admire, but it was sincere. However short-lived, however exaggerated it might seem, it was earnest, and callous must be that heart that could laugh at this intense emotion.

The fame of the negro preacher reached Ilanah. The bare fact that a negro could speak like an educated man was novelty enough to induce many of the residents to ride out to the meeting. Large parties were made up for the purpose, and many who went to laugh remained to pray, for although there was nothing remarkable either in the thought or delivery of the young negro, his own feeling was so earnest, it gave the power that touched hearts. The greatest revivalists have succeeded more from earnestness than from extraordinary intelligence. Thus it was with the negro preacher. Every word, look, action, as he moved among the people bore out his teachings, until the assembled negroes felt a genuine affection for him, and many a poor old creature whose heart was bursting with the wrongs and injuries of a lifetime felt the comfort of true sympathy when he had told his sorrows to his preacher. Hearing from his aunt Dinah the sad history of the O'Neal baby, young Lewis took a deep interest in Mammy and her charge. On the day preceding the close of the meeting, after the morning discourse was over, the preacher walked to Mammy's tent and asked to hold the baby. Mammy, delighted, stood and smiled upon the pair. The baby, who strange to say had gone willingly from her arms, now seemed to forget everything else but the preacher. With tears in his eyes the young man was looking at the helpless child whose short life was a record of so much woe. Overpowered by a sudden impulse, he fell on his knees and holding aloft the child said in reverent tone : " Child of sorrow, consecrated by the misery of your father and mother ; to God I dedicate your life ! May it be a sin-

less monument that will teach mercy to the cruel, justice
to the unjust!" And then rising, he sprinkled water
upon the infant's face and head in a baptism which was
unusual in the practice of his faith. Putting the child in
Mammy's arms he walked to his own tent, where those
seeking him an hour after, found him absorbed in prayer.
Mammy had been the only witness to the baby's baptism
and her sympathetic heart had been deeply impressed.
But not even the preacher's words and actions affected
her as did those of the baby himself. The solemn infant
seemed suddenly to have lost its gravity and lay clapping
its hands and smiling as if there were some lovely picture above its head. "Wha's de matter wid de chile?"
Mammy said to herself, and then seeing Dinah near,
called her into the tent. "Look dare, Dinah, see dat
chile. You tink dat's de sign ob deat'?" and Mammy's
voice sank to a low whisper at her superstitious fancies.

"Deat'," said Dinah, contemptuously. "Deat'! Why,
Mammy, we is among de tings ob life. Deat' am lef'
clar behind. Eternity am de aim. Deat' ain't but fer
de minit."

The woman had gained an unearthly look during
these days of prayer. She scarcely ate or slept; great
hollows had come around the fiery eyes. For her
nephew whom against his will she now called "Mister
Lewis," her affection had changed to idolatry. Ever
gentle with her, he yet sought to calm her religious excitement which at times almost mounted to frenzy. But
calmness to Dinah was as impossible as quiet to Niagara's
cataract. In the dead of night, at earliest dawn, all
through the day she wandered among the tents, now
kneeling in prayer, now sending forth her voice in
hymns, and adding by her own wild fervor to the influence of the preacher. She seemed to become taller and
thinner each day until on the seventh she looked more
spectre than woman. But her voice grew even more

13

prayerful, her eyes more fiery, and her swift, noiseless motions more full of intensity. Not one among the negroes but had " jined de church," and many a white listener from the town had taken away the sting of an awakened conscience. Through many a future would sound that black man's words calling to repentance, to reform.

It was the last sermon of young Lewis. In the evening another minister would preach, and on the morrow, the eighth day of the meeting, there would only be prayer and leaving-taking, when the three " laborers in the vineyard " would move to the south west to give another meeting in another district. Standing on the platform Lewis gazed on the people. Their number had much increased since its opening and he now looked upon over a thousand faces.

Every eye in that dense crowd was fixed upon him. Here and there among the negro faces gleamed a white one, while on the outskirts of the meeting there were several carriages filled with some of Ilanah's aristocracy. Policemen mingled with the worshippers, a few standing in a little knot outside of the crowd. But there was no need of their services. A congregation of the most refined could not have been more orderly, more quiet, fuller of absorbed attention, than these negroes. The ladies and gentlemen in their elegant equipages seemed moved by the same earnestness that held the humbler hearers. The preacher looked around. On his face shone a touching tenderness, in his eyes were tears. He and these people had prayed together, sorrowed together for their sins, and together resolved to strive for a better, higher life. Many whose past had been full of suffering and ill-treatment, whose present was a grovelling struggle for the barest necessities, and whose future held no earthly hope, had felt a stirring in their downtrodden souls as they listened to their preacher's exhortations.

There was comfort to these poor creatures in the simple words of the young man, who tried himself to live up to the doctrines he preached. Dinah looked on her nephew with adoring eyes. To her, his face was not black, nor his figure commonplace, but like those of a radiant angel. The woman was so eager, so intent, that she attracted the attention of a lady who sat in a carriage near her. "Look," said this dainty creature, "look at that woman's face. Negress as she is, she reminds me of the picture of Joan of Arc, so rapt, so intense is her expression."

"Ah yes!" calmy assented her companion, with a languid glance in the indicated direction. And then she turned away, settling herself more comfortably on the satin cushions, for the preacher was about to speak, and her friend had induced her to take this early ride to hear "something wonderful."

"'Come unto me all ye that labor and are heavy laden.'"

The blessed words lingered on the air. The preacher paused to listen to their tender invitation, and on the outskirts of the crowd a black man, tired, footsore and haggard, caught the sounds and quickened his wearied feet that he too might find some crumb of comfort. It was a negro with a skin of ebony and a tall figure, wasted by privation or disease. He leaned against a tree and looked around the multitude seeing many a familiar face. An exile, he had come back "to his own, but his own knew him not." He had been a prisoner and was now free. But what was freedom worth when he dared not breathe his name? And who could have recognized in that gaunt, emaciated figure the magnificent proportions of Tom O'Neal? Unknown himself, he knew those who once had been his friends, and he stifled his sobs as face by face they appealed to his memory. There stood a man who had been as a brother, here a woman, a friend to his Julie ; there knelt a child he had held in his arms, carried upon his shoulders. A child ! Was his own here—his child and its mother ? The tears that had risen to his eyes were checked in their flow. The sob that was bursting his heart, died at its birth.

The trees, the faces, spun round and round. This hope of seeing wife and child, which had been a staff off strength for his weakness, bread for his starving body, now at the moment of realization, was too mighty to be borne. He staggered and would have fallen but for a thin hand that grasped his arm and steadied him.

"Don' despair," whispered a voice he knew, " dere's hope fer de sinner."

"Dinah," he said.

But the fiery eyes which seemed to look through, not at him, showed no recognition. " Lissen to the words ob Christ," she said.

"Dinah, Dinah !" he whispered, "where's Julie, where's her child ?"

" Who am you dat 'sturbs de time ob prayer wid words of earthly seekin' ?" she answered looking full at the miserable figure before her. " Oh, nigger, dat chile aint no more Julie's chile. See him dar in de arms ob Mammy. De Lord foun' firs' fer him de riches ob kings, an' de preacher hab called him fas' to de Lord. See him de favored ob de Lord, dat baby sittin' under de eabes ob de Gospel catching de seed dat'll bar mighty fruit ?"

The weird eyes were looking straight ahead, the thin hand pointed to a spot near the platform where, held up in Mammy's arms, a baby smiled. O God, his own child ! Hungrily the father's heart yearned for the little creature, eagerly the father's arms stretched toward it, the father's breast panted to press to itself that soft little body. Forgotten were all the hardships of those toilsome months, the cramping pains of hunger. He did not see the hundreds of intervening faces—only Mammy's kindly

smile and that little copper-colored visage ! These made
the crowd for him. Even at that distance he noticed the
spotless white of his child's dress and the pretty wraps
that protected him from the air. They were better than
Mammy could give. Some kind heart had befriended
his child ! And the emaciated arms in exultation were
crossed over the rags that coverd his body. He looked
for Julie, but was content not to find her.

"She is at home, expecting me," he thought. She
would know him ! Her eyes of love could not look into
his without feeling he was her faithful husband.

"Come unto Me all ye that labor and are heavy
laden." Again the words fell upon the air; again
aching hearts felt God's tender love and the preacher's
arms were held in brotherly invitation. He advanced a
step and his lips moved. But no other words ever passed
those smiling lips, no other throb ever stirred that tender
heart. A loud report ! and before the people he had
served he lay dead—killed instantly by a shot from the
edge of the crowd.

"What was it ?" asked the ladies in their carriages, as
pale and frightened, they looked around.

"Drive home quickly," ordered the gentlemen, not
stopping to answer, and whipping up the horses, amid a
cloud of dust, feeling themselves "well out of it," the
fashionables returned to their own gay world.

"Ye strike at the shepherd, and the sheep are scat-
tered." In amazement the negroes gazed at the platform
and at the bleeding body of their shepherd. An old
woman with a baby in her arms climed up and leaning
over the fallen man, put her hand on his heart.

"Dead," she sobbed, and a mighty wail broke from
the multitude.

"Dead, dead, dead !" shrieked hundreds of voices.
Yet no one moved. Outside the crowd was a party of
young whites, laughing, chaffing, swearing, their faces

reddened by drink. And now their voices, heard above the wails and sobs, reached a woman's ears, a pistol brandished aloft flashed on a woman's eyes—eyes from whose wild depths sudden madness shone.

" Dere's de murderer !" she shouted, and pushing her way between the weeping, prostrate negroes she sprang upon the platform. She bent above the dead preacher. " My sister's chile, de preacher ob de Lord," she whispered. Tearing open his shirt, she pressed her hand upon the gaping wound. Then holding high above her head the crimsoned hand and arm she shrieked :

" Will you see de blood ob your preacher an' b'ar it like cowards ? Will you look on de deat' ob him who would hab died fer you an' not take de Lord's vengeance. God hab said 'an eye fer an eye, a toot' fer a toot'. An' you lets dat white debbil take de life ob dis man who has sabed you from hell fire ? Send him to hell, dat murderer ! Vengeance ! Vengeance !" Louder and louder she shrieked, and springing from the platform she rushed toward the group of whites followed by as wild and fierce a mob as ever stormed a Bastille or guillotined a king. This onset was so sudden, so unexpected, that it found the police, who dreaded some disturbance, quietly persuading the "young gentlemen " to leave the camp grounds. These " young gentlemen " were all well known. They were only " having some fun," and while, of course, an arrest would have to be made and some sort of examination held, the result was almost sure. No murder had been intended, and the negro's death would be put down to be " accidental shooting." It was " only a nigger " after all, and there seemed no injustice in it. But Dinah, wild-eyed infuriated Dinah, did not see the matter in this light. Like a tigress bereft of her young, she pushed aside the officers of the law and springing on the drunken youth, who still laughed as he brandished the pistol, she dug her nails into his throat until his blood mingled with that of the negro still red upon her hand. She dragged him back among the mob. "Ah!" she shouted with maniac laughter. "I hab yer." Even at that desperate moment when surrounded by the maddened negroes, each man's life was trembling in the balance, two of the police dashed among them and tried to pull Dinah away from her victim. But the thin fingers never loosened their hold until as a blackened corpse she threw him from her.

"Dere goes de pride ob de Eatons," she shouted, "gone to feed de flames ob hell!" There were a few moments when it seemed that each one of that little band of whites would fall under the fury of the mob they had excited. But the line was broken when Dinah, leading a charge, was caught and taken prisoner. To the surprise of the police she made not the slightest resistance.

" I hab done wid life," she said, and then called out, "Run, you niggers, de vengeance am satisfied!"

The negroes seeing Dinah a prisoner, and thoroughly frightened at their own temerity, fled like sheep. Some were captured, but the greater number escaped. Leaving the dead and dying, the police with their prisoners marched back to town, and "the gentlemen," lifting the body of James Eaton, bore it to the carriage which had so lately brought them "to stir up the niggers," as they had said when deciding to ride out to the camp meeting.

CHAPTER XXXVIII.

HAVE MERCY UPON HIM.

THE papers teemed with accounts of the "atrocious murder of James Eaton, the son of our distinguished fellow-townsman." Society hid its gay head under a sympathetic mourning veil. One of the handsomest houses in Augusta was closed for the season, and the Eaton family returned to the plantation just out of Ilanah, where they doubtless mourned, and certainly felt no blame was deserved by the young man himself who had only "gone on a little spree." It was an easily spoken excuse for the sin of drunkenness in whose wake had followed the murder of an innocent and helpful man. The elder Eaton longed for vengeance on the woman who had killed his son. Hanging was too good for her he declared, but hanged she should be and quickly too. Who would dare defend such an atrocious criminal? And Mr. Eaton's words embodied the views of the majority. Yet there was one who volunteered his services in her defense and went to the prison to see the half crazed woman. She seemed a ghost. A ghost in whose face were eyes of flame. She had no information to give, nothing to plead.

"My sister's chile, de preacher ob de Lord," were her only words. Yet these words, added to the facts he had gathered from one of the ladies who had driven in haste from the scene of the murder, made the lawyer resolve that spite of all consequences, he would defend the woman, and that this defense should be the crowning effort of his life. He set about his work the very day after the tragedy, and in thus espousing the cause of the negress cut himself off from the friendship of his own class. For the man who thus undertook Dinah's defense was one of the "aristocrats" of Ilanah.

"ILANAH, ——, 18—.

"DEAR UNCLE: I am about to enter a new army—the army of those who fight for the right. Black and white should be alike before law and justice. I have offered my services to defend the negress who killed James Eaton. It was a shocking death, but the woman's provocation was immense. Eaton was drunk, but not too drunk to prevent his taking deliberate aim at and killing a negro preacher who had been conducting a camp-meeting near Ilanah. As far as I can learn, the preacher was a worthy man, of some education, and rather eloquent. But if he had been a dolt, his murder was cruel and perfectly uncalled for. The cause that excited Dinah, as the woman is called, was, that this preacher was her nephew, for whose education she had been working for years. I think she is insane, and I cannot see how any one can do less than pity her, yet almost the whole town is against me. But I believe I am right and I hope you will agree with me. Affectionately, your nephew,

TALCOTT COLTON."

Thus wrote the younger Colton to his uncle, Dr. Colton, at Milton. He posted the letter as he rode out to the scene of the camp meeting, where he hoped to gather some evidence for his client. The sun had set and risen again since the preacher's death, and it shone through the leaves upon the platform stained with his blood as yesterday morning it had rested on his living face. Most of the tents were still standing and around them were gathered groups of frightened negroes, whispering, trembling, seeing in "every bush an officer." Talcott Colton spoke to several of them, but they were too much afraid of implicating themselves to give any satisfactory answers. Even his question: "What had

13*

been done with the body of the preacher?" was answered vaguely : "De Lord hab taken him away." Notwithstanding his pity, he was wearied with their stupidity and pleased to welcome in Brown, who had been sent out on special duty, an old acquaintance.

"Well, Brown," said Colton, "the shooting of the negro preacher seems to me a most cold-blooded murder. What do you think of it? You can speak freely, for I have espoused the negro's side."

"You have !" and Brown's face, which had been wearing its stolid "court-house" expression, changed to liveliest interest. "Wal, sir, I'm proud that one of our own Southern gentlemen has the pluck to stand up for the nigger. They is orful abused an' no mistake. An' no mistake neither, it'll reflect on us here in the South. It can't do me no harm, for I b'longs only to the poorer class. But it does my heart good to think of you."

Colton was surprised. He had known the man for years and had never before heard him speak a voluntary word. Yht here he was with fully fledged opinions, and those opinions decidedly opposed to the views held in his State.

"Why, Brown," he said with a smile, for it was only natural he should be pleased with the bailiff's indorsement of his own conduct, "you're a red-hot Republican. Your secret's safe with me, but I'm afraid your political head would tumble and I'd have to meet another bailiff, if you expressed your views publicly."

"No, sir ; no, Mr. Colton, I ain't no Republican. I'm a Southern man tooth an' nail, though I never did believe in slavery, not seeing the right o' a man's selling other men an' women. And now the war's over, an' the bloody shirt is buried, I don't see the good o' keepin' open the question with the bad treatment o' the nigger. Yer can't keep it secret, sir. It'll get abroad an' shame the State, sir, as we ought ter be proud on. Fer my political head, sir, I'll take it off myself. I ain't been nothing but a sneak ter stand by an' see the beastly injustice I seen in that same court house. I has done it fer my chillen. But gol darned ef I does it any more! I'm shamed, sir, actually ashamed to look them little innercents in the face an' hol' my tongue when I see the innercent sent to punishment. I hain't never been the same sence there was a nigger made a convict who was as innercent as my chillen, an' now I ain't goin' to stop an' see this pore devil of a woman hanged fer killing young Eaton. I was here a listenin' ter the preachin', an' I must say as the nigger preacher had a most uncommon persuadin' way. When I seen that man shot down like a dog an' the yaller woman like a wild tiger a yelpin' over his dead body, I'm darned ef I didn't feel like takin' a hand in it myself."

Brown took off his hat and mopped his head. Colton looked on more and more surprised, and, strange to say, found the man's words echoing in his own mind.

"I tells yer, Mr. Colton, yer'd a done it yerself. Ef yer thought anything o' family ties, yer'd a sprung on that young Eaton and ha' strangled out his rascally life."

They walked a little way without speaking. Then Brown turned with a twinkle in his eye. "I means ter resign, sir, but this I now tells yer is a secret. I was darned glad that I was too far off to help the others shoot the niggers. I'd not ha' done it, sir. A lot of pore devils who jest as they was happy prayin' to have their preacher killed! I'd not ha' fired upon 'em sir, not ef I'd been ordered to."

"Brown, you're a good fellow, and there's my hand," said Colton, holding out his handsome hand and taking Brown's plebeian one.

"Well, well," said Brown, laughing to himself. "I'm gettin' up. Fust thar's Mr. Day, and now it's the Southern blood." He straightened himself a little, giving Mr.

Colton a gratified smile as they turned to walk over the camp-meeting grounds. The shades of all the Coltons dead, and even the good old Doctor himself, would have been shocked and horrified could they have seen the last of their proud line thus confidentially walking with one of the class of "poor whites." But Colton felt not the slightest loss of caste and had rarely found himself more interested than now, while listening to the plain common sense of Brown. A new era was opening to this young man. Eaton's crime and death had awakened his sleeping soul. He too had "gone on many a spree" that had ended less tragically. But now when he looked on what might have been, he recoiled in horror.

On the spot where the shooting occurred, the bodies of several negroes still lay.

"They've just begun ter take off the bodies," Brown explained, and they walked on. Suddenly both men involuntarily stopped and took off their hats. It was a tribute to the power of misery, the majesty of death. Before them on the trampled grass lay the body of an old negress with a wound in her breast. In her arms was clasped a copper-colored baby. It, too, was dead. The same shot had evidently killed both. Kneeling beside them, more pitiful in his living than they in their calm sleep, was a gaunt and haggard man. His hands were clenched in each other and held down to the earth. His eyes were fixed on the infant's face. Brown recognized the man, and held his breath lest some one else should know in this skeleton the convict Tom O'Neal.

"Great God!" cried Colton, horrified at the sight. The man raised his eyes and looked at them. To their dying day both of those men remembered that look, that expression of the negro's face. It spoke of grief, immense, unfathomable.

"Brown," Mr. Colton drew the pitying "poor white" aside. At a little distance he took out his purse and putting it in Brown's hand said: "Give this to him, if you can speak to such misery." Mounting his horse he rode back to town. On the way he suddenly stopped, raised his hat and said as reverently as if in church:

"God have mercy upon him!"

CHAPTER XXXIX.

THE SILVER IN HIS CLOUD.

BROWN waited until the lawyer was well out of sight before he approached the negro. To no living soul dared he say that the miserable being was an escaped convict. It was a secret to be guarded if he would help the man; and help him he would—only he could not see the best way. He must first arouse him from this heavy trance of grief. Looking around in every direction and assuring himself no one was within sight or sound, he put his hand on the negro's shoulder.

"Tom O'Neal," he whispered in his ear, expecting to startle him. But the man did not stir, did not remove his eyes from the baby's face. Through days and nights of toil and starvation, while hiding in caves, creeping behind bushes, pursued, followed, tracked from place to place, he had been kept alive, made strong by the thought of the wife and child waiting for him. He had endured a thousand times the torture of death. And then at last to his famished soul had come the rapturous sight of his own child well and tenderly cared for. At sound of the shot that killed the preacher O'Neal dashed forward to reach Mammy and the child. Other shots would surely follow; but he would save them! Before him, around him surged the multitude forcing him back, pressing him against a tree. Wildly he fought and pushed; but those weakened sinews, that starving flesh, were not equal to his will.

"Let me pass, for God's sake, let me pass!" he cried, and threw himself forward on the crowd. But frightened, bewildered as they were, they paid no attention to his cry, and no man turned to help him. All were gazing at that silent figure lying on the platform.

"Let me pass," he shouted, striving to release himself from the tree where, pinned by the weight of hundreds pushing against him he endured a martyr's agonies without a martyr's hope. He saw Mammy, still holding the baby, climb on the platform and bend over the dead man, saw Dinah's gory hand rouse to fury the terrified people. He fought like a lion, but his struggles were useless. It was only when the crowd following the woman, rushed on the whites, that, panting and exhausted, he staggered forward. He was blind to all else but the figure of the old woman kneeling on the platform and holding a baby to her breast. Shot after shot was heard, moans and shrieks were coming from the black mob, but he did not heed them. He had no thought, no sight except for those two on the platform. He was almost within reach —they would be saved! "Mammy, lie down on your face!" he tried to shout the words. But his dried throat gave out only a hoarse whisper. The old woman could not hear it above the tumult and fury of that living sea. "Mammy! O God! too late!" A shot—the last that was fired—reached that faithful heart. On her face fell the foster-mother with the child, and O'Neal, climbing up beside them, bent in agony over the dead.

He lifted them, looked into the calm face of the old woman and kissed the still smiling mouth of the infant. The little one had gone without a look into his father's face! More terrible in his despair than Dinah in her fury, the man stood beside the corpse of his child. "Vengeance on his murderer!" he cried. And then there rose

before him Mary's face and he heard her soft voice :
"Endure to the end." He pressed his hands to his head ;
his hollow eyes lost vengeance in grief ; and lifting his
dead he carried them in his arms to a quiet spot beneath
a tree. There beside them he knelt unmindful of the
wind of night and of the morning's sun.

Somebody spoke to him—he looked up and saw two
men. They were nothing to him. Somebody was calling him ; what did it matter? The name of O'Neal belonged only to the dead, this infant, this—Suddenly
O'Neal looked up—He was going mad. He had forgotten Julie, his wife !

"Do you know where she is?" he whispered to this
stranger bending over him, and he felt no surprise when
he was answered :

"She is alive, Tom, but hasn't come back from the
Governor's where she went ter get yer pardon." "God
forgive me," Brown said to himself as he uttered this
half-lie. Indeed he felt delighted with it, when he saw
that its effect was to make the man rise from the earth,
while something like hope came into the suffering eyes.
"Look here," and Brown tried to follow up his happy
thought. "Your wife found a good friend the very day
of your trial. Mr. Day has supported her and your baby
ever since. Your house is all ready and fixed up. Mr.
Day has left money for you and your family. Mammy
gave it in my charge. If you'll go to your cabin I'll
bring it ter yer after dark and I'll drive yer in a buggy,
where it will be safe ter take the railroad ter the North.
As soon as your wife arrives she shall join you. Will
you go ?" Brown asked. "I will look arter Mammy an
the baby. They shall lie in my lot."

O'Neal did not speak—he put out his hand as the
blind do to be led, and then without a sound fell senseless in Brown's arms.

"Lord, lord, a livin' skeleton," Brown said, as partly

lifting, partly dragging the negro, he reached a covered wagon that during the camp-meeting had been used as a sort of lunch meeting.

O'Neal had begun to revive, and Brown finding some eatables in a basket, made him drink a little cold tea and eat something. When he was stronger, Brown helped him into the wagon and told him to rest until he could return with horses. "Then," said the kind-hearted fellow, "I'll take yer home fer my wife to nuss till you gets well."

O'Neal did not answer; he was too weak and ill to talk.

As evening approached Brown returned with horses and a bottle of home-made wine. Then, with the negro stowed away in the back of the wagon, he drove toward Ilanah. When the wagon neared the place where passed the little path that under the trees led to O'Neal's cabin, he touched Brown's arm.

" Sir," said the negro, " you have been very good to me. I'm stronger now and able to think for myself. I can't go to your home, sir, and I can't leave Georgia without my wife. I'll go to my cabin and wait there for Julie. There are places in the woods around I could hide in for a week. I know every foot of ground. No, sir, I can't go and bring trouble on a man who has befriended me," he added resolutely as Brown began to protest. Getting out of the back of the wagon he came to the side of it.

" I want to thank you," he said, "and that gentleman who was so good to my—my baby—and Julie. Thank—" But though he opened and shut his mouth there came no other sound than a dry gasp.

"Don't yer, now don't yer," said Brown blubbering himself like an overgrown boy. " Mr. Day don't want no thanks. As for me, I'm proud ter know yer, Tom O'Neal. I'll be ter yer house to-morrow. Won't come before I ken manage how ter keep sort o' sly. But

I'll be lookin' out fer yer, Tom, an' if I sees any one a
slippin' roun' I'll offer ter guide 'em, ter give yer time
ter get away. An' I'll sen' a message first, fer thar's one I
ken trust."

He wrung the negro's hand and watched the tall,
gaunt figure as after a low "Thank you, I thank you,"
O'Neal turned down the narrow path.

"By gol, he's had a hard time," Brown said, and he
pulled out his handkerchief to wipe away the tears of
honest sympathy.

Slowly the negro walked toward his cabin. Even in
the dim light of the evening he recognized every familiar
stone and tree. How many times along this very path
he had hurried, light of heart and foot, to his Julie! And
now like a dead man he was gazing where once youth
and joy had lived. Here was the tree under which when
newly married he and Julie had sat and talked of their
future ; and there was the place where, as his wife, she
had first looked on his cabin. He started and his heart
beat violently. Was it fancy or did the light shine from
their cabin window just as it used to do when he returned late from the market in Ilanah? He passed his
hands before his eyes. No! the light was steady. Julie
had reached her home, she was there waiting for him.
He hurried forwad and came unexpectedly upon a fence
that must have been lately built, for he had no memory
of it. And now his feet trod upon a ploughed field—
what did it mean? Here was where his cabin had stood
—surely he was not mad? Yet here was only a field,
while there, close to the woods, was the cabin. In a
strange bewilderment O'Neal hurried on until at the
cabin window he paused, looked in and saw—Was that
Julie? That pale, dying woman his young wife? He
leaned against the side of the house too faint to move.
Through the door which stood open he heard her voice.
There was no doubting that voice. It was Julie's sweet

and soft as when first he loved her. What was she saying? She was singing to a child. O'Neal could bear no more. Leaning his folded arms upon the wall he buried his face upon them and sobbed. His emaciated figure shook like a leafless tree in the winter storm, for she was singing to her baby, while that baby, O God! lay cold and dead. Still that sweet voice!

"Hush, my baby, hush."

He looked again, resting his head on the little casement. Julie had turned her face to the fire that was burning brightly in the stove. Her sad eyes were fixed dreamily upon the blaze. Her face looked thinner than before, with the hollows thrown into black shadows. O'Neal clinched his teeth that no sound could startle her —for in her arms, caressing it, kissing it, she held—a log of wood. Was she mad? Would she know him? softly he opened the door. Neat, as she had ever kept it, looked the little room; the table with its white cloth was laid for supper just as so often he had found it when Julie had welcomed him with smiles after his day's labor had ended. His step on the floor had made her start. She looked around, put the log on the bed tenderly as if it were indeed her child, and then not noticing him, went to the door and shading her eyes looked out and listened.

"Not yet come," she said to herself. "What keeps Tom?" And then she turned and faced him, looking full at him with the vacant stare of madness.

"Julie!" He uttered the pretty name tenderly. She trembled a little and he held his breath for fear. She came nearer, catching at his wrist with one hand while with the other around his neck she drew his face down to hers. Eagerly she scanned it, but even as there came to her eyes a gleam of recognition, she gave the hollow laugh of madness and turned away.

He did not groan, did not shed a tear, but falling into

a chair watched her with speechless misery as now singing to that log of wood, now looking out of the door and calling into the darkness, "Tom, Tom," and now bending over the stove she seemed to go through the routine of household duties.   But him she did not seem to see.   It was only after a violent fit of coughing, when, frightened at her suffering, he caught her in his arms, that she laid her head on his breast, looked into his face and gently said, "Thank you."   But even as in tender love he held her (shuddering as he felt how little of earth remained) she broke from him with a laugh, a fragment of song, and then with eyes fixed fearfully on something seen only by her madness, stood muttering incoherently.

Presently she coughed again, and this time in her exhaustion did not seek to leave his arms.   She smiled at him when tenderly he laid her on the bed, having, unnoticed, pushed the log aside.   She still smiled as she held his hand and leaning her cheek upon it, fell asleep.

And so he passed the night beside her, hearing now and again his own name, "Tom," murmured in her dreams.   In the morning when she woke he stood near with a cup of warm tea.   She drank it, smiled, kissed him and slept again.   Did she know him ? He could not tell, but it was happiness, saddest happiness to serve her.

It was past noon.   She had been lying tranquil, happy, clinging to his hand as a child might, and though her breath came short and quick with often a hollow cough, she did not seem to suffer.   He had called her " wife, Julie ;" she had looked lovingly upon him, but she did not speak. She seemed suddenly to have lost all strength, all desire for anything but to hold his hand and gaze on his face.   Her lips had moved but no words came.   She had closed her eyes, and so faint was her breath he had twice thought her dead, and agonized, had bent above her, feeling intense relief when she had opened her eyes and smiled. Finding some brandy in the little cup-board, he had put a spoonful in her mouth, but she had not swallowed it. She was dying, he knew she was dying! Would she go without once speaking to him? She had been lying some moments with her eyes closed and her cheek resting on his hand that was tightly held in hers— when a little girl, running along the path to the cabin, opened the door and entered quickly. It was Meg Brown. With sunbonnet off, with frightened face, and hair blown by the wind, she was most unlike her staid little self.

"Quick, run! Tom O'Neal they're after you!" the child gasped. The little voice sharpened by fright startled the woman on the bed.

"Tom O'Neal," she said, and though her voice was very faint the words were distinct. She raised herself in bed, clinging to his hand. She put her arms about his neck, looking into his face with eager eyes. Intently she gazed, while from his soul arose the prayer, "Let her know me, if but for one instant!"

Even as he prayed joy lighted her dying face. "Husband! Husband!" she cried, and fell upon his breast She had only a moment more of life, but that moment was the silver on the blackness of his cloud. She gazed into his face with joy and love, she questioned not the future nor the past, she was with him and felt no fear.

"Tom, dear Tom," were her only words. But as he called her "wife," she smiled, and when he kissed her lips she kissed him too. Then there came a moment's suffocation and—she was gone.

So quietly she went, with so few of death's tremors after her weary life, that holding her upon his breast, pressing his face to hers, he hardly believed she was dead until weeping Meg crept close up to him, resting her trembling hands upon his knee. In all the terror of her first sight of death the child remembered her father's trust and her quick ears caught approaching steps.

"Tom O'Neal," she whispered, "you must run!

Father says you must hide. He is coming with the others. He is keeping them off. Run, Tom, run. I'm Meg Brown."

He heard her words as in a dream, heard, too, the sounds of feet. What did he care now for liberty ? He did not even move when a voice, loud enough to have warned him called out : " He ain't thar, I tell yer he ain't." He knew the voice ; it was Brown's, and his heart stirred with gratitude toward the man who had been kind to him. He knew what was coming, but he could not move. Still he held to his breast Julie's fast-chilling body. Meg was on her feet pulling at his shoulder.

"Run, Tom O'Neal, run ! Father will meet you. Father will help you. Run !"

Faithful little girl ! She tried to push him to his feet, tried with her puny strength to force him away. But he did not move, did not loosen the clasp of his dead wife, until men's voices were heard at the very door. Then he kissed once more the dead face and closing the partly opened eyes, laid her on the bed. "God bless you, little missy," he said to Meg. "I don't want my liberty now." Standing on the threshold of his home he held out his hands for the manacles.

"I'm ready, Mr. Stern," he said simply.

But Stern did not move. For a second he stood shocked at sight of the gaunt figure before him. He had followed this man for weeks. Day and night he had thought, dreamed, only of his capture, and now when at last he had found him, there was nothing left but a skeleton ! It was only for a moment, however, that he paused. Facts and nature asserted themselves. The convict's recapture and the reward were two very agreeable facts to this man.

Brown had turned his back. He had believed the convict would not be retaken. Meg had had ample time to reach the cabin and give the warning and yet here was the man surrendering himself! He could not keep the stolid look upon his face. He felt like bursting into tears with Meg, who stood weeping just inside the door. It was to comfort his little girl that he entered the cabin. He saw the dead woman, and then like a flash the truth came to him.

"He didn't want ter escape," he said to himself, while Meg sobbed on his shoulder.

"I tried ter save him, but he wouldn't run. Poor man, poor man!"

"Never mind, Meg, don't yer cry, don't yer cry," said her father as he wiped away his own tears.

In a few moments O'Neal, manacled preceded by a policeman and closely followed by Stern, was walking along the little path to the road. After a look of gratitude to Brown he did not raise his eyes from the ground. When they reached the waiting wagon Stern placed the convict between himself and the driver, holding his pistol ready in his hand. Brown and the policeman sat at the back of the wagon and it rolled off, while little Meg under a tree at the roadside, hiding her tears with one hand, waved the other in sad adieu.

———◆———

CHAPTER XL.

TWO WOMEN.

ILANAH was much excited over the approaching trial of the murderess of James Eaton.

The angry father, the heart-broken mother and sisters were surrounded by sympathy. But this woman who in fury sprang upon and killed the young "gentleman "—did she deserve no pity? The newspapers in commenting severely on "this cruel murder," called Dinah a "tigress," but did not allude to the deed which had made her one. Numberless incidents of negro brutality were cited, the general degradation of the black race was made apparent, and any advance for the negro declared "impossible." Education for this very large class, it was asserted, was a crime, as it only added sharpness to the cunning of their low natures. The bleeding body of the black preacher, buried in his untimely grave, slipped quite out of sight, quite out of memory.

Dinah in her cell, gazed upon by curious eyes that from time to time peered through the grating, was unmindful of everything. She spoke to no one, answered no questions. Her attorney's visits were fruitless. Not even a word of thanks did he receive though he had in her cause "for justice's sake" cut himself loose from friends and associates.

She would sit for hours leaning against the wall, with hands tightly clasped and burning eyes fixed on vacancy. She offered no violence yet the jailer feared her and moved away if her wild eyes fell on him. Some negroes who had been her friends were brought to visit her by the lawyer. She showed no recognition or remembrance of them, even when they spoke to her. She mechanically answered when they said "Dinah," but even as they talked, turning her eyes on that memory which seemed alone to hold them, forgot their presence. A minister came to pray with her. He spoke of her crime and its terrible consequences: she neither answered nor noticed him. At last a lady came, the one who from her carriage at the camp-meeting had a few moment's before the negro minister's death, noticed Dinah's intense face. This lady, through all the crusts of fashion, felt a heart throbbing with pity for the "tigress" who had killed James Eaton, and being quite independent in every way, obtained a permit to see the woman, and one day drove up to the jail as Colton came out of the doorway.

Disappointed, disheartened, he was just leaving after a most unsatisfactory visit to Dinah, whom he had again failed to stir from her silence. He had had a hard time since he so hastily took up the gauntlet and entered the lists "for the sake of justice." Though he held his head high and seemed not to see, he felt keenly the cut direct, as old friends of his childhood, his boyhood, would pass him without recognition, and he would catch an occasional comment on the "nigger advocate." He flushed a little as he saw the lady. She it was who first excited his pity for Dinah, but since society had turned against him he had held aloof from her. He had not been her lover, yet there was a feeling that her scorn would be harder to bear than all the world's. "She shall not have the chance to cut me," he thought, and he looked the other way as he came down the steps from the jail.

"Mr. Colton," the lady was leaning from her carriage and smiling at him. In a moment he was at the side of the carriage, his face bright with pleasure. "You are forgetting your gallantry," she said, blushing, as she saw the light in his eyes. "Are you not ashamed to look away instead of rushing to help me from the carriage?"

"Forgive me," he said simply, as he opened the door and offered her his hand.

"You do not ask me where I am going, nor do you offer to accompany me, and yet you must do both," she said, as standing beside him she glanced up at him in a charming fashion.

He laughed more gayly than he had done for many days as he answered: "I'm willing to do anything you command; so 'where are you going, my pretty maid,' and may I go with you?"

"'I'm not going milking, sir, she said,'" the lady replied. And then the smile which had been so pleasant faded away from her fair face, and the dew of woman's pity rose to her brown eyes. "I am going to see the woman who killed James Eaton. And oh, Mr. Colton, I honor you for braving public opinion and standing by the right! Murder is fearful," and she shuddered, "but if ever murder could be excused it would be this murder. I feel deeply for the Eatons, but had you not undertaken the case I had intended to have engaged the ablest lawyers money could pay. As it is, I feel myself your debtor," and she smiled up through her tears, so charming in her emotion, that the man's heart gave a quicker bound.

He offered her his arm and they entered the jail together, the jailer marvelling much that Miss Belford, Illanah's pet heiress, should so honor the place.

At Dinah's door he uttered a few words of warning before turning the key. "She's dangerous, ma'am, she's dangerous," he whispered.

"Has she ever injured any one?" Miss Belford calmly asked. The man was silent and the lady entered.

"Dinah." The lady's voice was soft and kind; the lady's delicately gloved hand warmed with its touch the two thin dark ones clasped together. For an instant the fiery eyes came back from the dream-picture upon which they were ever gazing and looked at the lady. But she did not speak, nor did that corpse-like face brighten or soften.

"I'm so sorry for you, Dinah," said Miss Belford, still keeping her hand upon Dinah's. "I heard the preacher's words and I shall never forget them. He was God's preacher, and his death was a glorious martyrdom. I believe he is in heaven. I believe he is praying for you, for us all." The lady's eyes were glistening, the pretty face flushing with feeling. Miss Belford had never been

14

so truly lovely as now. Looking at her, Colton felt himself strangely moved. And Dinah? The flaming eyes lost their steady stare, she pressed her hands to her breast.

"My sister's chile, de preacher ob de Lord!" she cried, and sobbing violently fell upon her knees. Miss Belford knelt with her. Her dainty robes swept the cold stone floor, her delicate hands held those of the negress, and her trembling voice spoke the noble consoling words of a higher than earthly comforter. Colton's heart was moved as no eloquence had ever moved it, and from that moment his admiration for the charming girl changed to something warmer. When with kindly words of sympathy to Dinah and promises of soon returning, Miss Belford left the prison, she leaned on an arm that pressed her soft hand to a heart that had become her own.

If the fashionable world was angered at Colton's defense of the negress, it stood aghast at the report that Miss Belford went regularly to the prison to pray with "that creature." "Why should she do it? She is neither a minister nor a sister of charity," society said, and amused itself with shrugs, shakings of head and contemptuous smiles as it whispered "strong-minded," "eccentric," and even "insane." But the girl was serenely unmindful of society's disapproval, and went smiling on her way feeling more pleasurable excitement than a dozen balls could have given. These had rather palled on her taste, while "doing missionary work," as she smilingly called it to her guardian, made her "feel good, even if she wasn't." "It's variety, you know, guardy dear," she said in answer to his expostulation on her "imprudence." "And you know I always liked variety. So don't oppose me, that's a dear." And as Miss Belford from earliest infancy until now had always enjoyed her own sweet way, "guardy" did not oppose her. He contented himself with saying, "Don't carry it too far, Helen," and "here, now, I won't say a word," as Helen first pouted, then smiled, and then gave him a kiss. He patted her cheek and walked to his office congratulating himself that there was no wife to scold him for failing in duty to his ward by allowing her to do just as she pleased. As for the friends who took it upon themselves to remonstrate with Miss Belford's guardian, he would shrug his shoulders as he said :

"What would you do? Helen Belford is twenty-five, and mistress of herself and fortune. If she chooses to turn missionary it is her own lookout. But one thing is as well mentioned right here ; if any one does or says a rude thing to or of Miss Belford, I'll look out and shoot such a one at sight."

These words from Colonel Young were a timely warning. He was known to be a dead shot and high tempered. So the fashionable world became more circumspect in its remarks.

Miss Belford's first visit to Dinah was followed by many others. And thus being brought into contact with misery such as she had only read of and wept over in some thrilling novel, the girl was developing into a newer, higher womanhood. Religion with this favored child of earth had been more a matter of custom and fashion than of heart, and her church toilet a thing of far more interest than the sermon which almost invariably tired her. Partly out of curiosity, partly to keep a promise given to her colored maid who had "gone to der camp meetin'," Miss Belford invited one of her hundred friends and rode out to see "what they did." She had been greatly moved at the earnestness of young Lewis and began to feel a discontent with her life of utter selfishness, a desire to do something helpful. So often did she think of the sermon under the wide-spreading trees that she determined to go again. So calling for another of the hundred friends, they had ridden out to hear "Lewis's last sermon." How truly it was to be his last they little dreamed. At the sound of the shot Miss Belford, more courageous than women generally are, looked to see whose hand had fired it. The sight of the bleeding negro, murdered in a moment of prayer, filled her with horror, which increased, as through the crowd she saw the group of "young gentlemen," of her own class, and caught a glimpse of the pistol that in killing the preacher had maddened Dinah. Not waiting the word of command, Miss Belford's coachman, mindful of his mistress' safety, drove rapidly back to town. The pale and agitated girl remembered that less than a month ago the murderer had asked her to be his wife. She had refused him, partly because she did not particularly like him, and partly because she rather fancied some one else. And now she thought through all her horror that the man she did care for was probably in that group whose pastime had been the murder of an inoffensive negro. Just as she had resolved never again to notice that "some one," a horseman turned the corner of the street riding slowly toward her, and a pretty flush rose to her face as the "some one" thus proved his alibi and stood acquitted of crime. He raised his hat and rode at Miss Belford's side of the carriage while in an excited manner she described the murder of the negro. Possibly justice could not have found a fairer pleader, for when clasping her hands she had said, "I fear the negress killed James Eaton. It is murder, I know it is; but what a frightful incentive the poor woman had! It was all horrible, horrible!" It was then that Colton had felt himself fired with the desire to fight for the oppressed. And once having undertaken the work, he would not yield it to another. Being cut right and left, he stopped making visits, having become uncertain as to his reception. He even ceased calling on Miss Belford, who of all women was to him the most attractive. At first Miss

Belford was vexed, then grieved ; and then hearing how the world was treating him began to understand.

" Foolish fellow !" she said aloud, one day, while her maid was arranging her long beautiful locks.

" Did yer speak, missy ?" the woman asked. She had been for many years nurse and maid to the heiress, and between Southerners the tie of happy service is a strong one.

Miss Belford, who might perhaps have resented from any other the evident desire to enter into conversation, smiled as she said : " Polly, I was thinking of Talcott Colton."

Polly was delighted. " Lor', missy, I'se glad yer speaks ob him. I likes that gemman best o' all yore bows. But I'se feared he's foolish. He's goin' to defen' Dinah. An' missy, she's clean gone ; she won't speak ter no one. De oder day he 'vited some ob de colored ladies ter call on Dinah ter see ef she wouldn't talk, but not a word. She jest sat like a stone."

It was this that first inclined Miss Belford to visit the prison. She felt a certain responsibility as to the success of the young lawyer and determined that she would try her powers as collector of evidence. With some valuable knowledge gained for the purpose of serving him, she would reproach him for thinking that *she* could have treated him coldly, for espousing a cause she had herself urged upon him. Her plans were all arranged, but when the carriage stopped at the jail and she saw the young man turn proudly away, she could not resist her impulse to call him to her side. Nor did she regret it, though a little embarrassed by his evident pleasure. When in Dinah's cell the woman's corpse-like face and fiery eyes made her forget all her little plans in pity, she never thought of collecting valuable testimony for the lawyer ; on her knees she found herself repeating with fervor the only prayer she could remember.   The softening of Dinah's flaming eyes gave her more pleasure than anything she had ever known, more even than Colton's whispered words as together they passed out of the cell.

" You are an angel," the lawyer said fervently.

The girl went several times to the jail.   But while her compassion, added to her grace and beauty, made sad inroads on Colton's heart, she was not successful in obtaining any information that would assist the lawyer for the defense.   Except when the girl prayed, Dinah never spoke.   The dainties brought to her were untouched, unnoticed ; all questions went unanswered, unless a wild look, or some religious and perfectly inapplicable phrase, could be considered an answer.   There was no sullenness in the woman ; it was only that in gazing on the object that forever fixed her fiery eyes, she forgot everything.   But when Miss Belford would ask, " Dinah, shall we pray ?" the stiff figure would fall upon its knees, the long thin hands be clasped to her heart, and in the wildest rapture, the fiercest fervor, she prayed.   At every visit Colton was Miss Belford's escort, and each time she grew dearer to him.   He now went very often to see her. They rode together, drove together, and despite the cynical remarks of the hundred friends concerning his thrifty pursuit of her fortune, seemed not only very happy together, but very well matched.

The day for the trial came, and Ilanah turned out in full force.   So many ladies desired to be present that seats were especially reserved for them.   Dinah was the same in the crowded court-room as in her prison cell. With the same intense stare, with hands clasped tightly together, she sat rigid, apparently indifferent, as witness after witness testified against her.

The gay birds of fashion fluttered their plumage and bent their pretty heads together while in disgust they glanced at that " horrible creature " who had dared

attack a Southern gentleman. In their midst sat one
lady robed in deepest mourning, the twin sister of the
murdered man. Her black veil was thrown aside and
she kept her eyes fixed on the jury ; she was a more
potent argument against the prisoner than witnesses or
lawyers' eloquence.

Several gentlemen were called to the witness stand.
They had seen Dinah mount the platform and heard her
harangue the people—and they had neither seen nor
heard anything further. Under cross-examination by
Colton they acknowledged having heard the shot and
having seen the negro preacher fall dead. But they
could not say whence the shot came. James Eaton's
companions testified that never before having seen the
negro, Mr. Eaton could have had no real intention of
killing him. The cross-examination drew out the fact
that Eaton had uttered a threat of shooting the negro.
But the witnesses were unanimous in testifying to Mr.
Eaton's generally amiable nature, and to the belief that
at the time of the shooting any words of his could not
have weight as he was "somewhat under the influence
of liquor." One of the witnesses indeed, in an embarrassed moment, admitted that James Eaton had taken
deliberate aim at the negro. But a sob from the sister
of the dead man, which though not loud was heard in
the perfect silence of the court room, outweighed these
points in the negress's favor. With paling face Colton
saw that the case was going against him, unless by the
woman herself he could prove her actual insanity. And
Dinah, she for whom the gallows was making ready ?
She took no apparent interest in the matter. The prosecution had established a very strong case against the
fiery-eyed mulatto, but she heeded it not. Some negro
witnesses were called by the defense. They proved very
directly how "singler" Dinah had acted from the first
day of the meeting, strengthening the theory of her in-

sanity which was evidently the only plea of the defense.
Under cross-examination one of the negroes in quaint,
poetical, albeit ignorant, phrasing, described Dinah's appeal for revenge. It was then only that the mulatto
seemed to realize what was going on. She grew excited,
rose to speak, waved her arms to command silence, and
had she not been roughly pulled back by the new bailiff
who had replaced Brown, would doubtless have burst
forth in a wild harangue. The fiery eyes grew more
fiery, the rigid body swayed to and fro, and her mouth
working convulsively seemed unable to retain the words
burning for utterance.

Looking at the wild figure, evidently that of a mad
woman, Colton had almost resolved not to call his last
witness who herself had offered to testify, and to whom
his success in the case had become of personal interest.
But he had promised to leave no stone unturned, and
this stone was a diamond of the purest water. He looked
again at the negress, then scrutinized each juror's face,
and then with manifest reluctance the witness was
called, " Miss Helen Belford."   Faster and faster
fluttered the fans, and their owners whispered : " I did
not think she'd dare !"   " Well, that's too much !"
" Against the man who wanted to marry her !" sobbed
the black-robed sister.   Yes, Miss Belford's unencum-
bered thousands had been a tempting bait to more than
one young man whose principal love was self, and
whose chief aim was indulgence.   But the young lady
rated her thousands as only poor accompaniments to her
charms, and had resolved herself to be the attraction to
the man she should marry.   So she had given a decided
" no " to James Eaton and to many of his sort.   Now
flushing, now paling, she mounted to the witness stand.
Colton started forward, thinking she was about to faint,
and reproached himself for exposing her to such an
ordeal. She saw his motion, shook her head and tried

to smile and nearly burst into tears when with trembling lips she glanced at the sister of the dead James Eaton, as if asking forgiveness for what duty made her do. Standing near Miss Belford was her guardian, Colonel Young. He was very fond of the willful girl and had always indulged her every whim; but when she informed him of her determination to testify for the mulatto, he was astounded.

"My *dear* Helen—" he had begun. But she put her little hand over his mouth, and thus having him at a disadvantage, began to coax him, uttering meanwhile wise and determined words: "Now, guardy, don't say a word," which was unnecessary, as the Colonel couldn't speak, and then upon this adjuration Miss Belford kissed his cheek. "I *must* testify,"—another kiss—"Justice forces me to; and you must go with me to court—" two kisses in quick succession—"or, or, I'll—I'll feel myself as if I —I—were a wicked wo—wo—man too vain and—and proud to speak, and let another wo—man be hanged." Miss Belford's two hands were pressed to her eyes as she sobbed in earnest. Colonel Young looked first amazed, and then most uncomfortable; he tried to take his pretty ward in his arms, tried to soothe her with, "My dearest girl, Helen, my love—"

But Helen was not to be overpowered by petting. In the gentlest manner she drew herself away from him, and still sobbed in the most heart-broken way.

"No, no, I love you. I wouldn't do anything—ing to make—ake you miserable—able, not for all—all Illanah, and all—all the world—world. But you care—are more for gossip than for your own little—ittle Helen!"

That was too cruel in this fair Helen. But she kept on with her cruelty, sobbing until the kind old man became alarmed, and walking up and down, fumed, fretted, swore, and finally declared that he would do just what she wanted. Whereat in an astonishingly short time

14*

Miss Belford was resting her pretty head on his shoulder and calling him her "dear guardy," while he patted her cheek and felt delighted as well as vexed.

In consequence of Miss Belford's tears and kisses Colonel Young now stood near her as she waited to give her testimony. He frowned angrily at the hum of astonishment that greeted her appearance. There could be nothing so agreeable to the Colonel as to find any man who dared look disapproval of Miss Belford's action. He would welcome anything that would give him an excuse for a challenge.

Good old conservative! To him woman was a delicate being, made to ride in carriages, wear fine clothes and spend money, in all of which accomplishments Miss Belford excelled. But this new freak, this strong-minded notion of the fair Helen's vexed him all the more as between her tears and coaxings he was powerless to oppose her. Thoroughly angry with himself, he looked anxiously for some outlet for his feeling. While her guardian, very red in the face, was still seeking an excuse for striking somebody, Miss Belford, growing calm took the oath. Talcott Colton's eyes meeting hers said, " Helen, you're an angel," as plainly as eyes could speak, and the pink returning to Miss Belford's cheeks, her bright eyes answered the lawyer's glance very distinctly and satisfactorily. Questioned by Colton she testified to the perfect order of the negro meeting and to the strange expression of Dinah's face—an expression which had attracted her. She testified to the fatal shot, to seeing the pistol in James Eaton's hand and the sudden change in Dinah's expression to what appeared to her as violent insanity. She also testified to Dinah's conduct since her imprisonment, which must awaken pity, and left no doubt in her mind of the woman's insanity. Her testimony, which was not at all disturbed by cross-examination, created the first favorable impression for the prisoner in

the minds of the jury. So moved were those twelve free
and enlightened citizens that when Miss Belford in a
tremulous voice said : "She is not responsible," they
quite overlooked the fact that a witness's belief is not of
much value as testimony, and would certainly have rendered a verdict of insanity had they then and there delivered their unanimous opinion.

But the mulatto had to speak for herself and seemed
willing to do so. She had watched Miss Belford, and
though not seeming to recognize her face, had intently
listened to every word. Her expression had changed
from wildness to fury, and the flaming eyes no longer
fixed on vacancy moved from face to face, as if seeking
some particular one. She sprang up when she was called, eager to break the silence that oppressed her. Miss
Belford seated beside her guardian saw such pathos in
the wild figure of the negress that tears filled her eyes.
She put her hand on Colonel Young's arm, mutely
drawing his attention to Dinah, but the Colonel was too
angry with her for having made herself conspicuous, and
too angry with himself for permitting it, to notice the
pressure of her fingers. Helen did not feel slighted ;
she was engrossed in watching the negress, and very nervous at the probable result of her testimony. For, at the
question, "What is your name ?" the woman's voice,
clear and strong, rang through the court-room.

" Dinah !"

" An intelligent answer ; they will not believe she is
insane," Miss Belford thought, as she looked at Colton
and trembled for the result of the trial. Insanity's
phases were not among familiar subjects with the girl.
She could not understand the quick change from vacuity
to shrewdness, from memory's exactness to the wildest fury of unreasonable rage, and looked in wonder
at Dinah, whose answers quickly followed the questions of the lawyer. When the mulatto's excitement

had become evident, Colton had decided not to put her on the stand, but the lawyers for the prosecution asked it of the court, and now were, by different tests of memory, weakening the plea of insanity.

"What is your other name?" was asked.

"Ain't got no oder name," Dinah replied.

"What was your father's name?"

"Didn't hab no fader, was born before de freedom shone. Slabes faders ain't 'membered. Don't hab no daddies." Except for those fierce glances she had become calm, seemingly relieved by the sound of her own voice.

"What were you doing during the camp meeting?" asked the lawyer.

"Listening ter de words ob God, prayin' fer de sinner." She began to sway backward and forward. Her hands crossed themselves upon her breast, and on her face wrapt attention replaced wildness as if again under the great trees she drank eagerly of gospel wisdom.

"What disturbed your charitable prayers?" the lawyer's sarcasm was quite thrown away on the woman, but her eyes lost the far-away look, and once more grown fierce fixed themselves upon his face until they seemed to burn into his flesh. He repeated his question : "What disturbed your prayers?"

"De debbil." She uttered the words with perfect seriousness, and so prone to laughter is a crowd, that a titter passed around the stilled audience. It was quickly suppressed, however, as a sound of a woman's weeping was heard, and each remembered the dead man's sister. The prosecuting attorney glared at the prisoner. But no eyes could look down those fiery ones.

"Do you remember the circumstances of the preacher's death?" asked the attorney. A sound half-scorn, half-rage, like the muttered growl of some wild beast, was Dinah's only answer. Her eyes still on the attorney's face, no longer saw it. Before her another picture formed in shadowy and ghastly reality. Again she heard the soughing of the wind through the widespreading branches of the grove, again looked over the multitude to the preacher's gentle face. Again she heard the shot, and saw him fall, and through an opening in the surging crowd saw his murderer brandishing the still smoking pistol. Fiercest fury glared from those hollow eyes, her ghastly face was drawn in wild contortion, and she shrieked again and again for vengeance. She heard no questions, did not see the frightened faces in the crowded room ; she only answered that mysterious voice that forever called upon her.

"I'se killed him, I'se killed him, de debbil ! an' sent his soul to hell !" Then rose a cry almost as wild as her own, and James Eaton's sister was carried fainting from the court-room.

Aghast the jury looked at the self-confessed murderess. The prosecuting attorney shrugged his shoulders. The case was now, he considered, practically over.

Helen Belford's pale face was still turned to the negress, who was smiling triumphantly as she muttered :

"I'se done it, bress de Lord, I'se fired the gun fer freedom." It certainly was ungenerous in Colonel Young at that moment to whisper in his ward's ear :

"I hope, Helen, this has cured you of philanthropy." He tried to make amends, however, by pressing the hand she had left upon his arm. She did not notice this attention any more than she had his little taunt. She thoroughly understood his affection for her, and then, too, she had glanced from the mulatto's face to that of Colton, who was trying to reassure her with a look. Dinah had damaged her case, perhaps ruined it, but in every look, by every word, she had to him proven her insanity. That it took the form of self-justification was perfectly consistent with her mania. Talcott Colton had too much of what goes to make up true Southern

chivalry to fight the less valiantly for a losing than a
winning cause. Increase of difficulties would not excuse
relaxation ; on the contrary, it but stimulated to further
effort. He had prepared an exhaustive argument on
insanity, had, as thoroughly as could be done in so
few weeks, studied this peculiar phase of poor
humanity's ills ; and so armed with numberless instances, facts, references, he made a clever speech.

Dinah had returned to her former rigid attitude and
intent gaze on vacancy : she did not even glance at him
when in a burst of eloquence Colton plead for the woman's life, citing incident after incident, proof after
proof in support of the fact of her insanity. The Southerners, always susceptible to the magic of speech, listened
with breathless attention. Colonel Young whispered to
Helen : "I didn't know there was so much stuff in Colton." And the flushed and excited girl could hardly re-
frain from joining in the murmur of applause, that, totally
irrespective of unyielding prejudice, greeted the eloquence of Talcott Colton. Unpopular as he had made
himself he still moved the crowd.

With a deprecating smile and complimentary allusion
to the eloquence of " our young friend," with deep regrets that it was " enlisted in so bad a cause," the prosecuting attorney began his address. Drawing a picture of
the home circle made desolate by the " fiendish act of this
negress," he spoke forcibly of the danger to the community of not proceeding to the law's limit with the class of
dangerous criminals who seek shelter behind the plea of
lunacy. "The negroes—especially here in a country
where in numbers they far exceed the whites—must be
kept under the severest rule. Against the brutality of
the negro, gentlemen, you must protect our growing
children. Think of the valuable life this woman has
ended. She has cut off in the flower of youth the repre-
sentative of one of our oldest and most honored families.

Take the murder home to yourselves. What would be
your demand if your beloved son was to be strangled by
one of these negroes—these ex-slaves, who flaunt their
liberty in the faces of their impoverished owners? This
woman is an example all the more deserving of immediate punishment, since in the most incomprehensible
manner her cause has been espoused by one whom we
have been proud to call an ornament to Southern demo-
cracy." Not satisfied with this argument the prosecuting
attorney lengthened his speech until every listener became exhausted and wondered at his unfailing power of
wind and words.

Despite Colton's eloquence the majority of the jury
had inclined to a verdict of murder in the first degree.
This inclination was strengthened by the opening of the
speech of the prosecuting attorney, which in its appeal to
political prejudices was sure of awakening echoes in the
minds of the "enlightened twelve," who were all good
Bourbon Democrats. But as time sped and the speech
still flowed, rolling on with increasing sound, the jury's
attention began to wander and one kind-hearted old fellow, who had obstinacy strongly developed, fell to
watching the negress. Unmindful of the waning day
and of the voice of the man demanding her death sentence, Dinah sat erect and rigid, her eyes fixed on that
vacant place that for her held the dead body of the
preacher. So still she sat, so fixed were her eyes, that
the juror who had been growing drowsy began to find
a certain fascination in watching to see if she would
move. What fiery eyes ! what a corpse-like face !
Could she be sane and yet so perfectly indifferent to this
argument against her ? Her lips began to move, she
muttered something. Intently the juror listened, but
caught only the loud words of the prosecuting attorney.

"What motive could she have ? What motive ?" He
thundered out, having in reserve a fine point made from

Dinah's own words : "Revenge !" He paused to make
the point more telling and Dinah's mutterings became
distinct. Her low thrilling whisper was heard all over
the court-room making flesh creep with horror or hearts
thrill with pity :

"My sister's chile, de preacher ob de Lord !"

These words won to Dinah's side the obstinate juror,
and even to his adherents weakened the force of the
attorney's cry against "revenge !" Above his shout was
heard that thrilling voice : "My sister's chile, de preacher
ob de Lord." Her sister's chile ! The obstinate juror
wiped away a tear as for the first time the cry of the
womant's natural affection rang in his ears, making more
vivid the picture Mr. Colton had drawn of Dinah's devotion to and sacrifices for this negro preacher. Beasts
loved their young, had died in their defense ;—then why
not this woman ? Though the judge's charge was directly against the prisoner, the obstinate juror held to his
obstinacy. He would not concur in a verdict of murder
in the first degree. The only indifferent person in the
court-room was Dinah. She did not notice the filing out of
the jury, nor the hushed movements of the curious crowd
as it waited for the verdict. An hour passed—two hours,
three hours. A few lamps were brought in and dimly
illuminated the room. Four hours were nearly over ;
the judge had decided to adjourn the court until the
morrow, and a murmur of disappointment went around as
in an audible whisper he ordered the bailiff to take this
information to the room where the jury were weighing
in the balance a human life. But their deliberations
were over ; the twelve came back with the bailiff.
People pushed each other and stood on tiptoe trying to
read from the twelve inexpressive faces what they were
to hear in a moment. The foreman arose.

"Considering the extenuating circumstances and the
nervous strain under which the prisoner labored, we find

her guilty of manslaughter and recommend her to the mercy of the court."

Miss Belford, who had grown pale, now flushed rosy red and smiled triumphantly at Mr. Colton. What a compliment to his eloquence ! Ah, Miss Belford, pretty Miss Belford, all your lover's eloquence had not the power to move an obstinate heart like Dinah's thrilling whisper : " My sister's chile, de preacher ob de Lord."

How that one juror carried the eleven before him only juries can tell. But of all the twelve he who had brought them into such disrepute in this exciting case, cared the least about the judge's frowns, or the censuring whispers of the majority of the crowd.

Pushed up by the bailiff, Dinah stood to receive sentence.

" Gentlemen of the jury," said the judge, whose sympathies were directly against " the nigger," " your verdict has been the greatest surprise in a long legal career. It is not for me to question it. In accordance with law nothing remains for me but to pronounce sentence, which shall be to the limit of the law. Dinah Russell, for the murder of James Eaton, you are sentenced to four years' hard labor." Dinah was not dismayed. With the utmost indifference she looked alike on friend and enemy, and with the same ghostlike face and fixed stare passed out of the court-room. Next morning she was on her way to the convict camp Osmerillo.

Talcott Colton decided not to appeal the case. Dinah's insanity was of the erratic order which most puzzles and disconcerts a counsel, and he feared that should he appeal, her sentence would be even more severe. Knowing nothing of the convict camps generally, and being personally acquainted with the owners of Osmerillo Mine—men who were among the highest of Georgia's citizens—he believed that the sentence of the mulatto was not a hard one. So the camp meeting and its trag-

ical ending, Dinah and her trial, became things of the
past, and were remembered only for the sake of the influence they had had upon the fate of Talcott Colton and
Helen Belford.   Not many weeks after the trial the two
became one with due accompaniment of satin, orange
blossoms, bridesmaids and wedding breakfast.

CHAPTER XLI.

A CARPET-BAGGER.

NO news had been heard of Mary.   Miss Dawson
grew sadder and more quiet, and poor Janet
was a constant trial to the old doctor, who had
lived long enough to become philosophical over the inevitable.

" What is the use of this perpetual fretting, Jane ? "
The doctor, just returned from the wedding, had been
descanting on the charms of Mrs. Talcott Colton and
became disgusted with his unresponsive audience.   His
heart had bloomed into a certain youthfulness when
under the influence of Mary's beauty.   He had desired to
make her the head of the Colton family, but her disappearance, the months that had elapsed since the day she
so mysteriously stepped out of existence, and above all
the appearance of this handsome young lover, were
wonderfully calming to elderly passion.   He had experi-
enced a twinge of veritable jealousy when he saw what a
fine young fellow Dennis really was, and had en-
couraged his contempt for "carpet-baggers" generally.
But Dennis was charming in manner and feeling towards the old, and without feeling, manner is, after all,
like a piano without sounding-board.   He was, besides,

a man of force and ability, a natural leader, and would long ago have made his mark had he not been crushed under the weight of all the supposed crimes of carpet-baggers. In any other country than the South, a man like Dennis Day would have been a welcome citizen, and here, clouded over by the scandals forced upon the young Republicans of the State, was even impressing his good qualities upon one of Georgia's most uncompromising aristocrats. Dr. Colton, in the rebuilding of his mansion, had become a man with a hobby, and constantly found matters of absorbing and engrossing interest upon which he, the architect and the builders were so often at variance that he needed some strong, and decided adviser. This he found in the carpet-bagger. At first reluctantly consulted, and afterward eagerly sought, Dennis supplied a need in the old gentleman's life, a need, of which he had been only dimly conscious, but which soon became very keenly felt. Even Dennis's necessary absences were resented by the doctor. "For," the old gentleman argued, "Mary Hilton is surely dead. And the dead do not require any help, nor are they benefited by the labors of the living. As for myself, I would willingly give the half of all I possess to learn the fate of that lovely creature. But money is only wasted in this long and useless search. Do you suppose it is possible for a girl of Mary's beauty to be hidden anywhere, when there is a reward of $10,000 offered for her discovery? Here we are, nearly three months after Mary's disappearance, and except the red-headed girl who tried to persuade Dennis she was his promised bride, no one has answered the advertisement! My dear Jane, it is perfect folly to continue the search. This clinging to a delusion is killing you, and as for Dennis, I can hardly recognize in his haggard face the handsome fellow you presented to me, when you astounded me by saying in an undertone, ' No politics, he is a carpet-bagger.' I declare, Jane, I *was* astounded. For I really felt sure he was a gentleman. And I have quite decided he is one, spite of his unfortunate fondness for classing himself with a low set like that. He is a wealthy man. And all carpet-baggers are paupers who come here. Thank God, we are nearly free of the parasites !"

"You are always speaking of Mr. Day's wealth. Don't you remember that he told you he had only inherited this fortune a week before he heard of Mary's disappearance, and that up to that time he was the poorest relic a party ever had ? But there, cousin ! I have no heart for politics. My mind is absorbed on one topic, Mary Hilton. It seems to me I see that lovely face all day, and at night I dream of her, only to waken and find, my pillow wet with tears. Ah ! cousin, you have not self-reproach added to your cares. I feel that I have caused all this sorrow, and until Mary is found I shall never again be at peace." Miss Dawson had hidden her face in her hands.

"Jane Dawson." The doctor walking up and down the room was impatiently watching his cousin. She had always been his ideal woman. Her pride seemed no blemish to him who was as proud as she. This mourning with an unavailing sorrow was as annoying as it was unreasonable. "Jane Dawson, I am losing all patience with you. You spoke for Mary's good. You asked her to be your daughter. Certainly you could do no more. I am sure I cared more for Mary than you could possibly have done. For I intended to make her my wife, and had watched beside her during a tedious recovery from a painful injury. I could hardly tell which was most admirable, her wonderful beauty, or her sweet and uncomplaining disposition. Now you have never seen the girl but once, and then for only about an hour, and here you have been crying about her for months, while

I have accommodated myself to the inevitable fact of her death."

"She isna dead, she isna dead!" and Janet sobbing in violent hysterics fell at the doctor's feet.

This was really too much for the old gentleman, and he turned to leave the room. But as he reached the door there came a knock, and Dennis, hearing Janet's cry, entered hastily.

"Miss Dawson! Janet!" he looked around. From that cry, half-laugh, half-shriek, he had dared to hope that some news had been heard of or from Mary. And now pale, agitated, hardly more than the wreck of the handsome fellow of whose bright eyes Mammy had said that "Wid der sparkles I could a'most light de candle," he stood before them. The Scotchwoman, weakened and more colorless than before, was calmed by his presence and came back to herself; and seated in a great chair near Miss Dawson, she listened to Dennis's recount of the week's search. He had made only weekly visits to Milton, and these solely to report to Mary's friends. There was little now to tell, for though Dennis was seeing service more exhausting and continuous than during the war, he had not now as then success or gallant feat to cheer him on. Failure, heartsickness, disappointment —these were the only results of his protracted labor. And though as ever mindful of the women listening, he tried to lighten the history of his search, it was only necessary to look into his face to know the wearing troubles of the past months. He felt himself poor indeed without Mary. He would doubtless strive to make the best use of life, but in losing the woman he loved he had lost his chance of happiness.

"What do you propose to do now?" Dr. Colton asked the question, as having said good-night to Miss Dawson and Janet, to whom he had imparted a cheerfulness unknown to himself, Dennis and the doctor walked together down the broad hall to the stairway.

"Do!" Dennis turned on the doctor a very pale and determined face, "keep up the search until either I die or find Mary."

"Dennis Day," Dr. Colton spoke testily, "don't be a fool! Mary cannot be alive. It is absolutely impossible, my dear fellow. We don't live in an age when maidens are carried off and kept in dungeons; and nothing less than a dungeon of feudal times could thus long have kept Mary a prisoner. A brave man knows when to yield. I really believe you are too brave and too good a fellow to wear out your life tearing over the country, poking into every hovel, seeking what you will never find. Mary is an angel in Heaven, unless the whole scheme of Christianity is a myth."

"Yes, I believe with you," Dennis answered. "If Mary is dead she is an angel. But," and his face grew more resolute, his voice lower and more intense, "I believe she is alive. Death alone or the finding of her body will induce me to resign this search. It is the engrossing purpose of my life." And then to put aside discussion of a subject painful to him, he asked some questions about the new house. The doctor was full of his hobby. Five minutes later he had Dennis in his room sitting at a table spread with plans, figures and pictures, and was asking his advice on facades. After some deliberation Dennis gave his opinion and to the doctor's delight it agreed with his own. Now he would triumphantly crush both builder and architect.

"Aha! my dear boy," the doctor was never more decided about Dennis's ability. "You are a host in yourself. As for Jane Dawson, I never saw her take equal interest in any man. Why, it is really wonderful to see how she brightened up when you came in! Come oftener to town, can't you?"

Dennis thanked him heartily, but did not promise, for his time was dedicated to a purpose. Yet in all his own trouble he took thought for others. Hearing from Brown of the death of Mammy, of the baby and of Julie, and the recapture of O'Neal, he had grieved as for friends. For O'Neal he had interested Dr. Colton, who was one of the most influential men out of political life in the State. He strove also to interest him in his plan of making general war upon the convict system. But while the old gentleman admitted its horrors, his education had been strictly conservative, and he was a true Bourbon. To him it was a reasonable outgrowth of slavery, that laws should be different for criminals of different colors, those for the blacks being necessarily much more stringent than the laws for whites. Thus minor offences in a negro, such as stealing a chicken, would be visited by punishment more severe than manslaughter in the white. In vain Dennis demonstrated the injustice of such law. But for O'Neal's liberation Dr. Colton bestirred himself in good earnest. Owing, however, to the convict's having broken jail a pardon at present was almost impossible. Time must elapse and the negro be specially recommended for good conduct, before influence could obtain the release that justice and mercy had asked in vain. Therefore, although convinced that the convict in whose liberation Dennis Day was interested was identical with Miss Dawson's preserver, even Dr. Colton, with all the influence he had been able to command, was obliged to wait for the opportunity.

Brown, the ex-bailiff, wrote to Dennis that he was without employment, and a good position was straightway found for him as watchman of the factory nearest Seth Hunt's old home in Vermont. Thither the whole Brown family emigrated, and the head of it soon began to send Dennis enthusiastic letters concerning the advantages of education and political freedom. In his prosperity Dennis remembered all his poorer friends. Even Janet was made independent. "Take it for Mary's sake," he said as the Scotchwoman's pride resented the acceptance of what she had not earned.

"Fer Mary, fer my bairn! Ah, if she were here!" And then remembering that from the first Mary had loved "the one-armed mon," Janet accepted the competence he had settled on her. "As a loan," she said, with a slight return of her prim manner, and so, to spare her feelings, Dennis let it remain. Strangers, too, shared the bounty of the rich "carpet-bagger." Numberless little children were made happy, and hard lives brightened, and all through this inherited fortune that gave so little happiness to its possessor. For great as is the privilege of succoring human needs, it will not satisfy a hungry heart. Mary! Mary! Where was she? Where was she?

The Christmas holiday had passed, the joyful season that is so joyless to the unhappy. Except for giving largely in charity, ordering festivities at his distant Vermont mills, sending some flowers to Miss Dawson and a remembrance to Janet, the day for Dennis went as many that preceded and followed it; it found him in the saddle, riding over the country, seeking her of whom no trace could be found. He became so haggard, so worn by this perpetual anxiety, that he began to be pointed out by strangers as the "rich gentleman who was going crazy."

"Two months, nearly three, yet not a word, not a sign upon which to build hope! But I do hope, and will, until I die, or know *she* is dead," said Dennis, as with a pale and determined face he one morning rode away from Milton. The circuit for the search was now to be begun at a distance of forty miles from the city; and mounted on the best horse that money could buy he was covering the road at a rapid pace. Yet even the bounding beneath him of the noble animal, filled with a horse's best qualities, did not waken one spark of exhilaration in the man. Nerved with his purpose, weighed down with a sorrow more crushing than years of poverty and privation, Dennis's bright, happy nature was changed to sad gravity.

The men employed as detectives had long since abandoned any idea of finding Mary. They believed that Mr. Day had "lost his mind." But as their pay was regular and exact, and as faithful work was required, they attended to their duty.

Riding out to the appointed rendezvous, Dennis was as steadfast to his purpose as if the search had but begun. Projecting some minor changes of method, he was looking ahead with eyes fixed on the small point of brighter light at the end of the long avenue of overarching trees, when in the distance a moving object caught and held his glance. He still looked at it as lessening distance showed a woman clad in the homespun worn by the country people of the region. As she came nearer he still observed her without purpose or interest, and simply because she was the only living thing within range of his vision. Then something as he gazed began to stir at his heart, first fascinating and then almost terrifying him with a wild, glad hope. Suddenly his pulses seemed to stop, and then throbbed to bursting. His head swam, and partly to nerve himself for a fresh disappointment, partly that he might feel something firm beneath his feet, he sprang to the ground.

"Unreal, unreal! A phantom of my own creation— a mad fancy of my brain! Am I crazy? Or is that— is that—"

Breathless he stood, not moving a muscle, not once taking his eyes from that advancing figure.

15

CHAPTER XLII.

AMONG THE MOONSHINERS.

CIRCUMSTANCES in themselves ordinary enough have sometimes produced extraordinary results. That Mary Hilton should be alive and within fifty miles of Milton while a dozen men were scouring the country in search of her and rewards large enough to tempt cupidity were offered for the slightest tidings of her, certainly seemed remarkable, and yet the train of circumstances producing this result was only ordinary. Georgia, while it is one of the most prominent of the Southern States, has in its interior some wild counties and very rough people, who live, grow up, marry and intermarry without education or ambition, and who take little interest in anything outside their own community. Their principal occupation, illicit distilling, is the foundation of a sort of wild life that partakes of savagery. Their little colonies situated mostly in mountainous regions have rare communication with the outside civilized world. The rough country offers no chances for husbandry and few advantages of any kind for gaining support ; so the distilling business becomes a species of heritage that is transmitted from father to son, from mother to daughter. For the women engage in the business and are usually the mediums who convey the illegal goods to the neighboring towns. First one market and then another is sought, as the distillers have occasion to believe themselves objects of suspicion. On the day of the storm Betsey Scanlon, one of the most daring venders of the contraband goods, had driven into Milton with a load of whiskey. The kegs, hidden under potatoes and other country supplies, had been satisfac-

torily disposed of to some merchants who knew good
whiskey and could keep a secret. The storm was no
hindrance to this woman. She had passed her life in
brawls and contentions, and was undismayed by anything
less than a United States marshal with a posse of armed
men. Of late these visitors were becoming more and
more rare, for officials are not too fond of losing life in
inglorious warfare against moonshiners. Unless captured when selling goods, the distillers had been for
some time unmolested. The load of whiskey last sold
had, however, been seized, and the driver or vendor of it
was now in the State Prison. There was, consequently
more than a spice of danger in Betsey's expedition, and
there had been some hesitation as to the choice of the
vendor.

"I'll do it, boys!" Betsey Scanlon had said to the
heads of the band who were consulting over the
matter. And since Betsey Scanlon was strong as any
man, and moreover wily as a fox, she was unanimously
declared to be the first choice. So into Milton she had
gone, and had not only disposed of her own goods to
advantage, but now driving back at a brisk rate was
laughing to herself at the remembrance of the tools for
the continuance of their business which were concealed
under the bales of homespun and coarse groceries in the
wagon. The storm was in her favor. It prevented travel.
And thus without any chance of detention or inspection.
she chanted a rough song in a voice more man's than
woman's. "Lord, what a flash!" she said, when like a
sword of flame the lightning seemed to open the
blackened sky and struck the oak. Across the road fell
the tree, while fire ran along the branches, which most
sheltered from the storm, were least wet.

"Wot's to be done now?" Betsey muttered as she
sprang from the wagon and inspected the road by the
glare of the occasional flashes that were becoming less

frequent as the storm died away.   There was little space
to pass, and that was by the edge of a ditch and presented difficulties and dangers, too.   But what were
difficulties to a woman like Betsey ?   And as for danger
there was no danger to her but in suspicion of her
errand. So leading the horses, a pair of powerful blacks,
with a little judicious encouragement, she safely passed
the tree.

"Betsey's the gal !" she said in triumph—when
another flash, brighter than the preceding ones, showed
her something white lying under a smouldering branch.

"Wot's that ?"   She walked to the side of the tree
lifted the leaves that dripping with rain had probably
saved Mary's life, and dragged out the warm and breathing form of the girl.   "Well, I'll be shot ef it's not a
'ooman !—and purty, too," she added as another flash lit
up the delicate face.   "Wal, we're scarce o' gals, an' Ike
wants a wife ; so here, my beauty, as it's a choice atween
dying on the road or goin' ter be a moonshiner, I guess
I'll take yer wid me."

Without an effort she raised the girl in those mus-
cular arms used to lifting heavy kegs, and making her as
comfortable as she could in the wagon, mounted to her
seat, and driving rapidly, was well out of sight past a
turn in the road, when Janet beneath the fallen tree
found Mary's slipper.   On went the wagon.   Taking a
turn that led to the mountains, and travelling through a
wild rough country, it had made good fifty miles as day
broke.

"Hurrah for Betsey !" shouted the men, who, waiting
at her cabin, had been passing some anxious hours.
"All safe and snug ?" asked one, coming up to the wagon
side.

"Yes, snug an' safe as enybody could wish," Betsey
answered, throwing the reins to the man and springing
to the ground.   "But keep off ; no lookin' in the wagon!

Every feller shall have his share. But thar's an extra
thar for Ike. An' I don't want her frightened."

"Her !" A yell of derisive laughter went up from the
knot of men who as Betsey spoke all crowded to the
back of the wagon. But Betsey was there as soon as
they.

" Hands off !" she said sharply, and in the morning
sunlight, with her strong, heavily built figure and broad,
determined face, she looked equal to defending her rights.
" Ike's the only man as'll see what I've brunged him."

"Ike," a lazy, handsome fellow, dark as an Indian
and looking not unlike one, with his straight black hair
and regular features, stepped out from the group of four
or five others who, not altogether pleased at this decided
preference, moved away muttering. But Betsey did not
" care a snap," as she remarked in a sharp tone. She
was too valuable a comrade to offend, and in her way was
an authority that defied restraint.

"Wot's it, mother ?" Ike asked. For though Betsey
was childless, yet being the only woman who dared
oppose the lawless men in this lawless band, she was
generally called "mother" by them all—especially when
they wanted to conciliate her. Ike being flattered by her
prospective gift, desired in turn to flatter her. He put
his arm around her broad shoulders, that under a rough
pea-jacket looked like a man's and stooping pressed a
sounding kiss on her ruddy cheek.

"Look." She drew aside the canvas cover at the
back of the wagon. Ike was not quite prepared for
such a vision of loveliness. Lying on the dark blue homespun Mary seemed a pearl of whiteness. The jolting of
the cart had roused her from the stupor of the electric
shock, and now sleeping quietly and naturally, she was
awakened by the eager eyes fixed upon her.

"Ah!" With a start she sprang up, steadying herself
on the huge bundles around her.

"Thar! How do you like her?" Regardless of the wonder, even fright, in the girl's eyes, Betsey was complacently surveying Ike's flushed and agitated face. He did not speak, but gazed at the beautiful girl as if on earth nothing else remained for him to wish.

"Where am I?" Mary asked, trembling. For ignorant, innocent as she was, the dark face gazing at her had in it something that affrighted her.

"Whar are yer?" Betsey laughed a great laugh that to the girl's overstrung nerves sounded like a roar. "'Mong friends, that's whar yer are. An' the sooner yer gits ter feel it the better fer yer. Take her down, Ike. Why, boy, I didn't think yer'd be sech a fool. Standin' thar an' turning red, jest fer a bit o' white cotton."

Ike did not answer her, did not turn his eyes from Mary's face.

"Hurry, can't yer! or I'll do it myself." Betsey was losing patience, of which indeed she had not too great a store, and Betsey's favor was not to be trifled with. Without uttering a word Ike lifted the girl, and more gently than he had ever before touched anything, put her on her feet.

She looked around. The wild mountains covered with pines were not wilder or rougher than the group of men staring at her, and as freely commenting on her appearance as if she were a horse or other animal. They laughed, too, in a rough way, and shouted to Betsey to know how many more she'd got "aboord."

Everything was so wild, so strange to the girl reared among flowers, that she clasped her hands in a mute appeal, turning to Betsey, who, however unwomanly, was yet the only woman near. "Take me back to my father, to my friends," Mary said in low, trembling tones. So sweet was the sound of her voice that even Betsey stopped her work of unloading the wagon.

"Take yer back! Why, gal, that ll never be done.

Here ye are, an' here yer'll stay, 'less Ike should grow traitor and help yer away! Ef he did!" She tapped the pocket of her coat that showed the glitter of steel, and a threatening look drove away the broad smile with which she had turned to Mary. Thus repulsed, Mary looked timidly at Ike. His dark face was rendered darker still by the red flush, partly of anger, partly of a feeling that her beauty had inspired. He took her clasped hands in his.

"Don't be afeared." His voice had a tremble in it, that made the men laugh louder. But their laughter died away as with a wild imprecation he sprang before the terrified girl. "One more yell like that, an' I'll kill the fust man I teches!" He looked like a young giant as he towered above the smaller men who knew something of Ike's strength and something of his temper. They dared not irritate him further.

"Yer right, my boy." Betsey slapped him on the shoulder. "The gal's your'n an' yer right ter pertect her."

The men turned away. Ike and Betsey were too powerful a coalition for them to battle against.

From that moment Mary was saved from the violence, even the rudeness, of these rough mountaineers. She led a strange life among the pines and clouds, a life to which danger added a perpetual spice in the minds of these wild men, and whose freedom from all laws except that of force allowed strange license in speech and manner. In these altitudes she became far stronger and more robust than she had been in the plains among her flowers; and though she longed with all her sad heart for home and friends, she grew fond of those around her. Ike, who from the moment he beheld loved her, was tender and as respectful as he knew how to be. This young savage, whose only ruler had been his own wild will, now gained a certain dignity, even nobility, from his love for the "white girl," as Mary was called by the sunburned band of moonshiners. Ingomar was not the only wild man civilized by love ; and while the language of the old play is stilted and strained, the truth of the sentiment will keep it a favorite as long as players live, and people go to see them. Ike and Mary, neither of whom had ever read a romance in their lives, were playing as pretty a one as ever called forth maiden's blush or lover's sigh. But for the fact that the girl's heart had passed out of her own keeping it might have had as happy a termination. For who, not loving elsewhere, could note the daily proofs of love given by this young mountaineer and not grow tender toward him ? The wildest feats he would perform just to see the change in Mary's color, or gain a sigh or smile of wonder and approval. Although urged by Betsey, he had refused to force the girl to become his wife ; and even Betsey, rough Betsey, had enough of woman about her to like the divine spark of chivalry which had somehow found its way into the breast of this young hero of the mountains. Among these wild scenes Mary moved like an angel fallen from Heaven. Unconscious of her own charms, gentle, refined, no dove in a nest of vultures was more out of place. And yet she had a certain influence. The children loved her ; even the wildest of the young brood of law-breakers grew fond of the girl. The women modelled their homespuns after her dress. Soon she too had to wear homespun, for the cold made her own white robe unsuitable even before the briers had torn it. Thus habited like the others, and as much a prisoner as if in chains, Mary had to conform to the laws and rules of the band, who within themselves formed a little community. They had their pleasures and their pains. Women bore children, men fought, the young grew ; and so this small world into which she had been transplanted seemed likely to remain her home for life. One

month passed—two—and now in the third coming with
the promise of an early spring, Ike was growing weary
of the long waiting and wooing.

"Fool!" Betsey had said to him. "Don't yer know
these gals brought up whar time ain't nuthin', hes allus
ter be waited on, an' waited on. Take her like a man!
Women allus likes a master! An' though she's so soft
spoken she ain't no different from any o' our own
gals."

Ike pondered on these words and had half resolved to
act on them, when an event occurred that disturbed the
comfort of the moonshiners, and for a time forced them
from their accustomed haunts. A new marshal had been
appointed for this district of the State, and full of the
importance of fresh duties, resolved that he would scour
the mountains and find the stills that were so boldly de-
fying law and defrauding the Government. There is a
free masonry among these lawless bands that makes them
willing to warn even an enemy of danger when that
danger comes in the shape of enforced law. The little
colony in which Betsey Scanlon was a principal figure,
was yet in the enjoyment of luxuries procured with
money from the sale of their liquor, when one night a
boy arrived in camp. How he came or who sent him
was not inquired, at least not within the hearing of Mary.
All were gathered in Betsey's cabin around the open fire
of pine logs, whose flames, brilliant with pitch, lit up the
whole room, even the corner where Mary was seated.
At her feet lay Ike, as fine a model of vigorous manhood
as the country could produce. But the handsome, dark
face had lost some of its fire, and the black eyes fixed on
the girl were sad almost to tears. How strange that she,
so very gentle that a wounded bird made her weep, tender of everything, should be so hard to him! Would
she ever love him? Must he take her as Betsey advised,
and would her heart follow his command? He was worn

15*

out with this waiting, wearied by her constant "No,"—
shamed, too, by the half contemptuous laughter of the
woman who dared show what the men concealed. He
had nearly reached the limit of self-restraint. Despite
the power of love, tenderness was yielding to passion in
the dark face turned toward Mary. She was praying
within her heart—praying for strength, for light to see
God's will. She knew what was in store for her. There
were no concealments, no delicacy in the people around
her. As in a mining camp, morals were not high, and
children discussed what would shame many a man to
mention. From one extreme to the other, from sheltered
cottage to rough camp, the girl yet preserved the gentle
innocence of her nature. Even the knowledge that had
been thrown on her ignorance had not sullied the whiteness of her soul. Dennis had rightly named her, "a lily
sprung from mud," and here amid the loose manners and
looser morals of this mountain camp the lily kept its
snow. The man at her feet had sworn within himself
that willingly or unwillingly, Mary should be his by
every right recognized, both among the moonshiners and
the outside world. First here, according to their wild
ceremonial, she should be joined to him, and afterward
he would take her to a town, where for her own sake she
would be willing to have their marriage legalized by the
laws of the State. Still lying at her feet he was thinking
over his plans. He had not spoken a word, but his eyes
full of passion and determination had never left Mary's
face; she felt their influence, and trembled as she saw
the expression of the man who was literally her master.
Suddenly the door was pushed open and a boy rushing
in breathless and exhausted, shouted :

"Look out, look out, there are lights among the
mountains."

In an instant every man, woman and child was in
motion, and while the men with Betsey hurried out to

the stills to conceal, as far as possible, all traces of their
work, the women, equally busy, put out of sight every
suspicious object within the cabins. Ike had gone with
the men, not, however, before whispering to Mary, in
more authoritative tone than he had ever used to her :
" Don't yer go out o' the cabin. An' if strange men
come roun', keep hid ! D'ye hear ?"

She made no answer, and he did not wait for one, but
he turned at the door either for a last look or to be assured that she had not stirred. When the men went out
the children were sent to hide among the rocks with orders to be on the alert to give warning of the approach
of the officers of the law.

After seeing that Betsey's contraband goods were well
concealed, the women, not noticing Mary, went out of
the cabin. For the first time since her arrival in the
mountains, she was alone, and as even a dove will spread
its wings and fly, should the cage be left unbarred, so
this gentle, timid girl stole forth in the dark of night,
and afoot on the trackless mountains, started to regain
home and friends. They seemed nearer to her now than
during those weeks of captivity. When with Ike or Betsey, she had not dared to dream of the possibility of escape. Her mountain life had hardened her to exposure,
had accustomed her to walking, and while she knew that
among the rocks foxes, even bears, were found, she had
no fear. In her heart she carried the magic of love and
faith. Belief in God was a practical reality to Mary,
whose readings in the Bible had made her feel the surety
of visible help as an answer to fervent prayer. And only
to her own lack of fervor had she ascribed the long-
delayed answer to her prayer for deliverance. But now
she felt that a path had been made for her, and with exulting feet she walked, as if on air. Climbing over
rocks, tearing her hands with brush and brier, she lost
not one iota of her belief in this miraculous deliverance,

nor had she any doubt that the stars looking down upon her were showing her the way out of these mountain fastnesses. So sure was she of this, that she took for guide a line of stars spanning the arch above her head, and looking down only when some more difficult places required care to pass, kept her eyes fixed on these heavenly lights which were to lead her home.

The morning broke bright and clear. It found Mary tired, but still afoot. Puzzled now, with no starry ray as guide, she looked about her for a road broader and less dangerous. The little cabins of the moonshiners were far out of sight, and though the rocks and trees that surroundered her were similar to those among which she had passed the days of captivity. there were here no children to point out the easiest places, no Ike to lift her over the rougher ones. Cold, hungry and alone as she was, a stronger woman might well have been dismayed. But Mary, though now without the guidance of the stars, held to her faith in God's special providence. Even if it meant death, she was delivered. For she dreaded more than death the being recaptured and taken back to Ike's arms. Brighter grew the day, the sun gilding the brown rocks and brightening the dark spires of the pines that filled the air with fragrance. She broke off some of the smaller branches and tried to keep her mouth moist by biting the tiny spikes. Still bravely afoot she struggled on, growing unutterably weary. Perhaps if she rested now, the stars would come out by and by, and once more show her the way. Perhaps it was God's will that she should rest, for surely she feared she had not strength to go much further. So she stood for an instant praying, and then crept between some rocks, that jutting out, formed a kind of shelter. Exhausted, she soon fell asleep, still peaceful and happy in her faith that escape was certain.

CHAPTER XLIII.

IKE'S LOVE.

THE moonshiners had completed their arrangements for the reception of the marshal and his men. Some of the gang were stationed behind bushes and rocks, some were smoking before the fires in their own cabins. The children acted as scouts and each little brain was filled with excitement, each little heart longing to join in the possible mèlee. In all the confusion Ike thought of Mary. As the night was passing and no enemy had arrived, he left his post to seek her. He strode over to Betsey's cabin, which, since her arrival, Mary had shared with the older woman, and where he had ordered her to remain. He trembled as he opened the door, for he truly loved the girl and did not mean to be cruel. Beyond pleading that some word of her safety might be sent to her father and Janet, Mary had not spoken of her friends. Dennis, while constantly in her mind, was never mentioned, and thus Ike, not knowing of her love for this hero of her dreams, could not understand her persistent refusal of his affection.

After he had pushed the door open, he stood thinking and hesitating. His talks with Mary, her lessons of self-restraint, and maxims of religion, though weak in comparison with his life's lessons, yet had taken root in a heart naturally good. With an impatient gesture he brushed aside those last whisperings of a better self, and walked into the cabin.

It was forsaken. There was no sign of Mary, nor of any living creature.

She had disobeyed his order! A heavy frown, an

angry flush darkened his face, and Ike Huron became a savage—a savage so lost to humanity, so thoroughly brute that he was ready to kill the thing he loved. He walked to the nearer cabins, Mary was in none of them ; and the women all declared that she had been left in her own cabin asleep.

"She had escaped !" Ike muttered it to himself as he climbed the rocks, shading his face from the rising sun and with his practiced eyes seeking some moving object. Nothing was to be seen save the lights and shades of dawning day ; wonderful, beautiful effects for artist or lover of nature, but to this man with breast filled with rage, there was no loveliness on earth.

He cursed himself and his folly, and then quiet externally, controlling all but the heavy frown that marred the beauty of his face, he went back to Betsey. His post was with her at the most dangerous point, and both were pledged to die rather than to let the still be approached.

"She's gone." Ike spoke so indifferently that for a moment Betsey hardly understood what he meant. She was busy examining her pistols. "Who's gone ?" she said.

"Mary !"

"Ike !" Betsey's voice rose almost to a scream. "She'll peach !"

"No, she won't, for I'll kill her." The words were spoken under his breath, and the swarthy face changed to a ghastly yellow. "I've sent the boys to track her. They'll find the way she went, and then will come my time."

The day wore on. No marshal had arrived, and the men from the more distant posts came in to breakfast and joked about the scare. After a while it leaked out that "Mary had run away," and faces looked darkly at Ike. But no face was as dark as his own, no threats—and there were many—were so deep, so cruel, as his

who loved the one they believed a traitor. The breakfast was eaten while some of the men remained on guard
at the door of Betsey's cabin, which being the largest,
served for many uses. Though they believed that they
had been alarmed without sufficient cause, they still kept
watch, for it was the boast of this band that they had
never been caught napping. They had never had a
traitor either, until—and then in whispers they discussed
the probability of Mary's being found. While the women
were yet clearing away the remnants of the meal, and
the men formed groups near the cabin door, two bare-
footed lads ran up to Ike and spoke to him in low
hurried whispers. He had been standing alone, looking
moodily away to the distant mountain tops. A handsome
fellow, he looked picturesque enough for a model brig-
and, in his slouched hat and short coat fitting tightly
over broad shoulders and full chest. As he bent forward
in listening to the boys his hand involuntarily touched a
pistol in his belt. Even while the boys were speaking,
he started, looked the way they pointed, and then took a
forward stride. "I'll be back soon," he said to Betsey,
who, as the only one that dared to speak to him in this
wild mood, came up to him.

"Ike, 'spose yer caught?" she said, holding his sleeve
and detaining him. To this man alone did Betsey ever
show tenderness. A little lad, she had brought him with
her to the mountains, when, driven perhaps by some
crime, perhaps injustice, she had joined the moonshiners.
Then there had been no questions asked of their re-
lationship, and soon Betsey's daring ability and strength
had made her a leader in the band, and now no one
dared question her. She had been called "Mother Betsey," and he, "Ike Huron"; and that was all. Now
her face was working a little, and there was a tone of
pleading in the rough voice. As thus they stood close
together there was a certain resemblance between them,

but where the woman's face was coarse and homely, the man's was handsome. And his features were not without a certain air, that, under different circumstances, would have been called distinguished. "Don't go, Ike. I don't believe it was a false alarm. I believe the marshal'll be here soon. It they dare, let 'em come. But down thar 'lone, they'd kill yer, Ike. They'd kill yer fer I know yer. Yer'd never let 'em pass. The gal's not wuth the trouble o' findin'. I was a cussed fool to bring her ter darken yer days. But let her go; yer young an' handsome an' many a heart'll ache fer yer yet.

He had tried to pull himself away from her, but she had held his arm; and now having followed him to where a rock stood out and hid them from the eyes of the others, she clung to him with all her strength.

"Betsey, Mother Betsey." Ike's lips were trembling, and the great black eyes were softening at this tenderness from the rough woman to whom cursing was more natural than pleading. "I'd—I'd"—a gasp, almost a sob broke from him as he rushed away. He stopped, returned, caught Betsey in his arms, and for the first, the last time in his memory, tenderly kissed her. Then off he bounded, leaping down the mountain with the agility and strength of a practiced climber.

Betsey stood where he had left her. Her cheek was wetted with his tears, on her face still burned his kiss. Her eyes, too, were full of a softness no one had ever seen there, and her heart torn with the wild love, the fierce anxiety of a tigress for its young. She wanted to follow him, to help him, to die for him if need be; but she dared not desert her post. Who among those men would so well defend the pass to the still? "Curse that milk-faced girl!" she muttered. She watched the ravine where once more she had a view of that strong, bounding figure, and then with pride in his grace and beauty, exultation even in his fierceness, she brushed away the tears he had left on her cheek and walked back to her place seemingly the same good natured high tempered woman who had never loved anything so well as the whiskey still for which she was prepared to die.

The lads sent out by Ike had easily tracked Mary. A footprint on a bit of earth which, sheltered by a rock was dark and moist, a shred of homespun, were quite enough for these young terriers of the mountains. Following the stars on which her faith relied, Mary had gone over a mountain crest into another ravine, and though she had walked long and had been much fatigued she had travelled but a short distance from the moonshiners' camp. A half hour sufficed to bring Ike to the rocky nook wherein lay the girl who had softened his heart, and now fired his passion to madness. How fair she was! With a smile parting her lips she looked innocent as a new-born infant. He would kill her—upon that he had determined ; and yet even now as her sweet breath came softly upon his face, bending over hers, and he saw her bosom rise and fall in gentlest pulsation, he loved her! Sleep could not long withstand the fiery glance of those dark eyes. Mary stirred, wakened, and without a word opened full her eyes and looked into his. There was a deadly purpose in his face, a pistol in his hand. She had not for three months lived among these mountaineers without knowing something of their swift vengeance. She felt that her hour was come, and though cast in Nature's gentlest mould, the girl was no coward. " Mary, I am goin' ter kill yer!" Ike's voice was cold and harsh. In the dark eyes there lingered not one trace of the passionate longing with which he had gazed on the sleeping girl. "I loved yer, gal, I'd made yer as true a husband as any woman could hev. For yer sake, I'd hev left this lawless life an' settled somewhar that ye need not spend yer days in hiding an' yer nights trudging the mountains. But he war a traitor ; ye

runned away like a sneak in the minit o' danger; an'
whar I love I hates!"

She did not plead, nor shed a tear. Had she not seen
when once vengeance was vowed how useless were
words? Nor did she wish to live if life meant to be
false to father, friends—Dennis! The thought of him
she loved came unbidden. He would return to the cottage, would seek her; would he know how she had
loved him? Thinking these thoughts there came to her
face a dreamy beauty such as Ike had never seen there.
He believed that *he* had brought this fresh loveliness, and
throwing down the pistol caught to his breast the kneeling girl, for Mary's only answer when he had told her
she must die had been to kneel for prayer. But near as
was her pure life to the angel's, she had a woman's heart,
and that heart had flown to her beloved.

Clasped in Ike's strong arms, she trembled, blushed:
"No, no," she murmured, "not yours, never yours. I
cannot be." He sprang to his feet all softness lost in the
wildest fury of jealousy. For whom, then, had Mary's
face worn that love look? Who had won this girl he
craved? Surely there could be no satisfaction in knowing, since it was not he. Yet Ike, trembling in the throes
of the most fiendish passion, swore within his soul, not
only would he *know* the man she loved, but that that man
should not tread the earth! Death for both of them!
Death! It was nearer to him than he thought, for while
he drew from his belt the other revolver, a shot was
heard. Down the ravine on the path Ike had come two
men were running, followed in hot pursuit by five moonshiners. Five to one—great odds when the majority
were on their own grounds. The officers of the law
were making some show of resistance, firing as they fled
from behind every rock or bush that afforded temporary
shelter. "They've killed Betsey!" shouted one of the
moonshiners, recognizing Ike, who pushing Mary behind

him stood out in bold relief on the ledge of rock. With his private vengeance he would brook no interference, nor to it should there be witnesses. Seeing his own party conquerors, he had not intended to interfere ; but Betsey's death! that roused to madness the already half-crazed man.

"Killed Betsey! Curse yer!" He aimed and fired. One man fell on the rocks dead. The other turned, and seeing a foe in the rear and knowing that his own death was sure to follow upon his companion's fired instantly. The shot pierced Ike's side and the blood spurted on Mary.

"Oh, Ike! Ike! I am sorry." Mary was shaking with terror. Seeing Ike stagger she put her arms around him to steady him. He had his death wound, he felt it, and yet he smiled at the first voluntary embrace of this girl he loved. He drew a long breath, then fired again aiming at the man who had killed him. He saw him roll over a projecting rock, saw the moonshiners spring down the rocks and bend over the body, heard them shout, "Hurrah for Ike!" and then fell heavily backward. With her arms about him Mary fell with him. He turned his face to hers. All violence had left it, only love remained. "Kiss me," he said. She drew her arm from under him, raised his head on her breast and kissed his cheek.

"No! On the mouth." His voice was failing, his breath coming in short gasps. Again she kissed him, as a sister might a dying brother. His eyes were glazing fast, but still he looked at her, smiled on her. His lips moved, she bent her head to hear. "When—I—am dead, run ! Keep—to—the—right—across—the second—ravine. I love—"

His teeth were clinched, a little blood came to his lips, he shuddered, then stiffened ;—and Mary held the dead body of one who with half a chance would have been a strong and noble man.

"Ike! Ike!"   The mountains rang with his name.
Standing above the ravine down which the moonshiners
had leaped to assure themselves of the death of the
officer, they had not seen Ike fall, did not know he was
wounded.   But as he did not join them they began to
suspect some injury to him.   "Ike! Ike!"   The voices
were coming nearer.   There was no time to lose.   If she
should be found by these men there would be for her
only instant death.   Trembling less with fear than with
agitation at the scene through which she had just passed,
Mary looked for an instant on the peaceful face of him
whose living love had been her terror.

"God bless and forgive him," she murmured.   She
touched her lips to his brow in eternal farewell, and then
frightened by the steps which she already heard bounding along the rocks, she climbed to the other side of
the great stones that had sheltered her, and crouching
down was hidden before the moonshiners came up.
There was an exclamation of horror as they saw Ike's
body ; then silence, and then a few moment's parley-
ing.

"Dead !"

"An' Betsey, too !"

"Quar, warn't it ?   Both on em' dead the same
day."

"An' both died game !   Plucky devil Ike was.   The
fust feller's bullet must ha' struck him, but he never
died till he'd got two lives fer his'n."

"Wuth it, too !"

Then silence again.   And then the voice of one of the
older men.

"Wal, we'd better part.   One o' the men 'scaped
from Betsey.   Good ole gal, she tried ter kill him.   Ef
only we'd been on guard, faithful as her, she'd been alive
an' kickin' now.   Thar's nuthin, but fer us to look out
fer oursels till this has blowed over.   Pick up Ike, we'll

put him in the same hole with the ole woman, for I allus b'lieved they was mother an' son."

Mary heard their voices, caught most of their words. She listened, as with more regular tread they moved off with Ike's body; aud then giving them time to be well out of sight, she clambered down the rocks into a ravine, then up again on another ridge. There right before her lay a quiet and peaceful country. There was not a house in sight. She had no idea where she was, but with the beautiful faith of innocence believed that God would lead her. Still keeping to the right she soon reached a road. It was broad and shaded, and seemed well travelled. Without hesitation she turned into it, keeping still to the right. She had gone some distance and the day was advancing to evening. Tired and faint for want of food she walked on. Down the road some one was coming toward her—a man on horseback. Who was it? Could it be Dennis seeking her? It seemed most natural to this girl whose world numbered less than twenty persons that the man she loved had come to search for her. He had said he would return. Was this he? Inspired with fresh strength by this hope she ran forward. Ah! he had stopped! It could not be Denuis. He would hasten to her! More slowly now with eyes cast down, she walked toward the waiting horseman. In silent wonder he gazed at the girl, who with her short coarse dress, strong boots like a boy's, and hair woven in one long braid, looked more child than woman. What a marvellous resemblance to Mary! In every thing, but motion, this child might have been Mary's self. But the motion differed; for this girl moved with light, springing steps, and Mary's swaying walk had seemed a tender request for aid, for protection.

Nearer and nearer! The likeness grew yet stronger, and Dennis's heart unstilled by reason, throbbed to suffocation.

" Mary !"

Involuntarily he spoke the name always in his thoughts. The child stopped. Her eyes radiant with joy were raised to his. There was no doubt in his heart now—only love, perfect love.

" Dennis !" she cried, and sprang to his faithful breast.

CHAPTER XLIV.

" GUARD HER WEEL."

MARY found herself in a warm room, bright with flowers and sunlight, and Dennis at her side was calling her by every endearing name known to lovers.

"Dennis did you seek me long?" Mary asked, as her lover kissed her hands, and gazed on her with eyes that had taken back their youth and fire in the joy of her return.

"Long ! Love, we can't measure time by days or weeks. While I was searching for you, despair in my heart, and life endurable only because I believed you lived, centuries seemed passing. And yet now, holding you close to me, it seems only a night, a black, terrible night, since the moment when at your gate you fluttered your wings, my dove, to fly to the heart that worshipped you."

What more he would have said Mary must divine, for the door opened and Miss Dawson, Dr. Colton and Janet, entered.

" My bairn, ye are foun', I knew ye wad be, I felt it in my ain bones, that ye was alive somewhere. Ah, wad ye ever fin' a lover sae true, sae constant as this one-

armed mon who stole yer heart wi' his first words? I
hae changed my mind, Mary, he is bonny an' braw, and
I am weel content ye shall marry him."

Janet was on her knees by Mary's couch and in her
anxiety that Mary should have no chance to ask for her
father, would then and there have had her marry Dennis.

"He's rich an' powerfu' an' sae, sae true. Tak' him
noo, my bairn, my ain sweet bairn, an' then Janet can
die in peace, knowing there is a strong mon to guard ye.
An' strong he is, though they do say there's a bullet in
his side, an', more's the shame, he has lost his bonny
arm."

But while Mary, perhaps more than Janet, appreciated
all Dennis's attractions, yet Mary's nature was as constant as her lover's and she could never forget, never
cease to love, her father. Whatever his sin, he was her
father, and the sin was committed for her maintenance.
She smiled her welcome to Dr. Colton, returned Miss
Dawson's tender embrace, kissed Janet lovingly and then
while Dennis still held her hand asked :

"Where is father?"

It was a question each had dreaded. Dennis from the
moment that holding her in his arms, had mounted his
horse and flown rather than ridden back to the quarters
prepared for him, feared the wakening when Mary would
ask for her father. What should they say to her? How
answer her questions? Dr. Colton, wise on all but his
hobby, the new house, delivered his opinion to Miss
Dawson and Janet as they drove along the road indicated
by the messenger.

"Well, Janet, now that Mary is found, there is no use
in worrying over her father. For my part I don't believe he is her father. How such as he could have off-
spring like Mary is incomprehensible! Mary woman
like, feels obliged to love him. But," and here the doctor became embarrassed and less reasonable, "since Janet

affirms she loved Dennis from the moment she saw him, it is possible he will be able to convince her that it would be better to forget the parent, whom it would dishonor a man to call father."

"Loo'ed him! I wad ye could hae seen my Mary's eyes fu' o' tears at partin' wi' Dennis! Fule that I was. I tried to shame her out o' it. But the innocent is near God, an' sees better into men's hearts. She, puir bairn, saw that Dennis was true, an' loo'ed her weel." Janet delivered her views with the assurance of an oracle, utterly ignoring the fact that the same "puir bairn" loved and trusted her unworthy father.

"Pshaw!" said the doctor impatiently. It is not exactly an agreeable position for a lover, however old, to listen to the praises of a rival. And the doctor still clung to the idea of his being Mary's lover. But though Janet had always offended his fastidious taste, and it was impossible for him to understand Miss Dawson's indulgence to the outspoken Scotchwoman, to his credit be it known, that, annoyed as he was by the bobbing in and out of the carriage window of Janet's head, until her bonnet was awry and her smooth hair rumpled, he sympathized with her sentiment and managed to smile at the plain face of its unattractive exponent.

"Janet," said the doctor, "we rely on you to prevent Mary from too soon asking for her father." So Janet had hurried in, pressing Dennis's suit with even greater haste than the lover himself. He, contented with having Mary safe and well, would have waited and not wearied her by too hurried wooing. But now that she had asked that dreaded question, "Where is father?" each looked at the other. Dennis was left to reply.

"Mary, my darling, your father is well. Will not that content you until you grow stronger? You are exhausted, have passed through painful experiences; rest

now, or you may be ill, and then what will I do who
have lost so much of your sweet company ?"

Dr. Colton had turned nervously away at Mary's
question, dreading the result the answer might bring.
For if, as they all supposed, the knowledge of her
father's occupation had driven her from her home, what
would she do when she learned that not only did he per-
severe in his calling but that the cruelties of the convict
system were attracting the commiseration of the whole
country ? At Dennis's answer the old gentleman smiled
with pleasure. " The young scamp," he said to himself.
"He knows everything, from a facade to a woman's
heart. He deserves Mary. I yield all claim upon her."
These were sentiments none the less magnanimous because he had no claims. For the doctor had been so long
fed on the thought of his own power and importance
that he could not imagine himself to be an object of indifference to the one woman he had fully decided to
marry. Not even Dennis's ardent search and faithful
labor had won from the doctor a full resignation of his
fancied prior claim upon the lady. Even the new house
had been built with a view to its probable fair mistress.
Only after he had been convinced of her death had he
concentrated his feelings on the house itself. But now
Dennis's apt answer, low spoken though it was, had
charmed the doctor, and he voluntarily stepped back in
the race for Mary's hand. The fair hand was resting in
that of Dennis, and Mary's tender, truthful eyes were
striving to read his face.

"It could not injure me, Dennis, to see my father."

It is a hard matter to argue convenience with a soul
whose understanding stoops to nothing lower than great
principles and maxims. And thus, in the presence of
this child-woman, this pure, untarnished nature, these
men and women, so much wiser in the world's ways,
were nonplussed.

16

"Dennis, why don't you answer? Have I said wrong?"

"Mary, you cannot do wrong," was Dennis's prompt reply.

Mary, who smiled at this wise answer of Dennis's, was not to be changed from her purpose, Her eyes, fixed on his face, grew tearful with wistfulness, and he could not deny her silent pleading.

"Ah, Mary," he caught her hands and kissed them boldly. "I will do just what you desire!" Which answer so disgusted Dr. Colton that he walked impatiently to the window. It was high time some one interfered between this stupid man and his madness, thought the doctor, losing all faith in Dennis's wisdom and quite forgetting that in Dennis's condition the wisest Solon plays the fool. Mary was still smiling her pleasure when common sense in the person of Dr. Colton roused the lovers from their paradise.

"Miss Mary,"—the doctor was more elegant and precise than usual. In fact he could not enjoy this love-making in which he had no part, and with which Miss Dawson smiled in sympathy. "Miss Mary, if you remember, once before I was summoned by your father and intrusted with the care of you. Therefore allow me to represent your father." The doctor stopped suddenly. He had rather overstepped his intended remonstrance by thus admiting the fact of their differing ages. He looked a little blank, coughed, and then went bravely on. "As a father, as well as a physician, I forbid any more conversation. You have now overtaxed yourself. Deeply as I regret to interpose my command between Mr. Day and his very evident pleasure," here there was just a shade of stiffness, "I command absolute rest. I have lately seen your father and give you my assurance of his good health. And since Mr. Day has promised to do as you desire, you can see your father as soon as you wish after I have pronounced you able to be moved."

There is no disputing a doctor's authority. Dennis took a second place, and looked meekly enough for permission to speak. Mary's life or health in danger! That thought made a coward of him. He who had thought the doctor childish enough over facades was ready to do his lightest bidding.

This *coup d'etat* of the doctor enabled Mary's friends to form some plan for communication with Captain Hilton. A letter was dispatched by special messenger to the convict camp. It was returned with a line :

" I have seen the signature and refuse to read or receive any further correspondence.
To F. C. Colton, M. D.   " HENRY HILTON."

A consultation was held outside of Mary's room. What was to be done? With his usual impetuosity Dennis proposed to beard the lion in his den.

" Nay, nay! Ye mauna do that. He'd think nae mair o' killin' ye than ef ye was a dog, an' tho' the law might mak' him suffer fer killin' a rich mon, where's the law as could soothe Mary's heart?" Janet's reasons carried weight with them, as she, better than any one else, knew the man whom for eighteen years she had served.

" What do you advise, Janet?" The doctor himself asked the question.

"It's easier asked nor answered." Janet shook her head and then reluctantly, as if she were saying what she did not wish to say, added : " There's naething fer it but the bairn hersel' to catch him unawares. Ye maun prepare her mind fer the ruin o' her hame, an' tak' her there. Keep guard, keep guard." Janet had caught Dennis's arm and trembled with eagerness. " He's mair beast nor mon, an' wad e'en kill the lamb hersel', ef the fit was on

him. I hae met him at the cottage many times when I
ganged there, too sair at heart to stay away. I didna
speak to him. Wi' his glowerin' looks he didna tempt
speech. I doubt if he saw me, sae deep was he in gloomy
thought. But had he been anither, my heart wad ha'
ached fer him, sitting on the floor by Mary's window,
groanin' as if in pain. I think, an' ye guard her weel,"
again she caught Dennis's sleeve, emphasizing her words,
" she might wi' her tender voice waken the human i' his
breast."

So Dennis was left to tell Mary of the desecration of
her home, and soften as best he could the cruel facts of
her fathers conduct   How he told any part and did not
break her heart was a mystery to the doctor aud Janet.
Miss Dawson perhaps divined the power of a lover's tenderness, the endurance it might give. Nothing was
ever mentioned of what passed when Miss Dawson
closed the door upon the faithful daughter and her be-
trothed. Mary herself opened it to her friends. With
Dennis's arm about her, and very pale, she returned the
silent pressure of their hands ; felt and thus answered
their sympathy.

Shortly after, Janet, dispatched to Milton, came back
in all the pride " o' silken gounds " for her bairn, and
the little cottage was the scene of the first happy days
following Mary's return.

CHAPTER XLV.

" ONCE I SPARED YOU."

WHEN Doctor Colton pronounced Mary sufficiently strong, Miss Dawson and Janet rode back
to the city, whither the doctor had preceded
them, and where Mary and Dennis were to join them after
the interview with Captain Hilton. As it was impossible
to know what hour Captain Hilton would visit the cottage, Dennis, who was in some haste to have every legal
right to protect Mary, had proposed that they should
spend the day in the grove of trees near the cottage.
The carriage was stocked with every appliance of comfort, and they were to enjoy their first day alone.

O, men and women, whose life has fallen into the
commonplace, have you forgotten the delights of the
first day alone with the one you most loved? The
beauty of every shrub, the wonder in every stone!
Although the month was January, it was spring in Georgia. The lovers wandered under the trees, Mary listening
to reminiscences of Dennis's youth and occasionally
telling some of her own dreams. It had seemed a brief
waiting, when along the road at rapid pace came a horseman.

"Father!" and Mary grew pale. How often she had
watched for her father!—but never as now with nervous
terror struggling against love. Dennis did not know
that her father had driven her out into the storm, nor
that from her father's eyes murder looked on his child.
That interview was covered by the charity of his daughter's devotion; hidden even from herself by flowers of
tenderness, pity and prayer. But while he did not
imagine to what depths the fierce, unrestrained nature of

Hilton had fallen, Janet's warning, Janet's terror, were in Dennis's mind.

"Let me see him first, Mary!" Dennis plead. But Mary shook her head. She knew that she alone could touch her father's heart. As the horse stopped before the broken fence where once had hung the little gate, she started with horror. Could that haggard, desperate-looking man be her father? "He has suffered," she whispered, her breast filled with tender pity at this wreck of what she had so loved and honored.

Looking neither to the right nor left, Hilton threw himself from the horse, strode up the rough pathway and passed into the house.

"I will go to him," said Mary.

"I will go with you, Mary,"—and together they crossed the soft earth, entering the house a few moments after Hilton.

Mary was too much agitated to fully appreciate the ruin of what had been so dear. Yet she shuddered, when even her light step echoed through the empty house. She walked quickly to the door of her bed-room, whence in low moans came her father's voice. At the threshold she stopped, where once before he had paused to look on her. Then she was praying for him. And now for him, too, were the blinding tears that made his face indistinct to her vision.

He was standing by the window leaning against the broken sash. His eyes were fixed on something he held in his hand. Mary sobbed aloud when she saw it. Her little Bible. He had given it to her and had written in it, "To my dearest child, from father." He did love her, she had always known it. And now, he would welcome her back to his heart! Without speaking, with hardly a sound but the soft rustling of the dress, which she had chosen as most resembling those she used to wear, she moved to his side, fell on her knees, and clasping his waist with her arms, sobbed : "Dear father, I've come back to you."

Very slowly, like a man in a dream, he turned his eyes from the book to her. And then—as if some snake had stung him—he tore away those tender arms, threw her violently from him and fairly foamed in fury.

"You've come back ! Accursed viper that cast aside your father's love ! Once I spared your life, but now—"

Dennis had not an instant to lose. Just in time he dashed aside those fierce hands that caught at Mary's throat. Surprised to see this man who stood between him and his daughter, Hilton drew back. He passed his hand over his head as if he had been sleeping, and suddenly wakened had not quite collected his thoughts.

"I know that face," he said, as pale, resolute, not wishing to injure Hilton, but most determined to protect Mary, Dennis kept his eyes upon her father. It would have been an unequal battle between a one-armed man, who would not use a revolver, and that Hercules who in loss of flesh retained his hardened muscles. Mary, agonized, saw but one result—her lover dead by her father's hands.

But, muttering to himself, Hilton had lost desire to attack anything. He looked at the pair, as having risen and standing at his side, Dennis put his arm around Mary, Hilton's look changed to a sneer. He laughed—a bitter, hard laugh.

"Fool; fool," he said. "Fool, to trust a woman. Vipers all of them !" He threw out his hand, pushed them aside, rushed from the house, and mounting his horse rode furiously away.

"Darling ! Marry me to-morrow," Dennis said impetuously to the weeping girl beside him. And thus out of the ruins of her old life sprang a newer and more beautiful one.

Though blessed by a true marriage, Mary could not

forget her father. She could not go far from him even
when Dennis wished to take his wife to Vermont, desired
her to see the possessions which had for the first time
begun to awaken pride. He meant that the Hunt family
should see the grace and beauty of his Southern bride.
He wanted her to see his friends. But Mary's whispered :
" Not just yet ! So far from my father," settled the
matter, and he wrote to his lawyer, indefinitely postpon-
ing the visit which had been desired.

Dennis bought a charming place adjoining the grand
new house of Dr. Colton, into which he and Miss Dawson had moved shortly before the day when the cathedral
was decorated for the wedding of Mary Hilton. Dennis
would have the marriage as beautiful as music and flowers could make it. " My wife is my queen and shall be
so honored," he said. And fit for a coronation were the
magnificent adornments of the old church. The music,
the glorious music ! It filled Mary's heart, half with joy,
half with tears.

" A very small wedding party for so much preparation," thought the old priest, whose princely fee had
surprised him when on the previous day Dennis had sent
to him a note requesting that all arrangements should
be as imposing as possible. He opened his eyes in greater
surprise when he saw that besides the bridegroom and
the beautiful bride, there were only his two old friends,
Miss Dawson and Dr. Colton, and a woman who was
evidently some sort of domestic. Still it was no affair
of his, or of the organist's, whose friends peeping behind
the choir curtains, discussed the eccentricities of the rich
Northerner. For now Dennis was known to be wealthy,
the name of " carpet-bagger " was no longer given to
him. And yet the rich do not build up a state. The
poor men, those whose necessities educate and force
ability, are the sinews of a country. Those very men
whom the South call carpet-baggers, and the West

settlers, are a thousandfold more valuable citizens than the millionaire who generally spends a greater part of his wealth outside of the state and city that claims his residence. But true as this is, it is the rich citizen who is most esteemed ; thus the organist's friends commenting in whispers upon the eccentricity of the rich Northerner, forgot that he belonged to the despised class of carpet-baggers, and envied the bride her husband.

CHAPTER XLVI.

A FALSE ALARM.

DENNIS and Mary though married six months were still lovers. They were reading a letter now, a letter held in Mary's hands while Dennis's arm was round her waist. Thus ran the letter :

"Dear Mr. Day, and Mrs. Day too, how we all does want to see you. Nat has set up the garden jist beautiful, an mother's got another baby she's goin' to name Mary Dennis fer you. I has tried to write good, but I'm most afeard to send this, only if I don't, how will you know we all loves you, an' thinks of you, an' prays fer you every night. All of us, mother, father, all the chillern, an' your lovin'   "MEG BROWN.

"Nat sez I'm to tell you I'm orful handy roun' the flowers an' he does want orful to see Mr. Dennis an' Miss Mary, an' he hopes to see them oncet before his eyes shut up, but he do begin to feel old an' feeble."

Through open windows were coming sunshine and the fresh breeze laden with perfume. In vain by coughs,

16*

arranging the already perfectly arranged table and doing a great deal of unnecessary dusting, Janet strove to arouse the " bairns " as she called Mary and her husband.

" Love's a nice thing," she muttered, " nae doubt. But it's better after breakfas'."

Acting on this belief, and seeing Mary's hands with the letter drop on her lap, Janet ventured to disturb the group of husband and wife, more full of regard for the omelette than the graceful and tender picture made by the "bairns." " Weel, weel! an ye'll eat a little ye'll hae mair strength afterward."

Dennis rose, bringing Mary with him, and proceeded to relieve Janet's anxiety about their strength. It was only a "sham meal after a'," Janet said to herself, and with a shake of her head she watched the pair pass out of the low windows and stroll up and down the lawn under the trees. The Scotchwoman was still in the breakfast room trying to find occupation for her busy hands, when Mary, leaving Dennis, walked quickly to the house with light steps, which were her legacy from the months spent in the mountains.

" Janet, dear." She spoke in the same coaxing manner always used to her old nurse. " We are going to Vermont for a short visit. Would you like to go?

" Wad I like? Mary, I wad never mair lose sight o' ye. Nay, nay, 'til death, Janet Wilson is never again to leave the place where her bairn is."

So it was settled. Miss Dawson was persuaded to accompany them, and Dr. Colton decided to join the party. They reached Vermont as the old State was in all the glory of summer foliage. The picturesque scenery and flourishing towns delighted the doctor and his cousin who holding to their prejudice against Yankees, had never visited New England. Mary, in silent wonder, felt the magnitude of the great world of which she had only seen a little corner. At Newton they found the Hunts

waiting for them in full force. The mill operatives were
given a holiday and made a procession, the Browns were
drawn up in line before the old mansion, even to the
new baby ; and the beautiful grounds around the old
farmhouse blazed with bonfires.

" Why, Dennis, you're a king in your own land," the
doctor said, delighted equally by the riches of the man
and his modesty in never alluding more than casually to
his possessions.

Nat presented a huge boquet to " Mr. Dennis's wife,"
and the pretty cousin whispered to Miranda, "Why,
Mirey, she's not a bit common-looking nor sallow either
and speaks as good grammar as you do."

So, as it may be judged, Mary had made a favorable
impression on the Northern branch of the Hunt family.

" Well, Dennis," Dr. Colton said at breakfast the next
morning, "now I suppose you will leave Georgia and
settle among your own people."

"Leave Georgia ! No doctor. If when I was poor
and abused, called carpet-bagger and sneered at, I would
not leave, shall I now, because I am rich ? A carpet-
bagger I was, a carpet-bagger I am, just as much now as
then. Riches have not changed the man. I fought because I felt it a duty. I remained in Georgia for the
same cause that nearly cost me my life, and because I
believed that war would prove useless, unless a republican party grew up in the conquered section. One party,
one religion, will make bigots of any people. And a war
freeing any class is worse than useless, unless the newly-
given rights are protected, and the conquered, educated
in the principles of political freedom." Dennis flushed
a little, hesitated, and then more calmly but with great
ernestness added : "I am too obstinate to resign what I
believe a noble work. And I don't think any man has a
right to desert what comes to him as a duty. It seems
to me the first duty of our Government is to insure the

negroes protection in all their rights.   It is the first step
in educating and making them valuable citizens.   We
would draft them in war, then let us protect them in this
so-called peace.   No, indeed, Mr. Colton, so thoroughly
impressed am I with the greatness of this work that
I dedicate my life to it."

Bright days were spent in inspecting the mills and
the home for old people, Seth Hunt's legacy.   The
grounds surrounding the fine building were kept in a
state equal to those of the Hunt house itself.   The vision
of the kindly old faces of the couples who had herein
found a veritable home gave to Mary a pleasure great
and heart-warming.

"A magnificent inheritance," Dr. Colton called it,
when many days had been passed in riding over the possessions of Dennis.   He acknowledged even to himself
that the Yankees after all had a certain aristocracy, and
then felt, without saying it, that Dennis's manly character was a more true token of the noblest aristocracy than
all the wealth inherited from his eccentric uncle.

Well pleased with the stewardship of his uncle's
friend, Dennis left the property still in his hands, and
seeing in Mary's face a desire to be nearer her father,
this man who exulted in the name of carpet-bagger returned to Georgia with his Southern friends.

They found Milton in much the same condition as
when they had left it ; save that already in the sunny
South the trees and grass were losing in softest yellow
their brilliant green.   The negro cause was becoming a
little more prominent.   Some cruel murders had brought
committees of investigation from Congress, and several
fresh pens were taking up the horrors of the convict system, not only existing in Georgia, but also in several
other Southern states.

On their arrival Dennis rode out to Camp Osmerillo.
He was not, however, admitted inside of the grounds,

and after a few moments the card he had sent to Captain Hilton had been returned with some words written thereon in pencil :

" I neither desire nor will I receive any communications from you or any of the family. HILTON."

This had been all the comfort the long ride had brought to Mary.

" For all that," she said to Dennis, " I know he loves me, and I cannot believe that his heart is all hard or cruel. But," and her sweet voice had tears in it, " even if it were, I love him and always will. Is he not my father ?"

Dennis's reply was checked by seeing Miss Dawson coming toward them. She was walking through the opening cut in the hedge dividing the two lawns. Her affection for Mary and Dennis had increased with intimacy, and their mornings together were enjoyed equally by the husband and wife, who felt a filial love for the gentle woman. As usual they went to meet her, but Dennis saw something more than the ordinary greeting in her face.

" The doctor wants you, Dennis," she said, as she kissed Mary's cheek.

The old gentleman was in the habit of sending for the young one on every occasion, taking as much of his time, and feeling quite the same right to do so, as if he were a son instead of the man who had stolen his lady love.

" I'll be back in a moment," Dennis said to Mary, and filled with forebodings he walked quickly to the great house and entered the doctor's sanctum. Dr. Colton was walking up and down helping himself nervously to snuff, which was with him an invariable sign of mental disturbance. It was an anxious face he turned to Dennis.

" My boy, there's something wrong in the convict camp. That fellow Stern has just left my office. He had ridden into town on horseback—and a terrible ride it was, judging from his bespattered condition and the state of his horse.

"What brought him here?" Dennis asked, failing to find in this visit to a doctor's office sufficient cause for the agitation of the old gentleman.

His quiet tone annoyed the doctor. "What brought him here? You would not ask it so calmly if you could have seen the arm I had to set. A compound fracture, sir, one ot the worst my experience had ever met. And brute as the fellow is, I had to admire his pluck, for without a moan he underwent torture."

In his professional admiration, the doctor had almost forgotten his own nervousness until recalled to it by Dennis's words of heartfelt compliment.

"Doctor, your profession is philanthropic as well as scientific. No one could know you and not honor both great principles."

"Thank you, my boy, thank you. When I had set the arm I ordered perfect rest. 'Rest,' said he, 'I'd like to know how a man can rest when he is surrounded by a pack of black devils waiting to murder him.' And then without a thank you, he threw down some money and rushed out. I suspected something and ordered Jake to follow him. He has just returned saying that a company of militia and a police force has been ordered to Camp Osmerillo. They anticipate a revolt."

"A revolt! I don't believe it, doctor. Those unfortunate creatures are too well guarded. It is some cowardly fear of the brutes that ill-treat them. If it were not for Mary I would not object if they rose and killed their tyrants. I don't believe I'm at heart a murderer, but I swear I would kill any one who abused me as the law allows those convicts to be abused."

Dennis's eyes were dark with anger. The doctor caught the fire of this righteous wrath. "Well boy, I feel like helping the poor devils myself !" Thus these two gentlemen of independent fortunes and cultivated minds demonstrated a deplorable lack of veneration for the statutes of this sovereign State.

"And yet a revolt would only strengthen the laws that drive them to despair." Anger had given place to reason, as Dennis, with his back to the window, thought of the revolt in a new light. "Shall I tell Mary ?" He looked at the doctor, but before his opinion was gained the question was answered by Mary herself. Under the window with Miss Dawson she had heard Dennis's last words.

"Shall you tell Mary ? Certainly you must—everything." Standing on tip-toe she raised her fair face above the edge of the stone portico. Dennis flushed, smiled and jumping lightly to the ground stood beside his wife. "Dennis, were you about to keep a secret from me ?" She raised her hand in playful reproach.

Her husband took her hand and kissing it, kept it in his. Dr. Colton smiled down on the pretty picture of married life.

" Love—" Dennis began—and found they were alone. Miss Dawson was walking slowly toward the house and the doctor's window was closed. For a while they talked earnestly, and then, ruled by her husband's will, Mary at her open door bade him farewell. She did not complain, but on her knees prayed first for her husband's safe return, then for her father. And then she prayed for that negro, the " Lazarus" God had sent, whose life was so strangely interwoven with her own.

A half hour later, Dennis's voice under her window brought the roses to her face: " A false alarm, love." " A false alarm." Mary ran down to meet him, resting in his arms while Dennis told her that two miles from Milton the militia were met by a messenger from the camp, who reported all was quiet and no assistance needed.

CHAPTER XLVII.

OUT OF THE HOUSE OF BONDAGE.

TIME passed and there was no further sign of revolt in Osmerillo Camp. Since the scuffle, which had ended in Stern's broken arm and a convict's death, nothing had happened out of the ordinary routine. The convicts seemed as crushed as ever, and yet it was but seeming. There was a new spirit among those wretched beings—a spirit that had entered the camp with a woman, convicted of manslaughter. She was a wild-eyed, thin woman, apparently of little use in the ranks. "A clog," Hilton had muttered on seeing her. But she proved a wonderful worker, swinging a pick with the ease and rapidity of the strongest man. O Neal started, when, in the mine, he found this woman at work near him.

"Dinah."

At the whispered sound, she turned with upraised pick, looked at him for a moment, and then without recognition went on with her work. Dinah had seemed a link to his past happiness. He hungered for the sound of a friendly voice. But he could not recall himself to her memory. Although Dinah did not recognize her old friend, she spoke to him, called him "Broder in sufferin'." She tried to make him "jine in de work," as she called winning the freedom she predicted. After a little he saw she was mad, and pitied her. How she found her chances to speak, how her little phrases passed along the ranks of the convicts, and at night were whispered in the different cells, is one of the mysteries that only the cunning of oppressed prisoners can divine. Soon O'Neal noticed that a new impulse stirred the convicts. While no general revolt had begun, there was an evident change in those, who up to Dinah's coming had been completly terrorized. Lying awake in his bunk, with no desire now for life or freedom, O'Neal could hear the convicts whispering.

"Dinah sez de Lord sent her here ter lead us out ob de house o' bondage," a woman's tremulous voice said one night—a woman who the next day fell dead with fatigue as under the lash she bent to greater effort.

"Out of the house of bondage!" thought O'Neal when he saw the quiet figure.

That night another whispered conference had been held in O'Neal's cell.

"Dinah sez dat Jennie's deat' was de finger ob de Lord fer our delayin'. She sez ef we won't rise in a body an' kill de debbils, we'll all be killed. De Lord reproaches us fer wantin' de will ter fight de good fight." This time it was a man who somehow had caught a little of Dinah's tone. His words excited the tired creatures.

"We'se ready! we'se ready ter strike fer de Lord! When the signal come, by de Lord ob de chosen, dese niggers'll strike the blow!"

Like the wind the whisper rose to a groan as the negroes crowded together in an excited mass. It was too dark in the cell to distinguish faces and the black mass looked hardly human. But to O'Neal, he who knew how they had suffered, and how much more suffering would be brought upon them by an attempt at revolt, they were only too human. For him hope and desire were dead. But still there lived pity for his race, the will to help them. He knew better than these poor creatures, maddened by a false hope, how useless, worse than useless, would be revolt. For the convicts it would only bring more horrible cruelties. And yet, where or how could reason reach them? Quietly he watched their excitement, waiting a chance to speak. Finally the guard's regular tramp, tramp, came nearer the cell. Not a sound rose now from the crowd of negroes; silent, breathless, they waited until first passing the door and then moving on his round the steps of their keeper grew fainter.

"If de time's not come' spose we res' till the mornin'," said one, a quiet old negro whom O'Neal had noticed often wondering what had brought him to Osmerillo.

"Res'! Dat's Dinah's berry word! Res' 'til de mornin'. 'Til de mornin' ob de freedom! Res' 'til de signal, de signal comes from de Lord!" answered he who was evidently most in Dinah's confidence.

"Res' 'til de signal!" the negroes whispered it as a pass-word, and then were about to separate. Some of the most tired ones had already reached their bunks, when springing up O'Neal stood among them.

"Stop!" It was said softly, yet his tone of authority held them, affrighted them. Had they a spy in the cell? Was he going to betray them to Hilton? And that, before God was ready for the work? The more timid huddled together, the braver turned on O'Neal with threatening gestures.

"Curse yer! I'll kill yer fust!" said the negro who in tones and manner imitated Dinah. "No, sah! afore yer peaches on us, afore yer spiles de work ob de Lord's chosen, I'll strangle out your life!"

He clutched with O'Neal, and stout as he was, seemed likely to conquer this worn-out giant so fallen into decay. Nevertheless after a short, silent scuffle O'Neal rose victor. The negroes had left to them the small space between the bunks, and now on the floor with his knee on the breast of his antagonist, O'Neal tried to reason with the others. "My poor friends, don't you know I'd join you if there was a chance for freedom? Haven't I tried to escape? Don't I know that a revolt will only add to your sufferings? It's not only the officer and guards that are against you; it is the law—

the law that every man in Georgia will fight for! We can't kill them all. And to kill the guards would bring every one of these men against us. If I could go out now, be torn to pieces by dogs, and by this buy your freedom, I'd go and be thankful. Don't think I'd betray you! Only I beg of you for your own sakes not to revolt. Life isn't everything. There's a Heaven and a God, and after death we'll be white, free and happy."

His voice faltered and a sob broke from him; for to speak of Heaven to such starved, beaten, degraded creatures seemed an insult. They did not understand his words nor appreciate his tenderness, but they felt comforted in the certainty that "he wouldn't peach," as they whispered to each other while creeping off noiselessly to their bunks, for again the guard was drawing near. The rising moon shone through the chinks between the logs, and lit up the group of O'Neal and the conquered negro. The man had ceased to struggle now, and O'Neal held up a warning finger to the rest. Again perfect stillness. Tramp, tramp, at the door! The regular tread paused a second, a second whose passage made the cold sweat start out on the negroes. Would the guard open the door and find them still awake? They shivered at the thought of such a possibility. A second longer, and the guard passed on. Perhaps he had stood listening and was reassured by the perfect quiet. Perhaps he had only paused for a moment's rest. As his step grew fainter O'Neal rose and helped up the negro.

"Fool! don't you know a friend from an enemy! I didn't mean to hurt you," he said as the man took a step, then stopped, putting his hand to his breast, "but I had to speak to the others. Take care how you stir them up to a useless revolt. Their blood will be upon your soul."

CHAPTER XLVIII.

REVOLT.

THE spirit of revolt grow stronger. Reason, there was none. The word "deliverance" had pierced this black hell, and was it wonderful that to it clung the condemned? Half-crazed Dinah, this creature with a man's strength and maniac's cunning, had wakened their superstition. They believed that when the signal came they would find an easy victory and then "blessed freedom." Those with more intelligence and less supperstition, for there are grades even in the lower order of mind, saw in a revolt the chance for individual escape, and waited like the rest. Like them, too, they took to watching that pallid face whose fiercy eyes were fixed on the unseen. It was a long work, this stirring into excitement and then rousing to rebellion these chrushed, ill-fed, beaten convicts. But Dinah's enthusiasm never flagged, and now when Hilton's lash descended she listening exulting. Her words, her looks, her signals, travelled the length and breadth of the camp. Moses never felt greater zeal, greater inspiration than did this negro woman. In her ears voices were calling, "Chosen of God, deliver His people." Her unsettled brain grasped only this idea. The lash, of which she had her share, awakened only contempt. As from her Hilton would pass to some less enduring convict, she would whisper : "It's de 'strument ob de Lord ter gib fire an' strength," and the convict nearest her catching her words would repeat them. Those who shrank from that fearful lash, looked upon Dinah as a supernatural being. Since the hour when maddened with rage Hilton thrust his daughter out of her home, he had become self-absorbed and did not notice the hatred in the grimy faces turned from him as he passed them. His eyes, looking inward, failed to mark many a gesture that before would have been visited with severest punishment. Cruel as ever, pitiless in punishing, exacting beyond the endurance of human nature, he no longer held his slaves in subjection. Under his feet, slowly, slowly, the worm was turning, but he did not know it. Stern saw it, wondering at Hilton's apathy. But Stern and Hilton were no longer freindly. Hilton had never overlooked Stern's asking the assistance from the Mayor of Milton to quell disturbances in Osmerillo Camp. Before riding into Milton, when tortured with the pain of the broken arm, Stern had asked permission to do this, receiving for answer the taunt of " Coward ! If the nigger hadn't known you were afraid, he'd not have broken your arm."

"I am no more a coward than you, Captain Hilton. But it is for your safety as well as for the good of the property that I warn you I will disobey your orders."

After he had gone Hilton dispatched the messenger that prevented the coming of aid. On Stern's return to the camp he had expected his discharge, but since the interview in the cottage when he had left Mary in Dennis's arms, Hilton wanted some outlet for the bitterness of his thoughts and found relief in sneering at Stern, and so he was retained. For himself Stern had planned a future. He wrote confidentially to the owners of Osmerillo Mine stating the evident signs of an approaching mutiny and the neglect of Hilton to suppress the alarming symptoms. But Hilton's monthly reports being highly satisfactory, and the mine continuing to enrich its possessors, Stern's letter remained unanswered. Without any further interference Stern watched the growing rebellion, even encouraging it a little by a certain laxity and indulgence toward those most active in expressions of hatred to Hilton. Unnoticed by

the other guards, he nightly saddled his horse, ready for
instant flight, and slept with revolvers and saddlebags
at hand.   His arm was almost well ; it only occasionally needed the sling which he still wore.   He also began to watch Dinah, recognizing hers as the master-
spirit among the convicts.   He would stealthily sneer at
Hilton, calling him "Fool," under his breath, and hating
him more than he had ever hated any one.

Day after day, night after night, the convicts' miserable life went on, but the signal was not given.   Dinah
may have been experimenting in generalship ; the exper-
iment proved a success.   The hope of freedom which at
first had maddened the negroes now became a settled
purpose, and the killing of the guards grew to be an accustomed thought.   They slept with it, ate with it,
worked with it, and looking on some dead convict, swore
to it.   So matters stood when there came an evening so
glorious with flaming clouds, so fresh with rising breezes,
that even in this fearful prison its glories were not entirely lost.   Drawn into their accustomed line the convicts stood to be examined, when to the surprise of the
guard to whose duty it had fallen to pass the rods
through the chains securing the convicts in squads, the
rods were missing from their accustomed place.   The
hammer, too, was gone !   With a pale face the guard—
the same one who on his first coming had called O'Neal
"a statyer" and had given a drink out of his canteen to
fainting Nettie—touched Hilton to call his attention.
The captain was listening to the reports of the day's
work as the guards pointed out the convicts who had
failed in their duty.   In the annals of the camp there
never been a like report ; there was hardly a negro but
had failed in fulfilling his allotted task.

Hilton glared with rage.   "I'll teach them !" he said
brandishing his whip.

"Sir !" again the guard touched his arm.   "Captain,
Hilton !" he spoke aloud.

"What is it?" Hilton turned angrily.

"Something's wrong, sir! Order the convicts back to the mines and shut the door!" He whispered now.

"What's wrong?" Hilton was ready to be enraged with every one.

"The rods are gone. How, I can't tell. But the rods and hammer hev been hidden."

"Curse you!" was Hilton's answer. "I'll have you guards teaching the niggers to revolt! You've not looked for the rods. Who would dare to touch them?"

"I don't know who touched 'em, but I do know they're gone."

"Well, sir, you go to the blacksmith shop for a fresh lot, and the next time there's one missing I'll hold the guards responsible."

The young man walked off quickly; he looked back as he went and saw Hilton, glowering with rage, approach the convicts.

"Cowards! the whole lot of them have been demoralized by that fellow Stern," said Hilton to himself.

The words, louder than the whispered conversation with the guard, reached the man they were aimed at. He smiled sarcastically He might have told Hilton some things that would have made even him grow white, but he would not. "Not to save his life," he muttered to himself.

As if to tempt fate, Hilton, growing impatient, raised the whip and went up to the convicts. The first one failing in duty was a woman with child. She began to cry as Hilton came near. But that was of slight moment to him. She was only a beast of burden like the others, who unless bearing the burdens and accomplishing to the full their tasks, were to be punished. The woman's condition was a common one in the camp, and no favors were ever accorded it. Without a glimmer of pity up went the lash! Down it fell with a sharp whiz.

But in the woman's place there stood a man, a tall black man, who was much emaciated and who had all day been feeling a faintness unusual to him. Yet he could not resist the tears of the poor creature, and pushing her aside he stood in her place.

If the dead had risen, Hilton could not have been more amazed.   He looked for an instant at the negro, while his face grew ghastly in his rage ; then with a muttered curse he raised the whip, bringing it down with all his strength on the thin shoulders of O'Neal.   Under that fierce blow the negro staggered and fell forward, lying at the feet of the cruel executioner.

As if that had been the pre-arranged signal, a shriek went up.   A woman's voice called " Vengeance !" and stooping Dinah pulled off her chain, then rose, swinging it above her head.   In an instant the dogs were loosed and sprang upon the convicts, who, following Dinah's example, held each his chain for weapon—a dangerous one in such desperate hands.

At Hilton's command the guards formed into a square and, aided by the bloodhounds, kept the convicts in check.   But it was not for long, as Dinah having beaten off the dog that had torn her face and throat, dashed to their head shouting :

" Come ! de Lord calls yer !"

Above the confusion, the shouts of the rebels, the growls of the dogs, sounded this wonderful voice, firing into frenzy the excited crowd.   She rushed upon the unbroken square of guards, fastened her thin arms around one of the men, dragged him away and felling him, grasped his pistol.   Other negroes followed her lead, and though many were killed, others of the maddened creatures sprang into their places.   Overpowered by numbers and losing one after another of their force, the guards fought well.   Following the orders of Hilton, they were backing steadily toward the building, when suddenly out into the growing darkness shot gleaming flames, and on their backs they felt the heat of the burning barracks.

"We can't conquer them." Between incessant firing Hilton spoke to the man at his side. He was the young guard who had been sent for the rods, and who when Dinah had killed the first of the band had stepped in his place next the captain. He might have saved himself, but he was young and youth has more daring than judgment, so he would not desert his companions. "Pore statyer, there he goes!" he had said when O'Neal fainted; and then had been too busy with fighting to think of anything more.

"You're young," Hilton spoke without once silencing his revolver; "escape. Ride into Milton and bring out the militia." His voice was more kindly than the guard had ever heard it before.

"But, sir—" he said impulsively.

"Fool!" and Hilton wounded a negro who had sprung upon the guard when he turned. "This is no time for words. Go!"

This command the younger guard obeyed, and crouching, running, soon reached the stable which had thus far been untouched. The horses were gone—all but one, a newly broken colt that looked dangerous in its fright. But there was no time for hesitation; a greater danger was around him. He tightened the girth over the blanket, mounted, and at a full run went past the burning buildings out of the camp. The camp was brilliant with flame, and as he dashed past he saw a horse saddled and fastened to a pile of lumber not far from Hilton's private office.

"Whose is it?" he thought, and then it occurred to him that Stern had not been among the guards, and that the horse bore Stern's saddle. "The coward! He helped to madden the niggers, but he's afraid to face'em. Wot's

17

he waitin' fer?"   Racing along the road he looked back to see if any one were following.   Down in the hollow like a sea of flame lay the convict camp.

"Pore devils, they wos druv to it," he muttered, and then at full speed dashed on to Milton.

.   .   .   .   .

Around the flames in fantastic, horrible dance sprang and yelled the maddened negroes.   Stable, officers' quarters, cells, all one mass of scarlet light.   Many of the convicts had taken the first chance to escape, some infuriated maniacs threw into the fire coal, lumber and working tools, yelling as the flames leaped higher.   A few, and among these Dinah, continued the attack on the guards.   Only three remained of those who in power had been such cruel taskmasters.

Hilton seemed to bear a charmed life, but even he could not long withstand the settled purpose of a spirit like Dinah's.   Beaten off, wounded, again and again she came up to the front.   Through every distraction she held near her a few devoted followers.   She knew that once her iron arms were fastened around Hilton's neck she could kill him, but he divined her purpose and defeated each desperate spring.   Maniac-like she had forgotten the pistol in her breast, relying for weapon on the furious strength of those thin arms and fingers.   An instant she stood with blazing eyes fastened on the man she hated.   Then crying, "De dibbil is waiting fer yer!" she took surer aim and sprang at Hilton.   She clutched his throat and fell upon his breast as he staggered back. A mighty blackness rose before his sight, the fury died out in the man's soul, and he thought of his daughter. "Mary!"   As her name came to him the weight was lifted, his throat was loosed, and though barely conscious he heard voices.

"Leave him to me," said a man in faint tone.

"Is yer come fer his soul?" answered the loud

vibrating voice of the woman who had strangled him.

"Take him, den, to de pits ob hell. I'll git de one dat's lef'."

Wildly chanting she ran swiftly toward the burning buildings. Suddenly she stopped, saw something crawling near the ground, and with a cry, sprang upon it. The thing rose, throwing her off and then ran, ran with the speed and surety of an athlete.

It was a man! Stern! At the first cry of "Vengeance!" he had left the convict guard and made for the stable, secured his horse at the side of Hilton's private office, and entered. He had come for the money. He knew where it was kept and resolved that he would carry enough away to enable him to turn virtuous. The safe was of heavy iron; he tried to blow open the door, but the fuse wouldn't work. Securing another he was about to light it when the negroes came in a band to fire the house and he had been forced to hide. Not willing to leave the money, and momentarily expecting to be found, he periled his life for gain. When with wild cries the black figures moved away, he lit the fuse, crept to a safe distance, and waited.

The explosion was unnoticed in the confusion; and again he entered the now burning office. Blinded by smoke, scorched with flame, never hesitating, he felt his way to the safe and pulled out the money-bag which he had once seen Hilton open. Once more out in the air he looked around with exultation at the moment when, lit by flames, Hilton fell to the ground with the negress on his breast.

"Fool! I'm glad of it! he muttered, and hiding as well as he could from the brilliancy of those scarlet flames, he hurried toward his horse. He had nearly reached the lumber when with a shriek something sprang on his back. Rising, with a backward motion of his arms he threw off the woman he had recognized by her voice.

"That devilish mulatto!" he muttered, and feeling her hot breath, the touch of those long thin fingers, he ran. Strong and lithe, he ran well, distancing the pack of blacks that Dinah's shriek had called to the chase. Never stopping to look behind, holding fast to the money for which he had periled his life, he ran swiftly on. He passed the pile of lumber from which a broken bridle dangling told of the flight of his frightened horse. He saw him ahead, plunging and rearing. He was not far off. If he could reach him! More swiftly he ran. The chances were in his favor when suddenly remembering the pistol in her breast, Dinah drew it, fired, and Stern staggered, paused, and then ran on. But that instant's pause was fatal. With a leap Dinah reached him, clutching at him with her fierce hands.

"To hell fire wid de debbil!" she shouted. He struggled furiously, dropping the money and battling for his life. But struggles were useless. Surrounded, lifted from the ground with Dinah, who still held to him, he was hurried along.

"To de fire!" shouted Dinah, and with a rush they were carried to the still flaming houses.

"Help! Help!" Stern called, as he felt the burning heat and saw the blaze leap out to meet him.

"Into de fire!" shrieked Dinah, and raising him in her arms sprang with him into his grave.

Shouting "Hallelujah!" screaming, hurrahing, the negroes waited a moment expecting to see their leader rise triumphant from the flames. Then a cry, "Hilton lives!" started them with fresh impetus toward a spot where beside a black man gleamed one white face.

Strange to say, Dinah had been held in check by O'Neal. With the quickness of a disordered brain she divined that he was against her and believed he was by some peculiar supernatural gift able to thwart her plans. Several times she had been on the point of giving " de signal," when she felt upon her a steady look from those sad eyes and she could not speak the words the convicts expected. With wildest fervor she had prayed that the Lord " would eider make de nigger turn ter His work, or take him off by deat'." But she had grown weary of waiting, and resolving that her first act should be to kill " dah hindrance ob God's freedom," had by signs and tokens made the convicts while in the mines loosen each his chain. She it was who stole the rods. How she did it under the watchful eyes of the guard only a mad woman could tell. When O'Neal fell under the lash she believed that God had stricken down " de hindrance." " Dead ! De Lord's will !" then she raised her voice and gave the signal.

Although trodden on by the excited negroes, O'Neal was not killed. Gradually consciousness returned, and he raised himself on his arm and looked around. Where he lay, near the mine, all was quiet. Where were the guards ? Were they all killed ? And Mary's father ? This thought gave him strength. With weak, uncertain steps, a roaring in his ears, a mist before his eyes, he began to search for the father of the girl who had offered her life for him.

" A life for a life," he spoke to himself, looking around him with such failing sight that even the burning buildings, the wild black figures around them, were only dimly visible. He heard a strange sound at his feet. It was the man he sought, with Dinah on his breast and clutching at his throat.

" Leave him to me." It was the hollow voice, the face of one she believed dead. " Take his soul !" shouted Dinah, rushing off.

" Captain Hilton, Captain Hilton !" The sound of his

own name roused Hilton from stupor ; trembling hands were helping him up, urging him forward,

"Quick—run—I can't—protect you if—you are—seen—"

Hilton recognized the face of the man who was trying to save him. It was the negro he had made the special object of his hate—he who had that very night fainted under the lash. And now he was offering up life for him ; for turning at that wild cry, "Hilton lives," and stretching out both arms as if to keep off the crowd, O'Neal faced the wild black figures rushing toward them.

Was this a "nigger?" Were "niggers" beasts? The theory of a life was torn asunder, and Hilton was stunned. He thought not of the negroes yelling for his blood, thought not of accepting the offered sacrifice ; he forgot all but the heroism of the convict.

Still moving back, forgetting even the deep drain he himself had ordered, he suddenly fell into it, breaking his neck and dying instantly. Shrieking, cursing, shouting, over the ditch far into the marsh, leaped the negroes searching for Hilton. They left two new victims behind them, for their heedless feet had crushed the dying O'Neal into the trampled earth.

––––

Before morning Milton was filled with the news of the revolt at Osmerillo. The papers gave a full account and many horrible incidents of negro depravity. The butchery of the guards was especially held up as atrocious

Opening the morning journal, Mary's face changed to deathlike pallor.

"Darling !" Dennis's arm kept her from fainting.

"We will go at once," she said.

In the bright daylight the scene of the revolt was horrible. It was like some fearful battlefield upon which human beings had fought and died only to insure greater misery for the living. Mary, at her husband's entreaty, had waited outside in the carriage. Janet, who had come with her, sat motionless gazing on the white face and closed eyes of the woman to whom this shock might bring fatal consequences.

"The de'il. Why could he not ha' gane away an' died quiet-like," she thought, full of resentment against Hilton—a resentment that vanished, however, when Dennis with the man he had taken to help him came back bearing between them something very straight and stiff.

It was Hilton's body.

His face bore a look of strange calmness, almost peace. At least so thought his daughter, who kissed and wept over the still form that never again could welcome or repulse her.

There was another lifeless man that Dennis charged his servant to guard.

"A hero !" he had said, as just before the ditch where he had found Hilton he came upon the body of a negro whom in spite of rags, in spite of emaciation, he recognized as Tom O'Neal. "He offered his life to protect Hilton's ; I know it," said Dennis.

Out of his own noble heart he judged a noble man.

THE END.